Negotiating the *auteur*

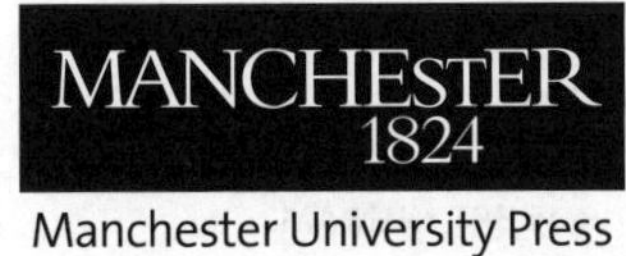

Manchester University Press

French Film Directors

DIANA HOLMES and ROBERT INGRAM *series editors*
DUDLEY ANDREW *series consultant*

Chantal Akerman   MARION SCHMID
Auterism from Assayas to Ozon: five directors   KATE INCE
Jean-Jacques Beineix   PHIL POWRIE
Luc Besson   SUSAN HAYWARD
Bertrand Blier   SUE HARRIS
Catherine Breillat   DOUGLAS KEESEY
Robert Bresson   KEITH READER
Leos Carax   GARIN DOWD AND FERGUS DALEY
Claude Chabrol   GUY AUSTIN
Henri-Georges Clouzot   CHRISTOPHER LLOYD
Jean Cocteau   JAMES WILLIAMS
Claire Denis   MARTINE BEUGNET
Marguerite Duras   RENATE GÜNTHER
Georges Franju   KATE INCE
Jean-Luc Godard   DOUGLAS MORREY
Mathieu Kassovitz   WILL HIGBEE
Diane Kurys   CARRIE TARR
Patrice Leconte   LISA DOWNING
Louis Malle   HUGO FREY
Georges Méliès   ELIZABETH EZRA
François Ozon   ANDREW ASIBONG
Marcel Pagnol   BRETT BOWLES
Maurice Pialat   MARJA WAREHIME
Jean Renoir   MARTIN O'SHAUGHNESSY
Alain Resnais   EMMA WILSON
Jacques Rivette   DOUGLAS MORREY AND ALISON SMITH
Alain Robbe-Grillet   JOHN PHILLIPS
Eric Rohmer   DEREK SCHILLING
Coline Serreau   BRIGITTE ROLLET
Bertrand Tavernier   LYNN ANTHONY HIGGINS
André Téchiné   BILL MARSHALL
François Truffaut   DIANA HOLMES AND ROBERT INGRAM
Agnès Varda   ALISON SMITH
Jean Vigo   MICHAEL TEMPLE

FRENCH FILM DIRECTORS

Negotiating the *auteur*

Dominique Cabrera, Noémie Lvovsky, Laetitia Masson and Marion Vernoux

JULIA DOBSON

Manchester University Press

MANCHESTER AND NEW YORK

distributed in the United States exclusively by Palgrave Macmillan

Published by Manchester University Press
Oxford Road, Manchester M13 9NR, UK
and Room 400, 175 Fifth Avenue, New York, NY 10010, USA
www.manchesteruniversitypress.co.uk

Distributed exclusively in the USA by
Palgrave, 175 Fifth Avenue, New York, NY 10010, USA

Distributed exclusively in Canada by
UBC Press, University of British Columbia, 2029 West Mall, Vancouver, BC, Canada V6T 1Z2

British Library Cataloguing-in-Publication Data
A catalogue record for this book is available from the British Library

Library of Congress Cataloging-in-Publication Data applied for

ISBN 978 0 7190 7218 5 *hardback*

First published 2012

The publisher has no responsibility for the persistence or accuracy of URLs for any external or third-party internet websites referred to in this book, and does not guarantee that any content on such websites is, or will remain, accurate or appropriate.

Typeset in Scala with Meta display
by Koinonia, Manchester
Printed in Great Britain
by TJ International Ltd, Padstow

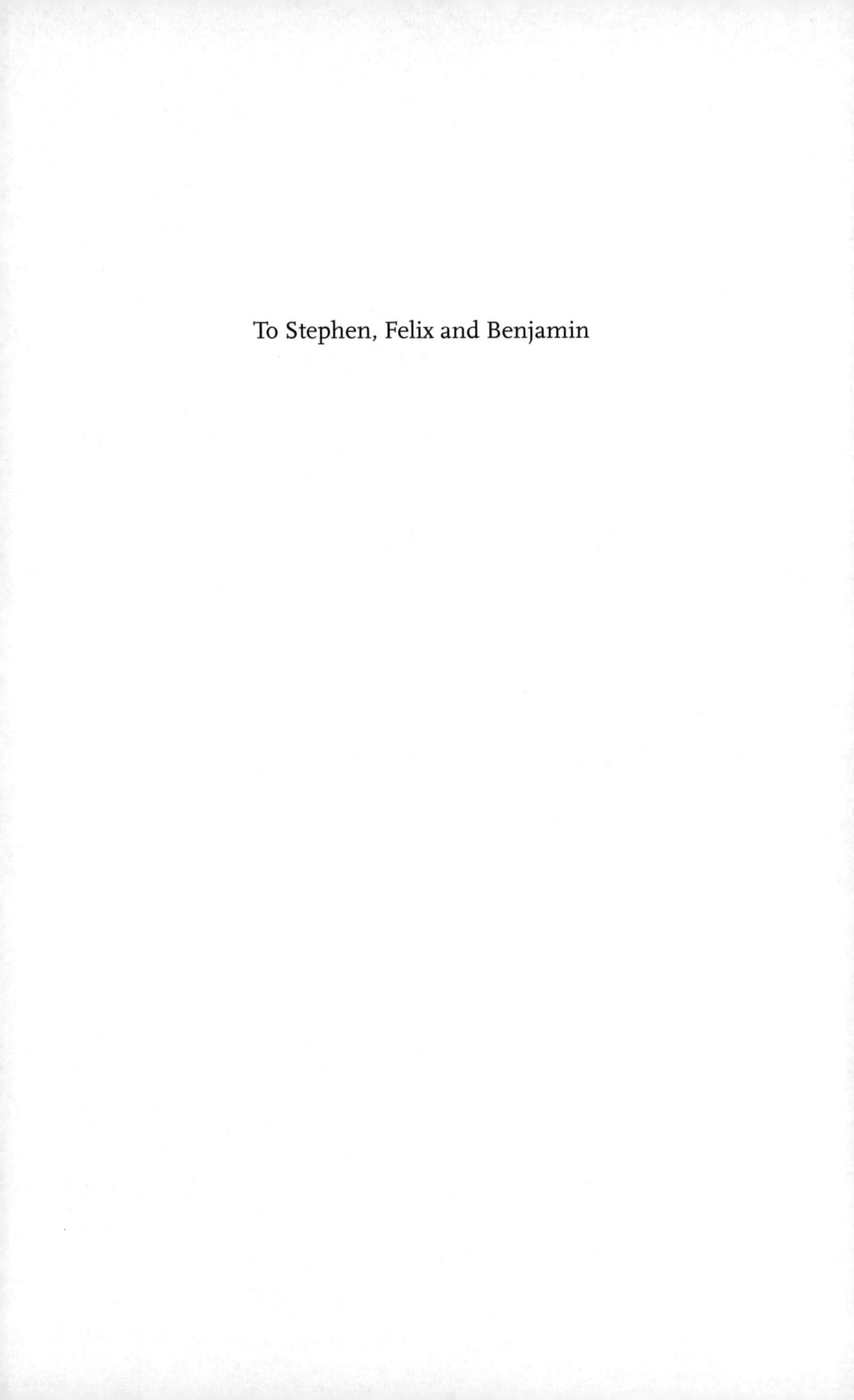

To Stephen, Felix and Benjamin

Contents

List of plates

Series editors' foreword

To an anglophone audience, the combination of the words 'French' and 'cinema' evokes a particular kind of film: elegant and wordy, sexy but serious – an image as dependent upon national stereotypes as is that of the crudely commercial Hollywood blockbuster, which is not to say that either image is without foundation. Over the past two decades, this generalised sense of a significant relationship between French identity and film has been explored in scholarly books and articles, and has entered the curriculum at university level and, in Britain, at A level. The study of film as art-form and (to a lesser extent) as industry has become a popular and widespread element of French Studies, and French cinema has acquired an important place within Film Studies. Meanwhile, the growth in multiscreen and 'art-house' cinemas, together with the development of the video industry, has led to the greater availability of foreign-language films to an English-speaking audience. Responding to these developments, this series is designed for students and teachers seeking information and accessible but rigorous critical study of French cinema, and for the enthusiastic filmgoer who wants to know more.

The adoption of a director-based approach raises questions about *auteurism*. A series that categorises films according not to period or to genre (for example) but to the person who directed them, runs the risk of espousing a romantic view of film as the product of solitary inspiration. On this model, the critic's role might seem to be that of discovering continuities, revealing a necessarily coherent set of themes and motifs which correspond to the particular genius of the individual. This is not our aim: the *auteur* perspective on film, itself most clearly articulated in France in the early 1950s, will be interrogated in certain volumes of the series, and, throughout, the director will be treated as one highly significant element in a complex process of film production and reception which includes socio-economic and political determinants, the work of a large and highly skilled team of artists and technicians, the mechanisms of production and distribution, and the complex and multiply determined responses of spectators.

The work of some of the directors in the series is already well known outside France, that of others is less so – the aim is both to provide informative and original English-language studies of established figures, and to extend the range of French directors known to anglophone students of cinema. We intend the series to contribute to the promotion of the formal and informal study of French films, and to the pleasure of those who watch them.

DIANA HOLMES

ROBERT INGRAM

Preface

One of the central aims of this book is to provoke increased interest in the work of the four directors discussed here and, although some of their early works have become more difficult to access, most of their films remain commercially available through French distributors. The translations in the text are the author's own unless stated otherwise.

Acknowledgements

I would like to thank the series editors Diana Holmes and Robert Ingram for their sustained encouragement and detailed attention to this volume, and Matthew Frost at Manchester University Press for his patient professionalism.

My thanks to the many friends, experts and expert friends who have inspired, entertained (and endured) conversations that kept this project alive – especially to Guy Austin, Martine Beugnet, Elizabeth Ezra, Diana Holmes, Martin O'Shaughnessy, Gill Rye and Carrie Tarr. My thanks also to colleagues and students in the Department of French at the University of Sheffield, to the team at the Forum des Images, and to Dominique Cabrera and Laetitia Masson for generous help with access to images.

My great thanks to Stephen Walker for his boundless faith and support.

Introduction: continuing negotiations

L'art travaille à mettre en lumière un effort qui révèle des contradictions vitales: le savoir intime et la compréhension universelle, la construction et la destruction, la tentation d'accession à une place idéale et le nomadisme, la marginalité et la collectivité. Ces contradictions doivent mener celui ou celle qui regarde à prendre d'autres positions ... à se mettre en mouvement individuellement et collectivement.[1]

(Stoll 2004: 33)

The recognition of the inherently discursive functions of art provides a central context for the multiple aims of this volume. Framing its primary wish to trigger greater critical engagement with the work of the four directors discussed is the desire to recognise and articulate the functions of work that does not mesh neatly with dominant critical discourses. The inbetweenness of these films may spoil their potential canonisation, yet their positive and dynamic negotiations of apparent contradictions and oppositional forces (across frameworks of production, performance and reception) to create inclusive synergies of the pleasurable, the personal and the political remain powerful and important. The central tensions enumerated in Stoll's list will echo throughout the Introduction and the following chapters, as the diverse range of films discussed perform complex negotiations between the intimate and the universal, between the construction of

---

1 'Art strives to shed light on work that reveals vital contradictions: between intimate knowledge and universal understanding, between construction and destruction, between the temptation of securing an ideal place and nomadism, between the marginal and the collective. These contradictions must lead those watching to position themselves differently ... to set themselves in motion individually and collectively.'

new narratives and the undermining of generic and gendered conventions, between the assertion of autonomous creative agency and the recognition of shared collective heritages and desires. Indeed this Introduction constitutes a set of serial negotiations between shared contexts (discourses of *auteurism*, gender, genre and the political) and the focus, in the following chapters, of the individual specificities of the respective oeuvres of Dominique Cabrera, Noémie Lvovsky, Laetitia Masson and Marion Vernoux (as enshrined in the *auteurist* trope of singular creative agency). These positions of negotiation, and the resultant intermediacy, are here perceived not as compromised and responsive dilutions of opposing terms but as a positive and proactive dynamic of ambiguity and openness, which produces the challenging nature of the knowing negotiations of boundaries central to these films.

The volumes in this series have focused predominantly on the work of a single, internationally recognised director. The separate chapters of this volume, however, will address the work of Dominique Cabrera, Noémie Lvovsky, Laetitia Masson and Marion Vernoux in turn. The multiple focus of this volume, although not intended as a formal 'companion' volume to Kate Ince's edited volume *Five Directors: Auteurism from Assayas to Ozon* (Ince 2008), shares its stated aims and the imperative to provide critical material on outstanding, contemporary directors whose films are not (yet) assured of critical recognition. Beyond this general principle, the motivations for the choice of directors featured here remain multiple and, whilst I do not suggest that these four directors constitute an exclusive group identity, nor that their work shares either clear didactic objectives or formal concerns, it has evolved within shared socio-economic, cultural and film industry contexts. The four directors under discussion are not new arrivals and began making films in the early 1990s, yet they have received scant critical attention in both popular and academic film criticism. They share similar profiles in terms of box office success, number of films made and generational affinities and, whilst their respective reputations have been established through the public and critical acclaim afforded their documentaries, shorts and feature films in France, their filmic output has not, at this point, received the distribution which they merit beyond those national boundaries.[2]

2 A wider selection of directors with similar profiles could include Pascale Ferran, Tonie Marshall, Laurence Ferreira Barbosa, Emilie Deleuze and Agnès Jaoui.

Cabrera, Lvovsky, Masson and Vernoux all make films that straddle boundaries of categorisation and therefore escape the quickly established and self-perpetuating groupings that serve as powerful frameworks for popular access via DVD distribution, critical canonisation and academic curricula. These films problematise the divide normally perceived between *auteur* and 'art house' and popular, genre-based cinema in terms of both their production and their reception – a divide which is clearly rendered more complex as it shifts to accommodate the consideration of the different modes of distribution afforded to French film in an Anglophone setting. Thus these films do not form part of the canon of contemporary *auteur* production, nor are they studied as examples of popular cinema – the latter being largely restricted to examples of the comedy, thriller or biopic which, increasingly, have succeeded in breaking through to multiplex distribution in Anglophone markets.[3] I want to present now several important contexts which frame the readings of these specific directors and their films and which engage with wider negotiations of oppositions within French cinema and Film Studies. These oppositions reveal the complex interactions between the trajectories used to address (their) cinema and include: the continuing and recently reasserted dominance within French Film Studies of constructions of the director as *auteur*, the particular debates around the female *auteur*, the opposition between contemporary *auteur* film and popular genre production and the location of the political in contemporary French film.

Directing *auteurism*

The *auteurist* approach, which has long enjoyed a privileged position in Film Studies generally, and in the history of French cinema in particular, asserts the director, as *auteur*, as the 'unifying principle in the production, interpretation and reception of an artwork' (Maule 2008: 13). Its persistent influence reflects a historically diverse set of needs which include the desire to assert the cultural status of cinema as art-form through the fostering of constructions of artistic agency dominant in other domains, to the protection of intellectual property

3 Recent examples include: *Ne le dis à personne* (Canet, 2007), *Ils* (Moreau and Palud, 2006) and *Coco avant Chanel* (Fontaine, 2009).

and the exemption of cinematic production and distribution from wider trade agreements and the projection of nationally specific cultural production. There is no space or need for a detailed history of the emergence of the *auteur* here yet, although its origins clearly predate French critical discourse of the 1950s, it remains identified with the '*politique des auteurs*' first articulated by François Truffaut and largely defended by the critics of *Cahiers du cinéma* in the 1950s.[4] It retains close associations with a rejection of the high-budget, studio-based, literary adaptations of the '*tradition de qualité*', the adoption of the formal innovations of the Nouvelle Vague and the identification of a new generation of filmmakers. This historically specific example clearly reflects wider cultural strategies that accompany generational shifts in cultural production and serve ultimately to protect investments in new articulations of cultural and economic capital. As Bourdieu points out:

> [les] plus jeunes, qui sont aussi les plus démunis de capital spécifique, et qui, dans un univers où exister c'est différer ... parviennent à affirmer leur identité, c'est à dire leur différence, à la faire connaître et reconnaître ('se faire un nom'), en imposant des modes de pensée et d'expression nouveaux.[5] (Bourdieu 1992: 54)

The strategy or policy (*politique*) of *auteurism* advocated the identification, throughout a film maker's oeuvre, of a formal unity of *mise en scène* (personal style) and of recurrent thematic motifs, thus privileging the creative agency of the director above the work of an inherently collaborative team, whilst also focusing on the perpetuation of the trope of transcendent genius at the expense of engagement with the socio-economic and cultural contexts of the production or reception of a given film. Constructions of the *auteur* have evolved through the idolisation of a select group of Hollywood directors (Fuller, Hitchcock, Sirk), who were lauded for the quality of their production within the constraints of the Hollywood studio system, through its interpretation

---

4 Recent works by Jeancolas, Meusy and Pinel (1996), Rosanna Maule (2008) and Virginia Wright Wexman (2003) provide excellent detailed analyses of the evolution of the figure of the *auteur*.

5 'the youngest, who are also those most lacking in specific cultural capital, and who, in a universe where to exist means to distinguish yourself from others ... succeed in asserting their identity, that is their difference, in making it known and recognised ("making a name for themselves"), by imposing new modes of thought and expression.'

as primary marker of prestige and canonisation (see Sarris 1968), to a structuralist incarnation reifying central oppositions that structure the director's work in order to assert their worth 'not only in their universality (what they all have in common) but also in their singularity' (Wollen 1970: 60). In line with wider shifts in literary and critical theory, critical discourses on film after the mid-1970s have challenged the dominance of *auteurism* by foregrounding the construction of an individual text and shifting the location of meaning from production to critical reception (thus demoting issues of directorial agency, holistic readings of an oeuvre and cultural hierarchies of production). Yet the striking persistence of the continuing status of *auteurism* in France should be recognised as a symptom of the strength of its wider ideological function in asserting the place of cinema within the *culture légitime* rather than only within the *culture de masse* or popular culture (Bourdieu 1979). Indeed Blewitt, glossing Bourdieu, concludes that '[A]uteurism dominates the aesthetic consciousness of the middle classes' (Blewitt 1993: 368) and, as such, continues to function as a prominent example of the masked articulation of social and cultural power relations, through the institutionalisation of taste operated primarily through classical film criticism in France.

Other, more specific, factors must be signalled, however, in relation to the reassertion of the position of the *auteur* within French cinema over the last twenty years. The successful French negotiation of the arguments 'for' in the GATT trade agreements of 1993, which ensured the protection of national film production and distribution, drew upon the figure of the *auteur* as a central element of its construction of the identity of French cinema (often still posited in opposition to that of Hollywood production systems) and the securing of its status as 'exception culturelle' (see Creton 1997: 23–5). The same period also saw the strengthening of the intellectual property rights or 'droit d'auteur' of the director over the rights of the producer and other interested parties (see Jeancolas et al. 1996: 160–5). Maule's excellent historicised account of the development of the *auteur* in European cinema asserts that, in the twenty-first century's crisis of (independent) national cinemas, 'the *auteur* remains an important marketing figure and emblem of independent cinema as counter-hegemonic realm, entirely consonant with European cultural policies and institutions' (Maule 2008: 18). Indeed much contemporary criticism in France continues to frame the director's centrality as part of a heroic struggle against a globalised film industry in its assertion of 'une certaine fidélité à des convictions artistiques qui font de lui l'unique "propriétaire" de son oeuvre' (Vasse 2008: 243).[6] Ince identifies the wave of critical re-engagements with the figure of the *auteur* that accumulated throughout the 1990s and which revalorised its historical function in the context of a globalised film industry, such as the emergence of comparative studies of film and painting and the marking of the centenary of cinema in 1995 with the commissioning of a history of the *auteur* (Ince 2008: 6).

That the revival in critical fortunes of the *auteurist* approach should coincide with the emergence of a new generation of filmmakers (42 per cent of French film production in 1992 was of first films (Brassart 2006: 3)) is not surprising as it echoes the mutual dependencies of the twin arrivals of the *politique des auteurs* and the Nouvelle Vague in the 1950s. This parallel model can be extended to a link between the Nouvelle Vague's rejection of the 'tradition de qualité' and the reinvigoration of the *auteur* figure in the mid-1990s, critically framed as a reaction to the production-led *cinéma du look* of the 1980s and the high-budget, literary adaptations of the heritage cinema that dominated film production in France (and in the UK) in the early 1990s. Wider contexts support this development as the evolution of the European media landscape saw private television channels, mainly Canal + and Arte, begin to commission films at this point (rising to 80 per cent of French film co-productions in the mid-1990s (Brassart 2006: 3)) which consequently sanctioned the identification of new *auteurs*.[7] Modes of training and institutional changes remain significant, and IDHEC's successor FEMIS[8] has been singularly influential in producing close-knit, collaborative cohorts who frame their professional identity as directors in artistic rather than technical discourses (Brassart 2006: 4).[9] Of the four directors discussed in this volume, only Masson features regularly in (longer) lists of contem-

---

6 'a certain loyalty to their artistic convictions which make them the sole "owner" of their work'.

7 Others have seen such practices as stifling the personal vision deemed necessary to a sustained *auteur* cinema (Vasse 2008: 93).

8 Institut des hautes études cinématographiques (1944–1985), Ecole nationale supérieure des métiers de l'image et du son (1985–).

9 Of the four directors discussed in this volume, three graduated from these schools Cabrera from IDHEC in 1981, Lvovsky from FEMIS in Scénario (1990) and Masson in Image (1991).

porary French *auteurs*. Both Lvovsky and Masson are included in a recent list of 37 contemporary French *auteurs* (Vasse 2008: 5) and in Ciment's recent defence of the rich diversity of contemporary French cinema (Ciment 2010: 1). The absence of Cabrera and Vernoux (and others) from such lists can be framed not as a qualitative judgement but rather as a reflection of the relative resistance of their profiles to such labels through practices of working across divergent fields (Cabrera from publicly funded documentary to historical drama) and in genres which occupy lowly positions in the hierarchies of filmic production and critical reception (Vernoux and mainstream comedy).

Negotiating gender

The four directors whose films are discussed here are all women and, whilst studies of cinemas past and contemporary continue to field predominantly male lists with scant reflection on their claims to universality of coverage, there is need for further comment here. Women are widely involved in all aspects of filmmaking in France today and, whilst there is not room here for a historical overview[10] or for discussion of this wider group of professionals, it is important to restate that the landscape of French cinema of the past forty years bears witness to the combined impact of socio-political change (successive waves of feminism) and technical advance (the lowering of production costs and access to alternative cheap means of distribution) on the participation of women in filmmaking. The emergence in France in the 1970s of a significant number of women directors, who articulated new representations of female subjectivity, agency and gendered identities, both through a challenge to dominant modes of filmic representation through formal intervention (Akerman, Duras, Varda) and through an engagement with the codes and conventions of popular generic forms (Serreau, Kurys), has continued. The 1990s witnessed an increase in the prominence of women filmmakers in France as the number of women filmmakers who received funding from the State system of *avance sur recettes* (advance funding recouped through box office returns) approached a quarter of the total annual

10 For extensive and detailed coverage of contemporary French women directors see Tarr with Rollet 2001.

applications.[11] Films directed by women now represent almost 20 per cent of French film production.[12] These figures support claims of a new visibility of films by women (Sellier 2003: 213), whilst such sustained growth provides further evidence that 'the gender configuration of French cinema is shifting' (Wilson 2004: 217). French women filmmakers retain striking and sustained levels of funding and productivity that remain markedly absent in British and Hollywood film industries (both industries failing to improve on a stagnant 6 per cent share for women directors). Yet, as Ginette Vincendeau argues, the picture in France remains more nuanced as the achievement of near-parity in admission to the directorial track at Femis, and improvements in parity of funding (of first films at least) are countered by the continuing dominance of men as the 'gatekeepers of cinematic prestige' through positions of critical and institutional power (a marker of this is that only three of the 53 films included at Cannes in 2010 were made by women) (Vincendeau 2010).

The choice to focus the following chapters on directors who are women is clearly deliberate, yet it is not motivated by a perceived need to legitimise, defend or protect the oeuvres of these four filmmakers *as women* before all other considerations – their work requires no such strategy. Whilst tracking the engagement of women in all male-dominated forms of cultural practice remains politically valuable in raising consciousness, building solidarities and effecting change, many remain wary of the risks of an approach which privileges sexual difference as the (over)determining factor in a consideration of their work, a strategy which risks repeating the mantras of conventional patriarchal discourse in its reduction of the lived experience and (self)representation of women to the projection of a mythical, homogenised model of Woman. Neither is my choice of directors founded on the view that it is the sole privilege of women filmmakers to represent female subjects or indeed to challenge the conventions either of the definition of Woman, the representation of women or the wider constructions of gendered identity. I am not suggesting a reinstatement of reductive and unhelpful categories such as 'films de femmes / women's films', nor am I suggesting that specific formal or

---

11 In 1997, 12 out of 52 awards went to women directors, and 12 out of 55 in 1998 (Sellier 2003: 213).
12 CNC figures show that this rose from 15 out of 112 in 1990 to 35 out of 181 in 2009: www.cnc.fr/Site.

aesthetic elements common to all four directors constitute evidence of a wider, gendered authorial subjectivity or cinematic style which could subsequently be applied to all women wielding cameras. What interests me here is the work of these four filmmakers as instances of the continuing negotiations of a male-centred heritage of dominant cinematic conventions, codes, narratives and representations through which, inevitably, run central questions of gendered identity.

Many, indeed most, French women directors resist the formulation of such wider groupings, wary of their association with perniciously concessionary and reductive discourses. Laetitia Masson rejects the notion of a gendered authorial identity, stating that, although she admires the work of Claire Denis and Patricia Mazuy, she recognises no common affinity or themes with women (directors) as a collective identity (Audé and Garbarz 1998: 32). Masson indeed goes further to reject an authorial identity determined by either sex or nationality, stating that she doesn't see herself 'as a woman who makes French films, but as someone who makes films and leaves as much open as possible in order to communicate something to the audience' (De Bruyn 2000: 25). Whilst Cabrera attests her sanguine awareness of the discriminatory treatment of women in all areas of the film industry (see Chapter 1), she rejects the suggestion that the process of her filmmaking is determined by sexual difference or a gendered creative identity, asserting provocatively that 'je n'ai pas le sentiment que c'est seulement mon utérus qui pense quand je fais un film'[13] (Puaux 2001: 179). The rejection of the title of woman director, in favour of the perceived gender-neutral label of *auteur* can result in a concomitant distancing from feminism (Tarr with Rollet 2001: 10), yet the resistance of these filmmakers to any categorisation of their creativity and their work as defined by their sex must also be seen within the specifically national context of the construction of identity. Dominant social and political discourses in France contain the deeply embedded notion of a universal equality of the individual citizen before the State, and contemporary feminist discourse in France continues to focus on notions of *parité* and equality rather than the construction, defence or privileging of (sexual) difference.

This powerful trope is overlaid further, in this specific cultural context, by the dominant model of *auteurism*, which, in addition

13 'I don't get the feeling that it is just my uterus that does the thinking when I'm filming.'

to its perpetuation of patriarchal models of filiation and authority, privileges the role of the transcendent individual above all potential collective identities and practices. As Vincendeau asserts, this emphasis is 'une stratégie qui occulte d'autres aspects déterminants (dont le sexe de l'individu en question)'[14] (Vincendeau 1989: 99), and results in women filmmakers' assertion of their equal status with male *auteurs* rather than an assertion of difference. The assertion of the critical status of some women filmmakers as *auteurs* is evident although its bestowal remains strikingly rare and is repeatedly applied to a small number of central figures, namely Marguerite Duras (already a seminal literary author), Agnès Varda, Claire Denis and (more recently) Catherine Breillat. This Manchester University Press series reflects this common stance in its inclusion of single volumes dedicated to these four directors (*Chantal Akerman* (Schmid-2010), *Catherine Breillat* (Keesey 2009), *Claire Denis* (Beugnet 2004), *Marguerite Duras* (Gunther 2002) and *Agnès Varda* (Smith 1998)) and presents an important extension of this list to include female directors associated more strongly with genre films: *Coline Serreau* (Rollet 1998) and *Diane Kurys* (Tarr 1999). In relation to the generation of filmmakers discussed in this volume, Françoise Audé's second edition of *Cinéma d'elles* (Audé 2002) asserts the *auteur* status of Dominique Cabrera and Laetitia Masson, yet recent studies of contemporary French cinema have made a decisive move away from presenting separate chapters devoted to women filmmakers (see Prédal 2002 and Trémois 1997). Vasse's list of 37 contemporary French *auteurs*, compiled in 2008, includes ten women.[15]

Feminist critical discourse adopts a divergent range of positions in relation to the possible relationships between women filmmakers and the figure of the (female) *auteur*.[16] Since the 1970s, much feminist criticism has rejected dominant constructions of genius as inherently linked to patriarchal order and gendered constructions of creativity, in their sustained association of creativity with masculine virility, solitude and the heroic transcendence of the familial and the domestic

14 'a strategy that occults other determining factors (including the sex of the individual in question)'.

15 These are Chantal Akerman, Sophie Bredier, Catherine Breillat, Claire Denis, Pascale Ferran, Noémie Lvovsky, Laetitia Masson, Patricia Mazuy, Mariana Otero and Marina de Van.

16 The term *auteure*, proposed by the ministerial decree on the feminisation of professional titles, is rarely used (Sellier 2003: 213).

(Battersby 1989). The critique of such tropes of creativity was accompanied by a recognition of the reductive readings of women's cultural production as unmediated and unvalued personal discourse to include a rejection of the 'reductive reading of film as autobiography; the repression of complexity in the desire to identify an overriding stylistic or thematic unity' (Tasker 2002: 3) that is commonly associated with *auteurism*. The romanticisation of the filmmaker, perpetuated through the figure of the *auteur*, serves to mask not only the 'status of cinema as a social practice based on collective and commercial activities' (Maule 2008: 13) but also its corporate structures, which include cultures of direct and indirect discrimination that continue to obstruct the full and equal participation of women.

Other critics however suggest that, as much of the historical impetus behind *auteurism* must be recognised as pragmatic, it is acceptable for the assertion of women *auteurs* to provide both a vital counterpoint to the historical neglect and exclusion of women filmmakers (Martin 2003: 30) and a valuable practice which secures 'position and power within the institutional frameworks and reception' (Rabinovitz 2005: 23). This empowerment through inclusion and critical valorisation is central to the argument that the designation of female *auteurs* is an important move in its ability to contest systems of oppression that confine us to 'the status of alienated female consumers of a subculture from which men emphatically distanced themselves in an affirmation of both their cultural and their social dominance' (Sellier 2003: 219). Given the continuing status of the *auteur* model, the construction of a female *auteur* does, paradoxically, assert parity of creative agency. Its accordance of agency, subjectivity and cultural visibility to women directors further reveals tensions at the heart of cinematic conventions in the context of reductive representations of women through the narrative and representational strategies of mainstream cinema and wider cultural discourse. As Mayne argues 'the articulation of female authorship threatens to upset the erasure of "women" which is central to the articulation of "Woman" in cinema' (Mayne 1990: 97).

Recent criticism of the *auteurist* approach, which aligns it with critical disappointment at the state of contemporary French cinema, presents its long-established characteristics, 'fragile, changeant et pluriel' (Prédal 2001: 37) (fragile, unstable and plural), as wholly negative and decries the banality of its central function as the self-fulfilling mythologisation of a select few by an elite group (De Baecque

1997).[17] Yet, if we accept that the *auteur* has always been 'a fiction, a polemical device used to promote a certain kind or reading rather than a particular kind of writing' (Forbes and Kelly 1992: 4), then its malleability is open to more positive configurations through a demystification, rather than a defence, of authorship (Mayne 1990: 98). A further recognition that the central paradox of the *auteurist* trope has always resided in its reliance on the formation of collective identities and filiations (generational, national, generic) that it works so hard to disguise, suggests that a recognition of the *auteur as* a 'nexus of communicative alliances' (Dobson 2008: 57), that permits shared positions built on patterns of simultaneous innovation, recognition and repetition, may also provide a model of intermediacy and negotiation that accommodates the specific socio-cultural inheritances of women filmmakers.

Negotiating genre

The evocation of patterns based on repetition, recognition and innovation immediately recalls the function of cinematic genre and its central role in configurations both of the *auteur* and of gendered cultural production and reception. Seminal sociological work on art as collective and collaborative activity reminds us that all artworks rely upon shared conventions and that the repetition or difference from such conventions plays a pivotal role in setting the social parameters of reception (Becker 1982). Despite its origins in an appreciation of directors praised for sustaining a personal cinematic vision whilst working within the genre-led Hollywood studio system, the figure of the *auteur* continues to be associated with an opposition to popular genre cinema; indeed a dominant and defensive critical reluctance in France to engage with genre exacerbates the reliance upon discourses of *auteurism* (Vincendeau 2005: 140).

The disdain shown by classical criticism in France to the projected *académisme* (formulaic conventionalism) of genre cinema, whilst having little impact on the commercial prioritisation of genre in the film industry, does, nevertheless share with it the accommodation of projected hierarchies of genre that, in line with all modes of

---

17 As Ince points out (Ince 2008: 9), such attacks have been less successful in proposing viable alternative discourses of contemporary French film criticism.

mainstream cultural production, perpetuates ideologies of gendered identity. Such hierarchies have historically served to elevate genres associated with the masculine – the thriller, historical film, war film and western (although the latter remains extremely rare in French cinematic production) – above those conventionally associated with the feminine (romance, romantic comedy, family drama and melodrama), with female directors and with a projected and homogenised female spectatorship. The reductive parameters of such associations have a clear (if unquantifiable) impact on the generic choices of women's filmmaking, yet a converse trajectory can also be suggested as these same associations can be exploited in order to get financial backing for projects which are perceived in terms of their gendered genre, but include thematic and narrative elements that might be rejected outside of these frameworks. Such engagements with generic templates and expectations are evident in Masson's use of romance and detective narratives in order to debunk the former and subvert the later (as discussed further in Chapter 3). Altman's seminal reworking of genre theory, which asserts the inherent hybridity, evolution and ideological functions at stake in the multiple investments in genre production and reception (Altman 1999), paved the way for a radically flexible critical approach to genre as 'whatever we collectively think it is' (Moine 2002: 172). The perceived boundaries between *auteur* and genre-led production are increasingly blurred and subject to more explicit reconciliations. Moine reveals such an operation within the dominant generic field of French comedy in her identification of the shift in the cultural hierarchy of genre through the emergence of a *comédie d'auteur* (itself set in strategic opposition to the Holly-wood model of a *comédie d'action*) (Moine 2005: 224). This arrival has multiple functions in its widening of an *auteur*'s popular box office success and its rehabilitation of constructions of French national comedy through the authenticating labels of a mutually valorising directorial identity and national brand (ibid.: 228).[18]

The conventional distinction between *auteur* and genre-led production is embedded in the projected opposition between popular cinema (popular in the sense of its targeting of a wider public) and *auteur* cinema. Attempts to delineate these boundaries, such as Prédal's confusing claim that 'Le cinéma d'auteur n'est pas populaire car il

18 One of Moine's central examples is Vernoux's *Reines d'un jour* which is discussed further in Chapter 4.

s'adresse aux individus plutôt qu'aux masses'[19] (Prédal 2008: 44), serve merely to reveal an over-investment in the figure of the *auteur* and the mutual dependence of much of the critical establishment and *auteurism*. In an angry response to *Cahiers du cinéma*'s inclusion of only three contemporary French *auteurs* in their review of film production of the 2000s, Ciment describes the pernicious perpetuation of such stark binaries as 'le fléau de la vie culturelle française' (the scourge of French cultural life) fuelled by the obsessive reporting of box office results that almost entirely excludes less profitable films from popular media coverage (Ciment 2010: 1).

The increasing polarisation between projects with vast budgets and more modest productions produced on diverse media platforms has brought about a crisis in the funding of mid-range budget films or *films du milieu* in France. In an impassioned speech delivered at the Césars award ceremony in 2007, the director Pascale Ferran criticised current funding arrangements which, had they been in place in the 1960s, would, she argued, have blocked iconic productions by Truffaut, Demy and Resnais. The subsequent formation of the 'Club des 13', a lobbying group including scriptwriters, directors, producers and distributors,[20] led to the publication of a 2008 report which criticised the transfer of commercial power from cinema producers to distributors (television and global distribution) and the resultant prioritisation of the potential mediatisation and fit with prime-time programming of a product rather than its qualities as a film (Ferran 2008: 7). The squeezed but diverse middle ground identified in the report, described as 'des films ambitieux à vocation populaire ... pour les budgets moyens – 4 à 7 millions d'euros'[21] (Ferran 2008: 23), dropped from an annual production of 49 in 2004 to 19 in 2006 (ibid.: 23). Lvovsky's profile (her work having broken the threshold of one million admissions with the commercial success of *Les Sentiments*) escapes this bracket, yet the other three filmmakers discussed here fall exactly within this category and continue to struggle to secure funding for

19 '*Auteur* cinema is not popular cinema as it engages with individuals rather than with the masses.'

20 The founding members of the Club des 13 (which now has over forty members) were: Cécile Vargaftig, Jacques Audiard, Pascale Ferran, Claude Miller, Denis Freyd, Arnaud Louvet, Patrick Sobelman, Edouard Weil, Fabienne Vonier, Stéphane Goudet, Claude-Eric Poiroux, Jean-Jacques Ruttner and François Yon.

21 'ambitious films aimed at a popular audience ... with medium-sized budgets of €4–€7 million'.

their films. The reflexive narrative of Masson's *Pourquoi(pas) le Brésil?*

formulates an explicit engagement with the unwelcome intervention in the creative process that accompanies the search for funding. The financing structures of the most recent films by Vernoux and Cabrera reflect a more nuanced reading of the relationship between cinema and television in contemporary French film production as they reflect a growing recognition that greater artistic freedom is maintained when working with certain private television channels (notably Canal plus and Arte) than for mainstream cinema production companies in collaboration with mainstream television partners.

Le jeune cinéma français: locating the political

The final negotiation that I want to broach here, and which remains inherently linked to the consideration of the relationship between *auteur* and popular cinema, is that of the location of the political in contemporary French film. This Introduction has situated the following chapters within the historical and commercial contexts of *auteurism*, genre and commercial process; however, it is also necessary to address the specific background of the hailing of a *jeune cinéma français* (young French cinema) that has dominated critical reception of films made in the 1990s in France, as evidenced in the volumes which address this phenomenon (including Prédal 2002, Marie 1998, Trémois 1997, Chauville 2000). The four directors discussed here all made their first feature films in the mid-1990s in the context of a generation of filmmakers whose work witnessed a return to a filmic and extra-filmic engagement with the socio-political realities of contemporary France and has been labelled as 'le jeune cinéma' or even 'la nouvelle nouvelle vague' (Grassin and Medioni 2005: 5). The emergence of such a model triggers comparison with the Nouvelle Vague, as discussed earlier and reveals a parallel overinvestment in the trope of the new (Nacache 2005: 63) to claim a unity and coherence deemed necessary to guide popular reception and valorise critical discourse. Nacache goes further to identify the terms of 'new' or 'young' as key 'opérateurs génériques' (genre-forming terms) (Nacache 2005: 58) in French cinema, traits which differ from standard understandings of genre in their foregrounding of shared function rather than comparable content. This construction is contextualised by a dominant critical discourse that rejects national tropes of cinema and marginalises analysis of constructions of national identity in contemporary film.

The identification of this new tendency, supported by a rise in the number of first films made, has no clear collective definition but markers include a return to codes of realism (after the dominance of the heritage film), a re-engagement with socio-political discourse and a narrative focus on marginalised protagonists whose identities are marked strongly by their situations of social and financial precarity. Martin O'Shaughnessy's important and lucid account of the reassertion of the political in contemporary French cinema, through films which disrupt 'the surface calm of political consensus, bringing struggle back to the surface, restoring grounds for critique and demonstrating the necessity of resistance' (O'Shaughnessy 2007: 179), identifies new articulations of a committed cinema following the collapse of funding networks for didactically oppositional political cinema. Whilst closely aligned with the identification of 'fragmentary stories of small groups and marginalised individuals evicted from broader solidarities, stripped of a public voice' (ibid.: 3), these films do not foreground the central characteristics of what might be broadly termed 'oppositional cinema'. These studies of *déliaison sociale* (societal breakdown), often located geographically in the struggling, post-industrial towns of northern France or in settings of rural desolation, enact a parallel remapping of the 'psychosocial territory of France' (Trémois 1997: 10). The focus on the plight of marginalised individuals, rather than social groups, and the emphasis on the impact of such struggle on individual subjectivity rather than on collective social discourse constructs a 'réalisme intérieur' (internal realism) (Prédal 2002: 73) in response to a consumer culture that triggers 'intense emotional experiences shaped by anxiety, alienation, resentment, and a detachment from others' (Denzin 1991: vii).

Whilst O'Shaughnessy includes Cabrera and Masson amongst 'less prominent figures ... whose work has played a central role in the re-emergence of commitment' (O'Shaughnessy 2007: 5), the output of the four directors discussed here, whilst exhibiting many characteristics of the 'jeune cinéma', remains absent from the already canonised films associated with this tendency. Most of the films discussed in this volume engage, through varying degrees of explicitness, with issues of socio-economic exclusion, the perpetuation of reductive gendered roles and the fragmentation of collective identities, yet the fact that this is often combined with and contained by a strident use of popular genre forms has seemingly excluded them from analysis. The knowingly formulaic foundations of genre film provide exaggerated reflections of dominant socio-cultural discourses and, as such, are capable of presenting a universally recognisable template against which challenge and subversion to such norms can be framed effectively. The consequences of such exploitations of mainstream and commercially favoured generic forms are largely underestimated in their potential to contest powerful assumptions, including the assumption 'that women are unfunny as well as non-violent, domesticated and outside history' (Rollet 2003: 130), and have the potential to reach wider audiences than films which foreground an explicit political engagement. Masson's use of the overstated generic templates of the romance facilitate an acute feminist critique of the socio-economic position of women, implementing 'excess as self-reflexive commentary on the genre' (Grant 2008: 289) and critiquing a generalised tendency towards the (neo)conservative reification of nostalgia and the common misogynist blindspots of postmodern discourses (see Denzin 1991). This exploitation of genre forms fits helpfully with the functions of a *cinéma social* working through its 'capacité de résistance aux images face aux attendus de la représentation' (Osganian 2003: 51) (capacity of resistance to images in the face of representational expectations) and encouraging reflection on the ideological apparatus of mainstream cultural production.

Critical revalorisations of cultural discourse that espouse radical form and formal innovation as a measure of political intent also work against inclusion of these films in canons of contemporary French cinema. Rancière's denunciation of the absence of formal innovation in political film in the 1990s (Rancière 2000) is founded on a critique of the narrative recipe of a confirmation of spectatorial expectations and the unexpected to form the 'réel de la fiction' (the real of fiction). Rancière's preferred mode, 'fictions politiques du réel' (political fictions of the real) relies on the combination of complex layered structures and documentary style to explore the nature of truth (Rancière 2000: 63), his central example being Godard's *Histoire(s) du cinéma*. Whilst no one would contest the inherently political nature of film form, it remains clear that the conventions of the 'réel de la fiction' (including generic templates) can themselves function as devices of demystification to open up the simultaneously constructed spectatorial discourses of pleasurable recognition *and* critical *distanciation*. The desire to characterise and construct the history of contemporary French film is already asserting the twin dominance of the divergent threads of a return to political realism and the foregrounding of explicitly political content (Laurent Cantet, the Dardennes, Bruno Dumont) and a radically haptic cinema of sensation (Claire Denis, Philippe Grandrieux). The oppositional exclusivity of such threads is superficial (as shown in Beugnet and Ezra's dazzling reworking of French film history (Ezra and Beugnet 2010)) yet still powerful in its moulding of popular and academic production, reception and cultural longevity. The films under discussion in this volume have not been included in either thread.

Social intimacy

The shift, identified by critics of *le jeune cinéma*, from a political focus on the social collective to the crises of individual subjectivity is of course but one example of the cultural articulation of the late capitalist insistence on the primacy of the individual, empowered to construct their unique identity through material consumption and lifestyle choices. The lack of access to metanarratives of political change and identity has been contrasted with an exclusive focus on the personal that goes beyond the emergence of identity politics to risk the denial of social and historical consciousness. Yet, rather than receiving such shifts as the articulation of an unbreachable divide between discourses of a systemic political and those of the personal, an acceptance that the feminist insistence that the personal is always political constitutes a two-way dynamic and thus enables us to recognise these films as asserting, rather than denying, the inextricable nature of relationships between the political, the social and the individual. The personal remains political and the individual is always already social.

The negotiation central to all contemporary constructions of the political and which remains most striking in its permeation of every one of the diverse films discussed in this volume is that of the boundary between the public and the private, between the social and the intimate. The central problematic of the bleeding of socio-political discourse into the realms of the private is clearly at stake in several films in this volume that critique the individualist escapism of the romance narrative and the reduction of relationships to commodity exchanges (Lvovsky's *Oublie-moi*, Masson's *A vendre*, Vernoux's *Rien à faire*) and reveal the connections between personal crisis and social malaise (Cabrera's *Demain et encore demain*). In the same way that O'Shaughnessy recognises the potential for melodrama, despite and because of its focus on the individual and the familial,[22] to stage an 'acerbic critique of individualism' (O'Shaughnessy 2007: 3), so the different genres represented through the films in this volume (particularly romance and comedy) problematise such discourses and, through the adaptation of both form and content, challenge conventional boundaries between public and private realms.

Whilst the sustained critique of dominant discourses remains a powerful tool, I want to argue that the films discussed in this volume go beyond a challenge to oppositional discourses of the political and the personal, the social and the intimate, to create a strikingly coherent formulation of an intermediate term, a radical combination that I will describe as social intimacy. Avoiding the dominant model of the *jeune cinéma* which foregrounds a 'non-reconciliation absolue entre individu et société' (Osganian 2003: 52) (an absolute lack of reconciliation between individual and society), these films tend to ambiguous or hopeful interventions. The final sequences of many of the films discussed in the following chapters suggest narrative resolution not as closure but as an opening to the social. The final sequences of these films show their respective central protagonists, from the broken-hearted Marie-Do in *Rien à faire* (Vernoux, 1999) to the reflexive director-protagonist in *Demain et encore demain* (Cabrera, 1997), from the uncanny romantic dreamer of *Love Me* (Masson, 2000) to the new mother embracing social heritage in *Faut que ça danse!* (Lvovsky, 2007), embarking upon uncertain alliances that assert the necessary power of the social. Such constructions of a social intimacy chime with other articulations of a political discourse that Baqué identifies as best articulated in the field of contemporary documentary (discussed further in Chapter 1), that of an 'être avec' (a being with) which in addition to its ability to 'mettre au jour les dysfonctionne-

---

22 The dominance of the *cellule familiale* (family unit), seen as the politically conservative and nostalgic main unit of social organisation of contemporary French cinema (Frodon 2005: 74), is shown as an inadequate framework, incapable of supporting identity in isolation from wider communities and social groups.

ments d'une société malade, éveiller les consciences et construire le témoignage'[23] (Baqué 2004: 281) articulates the continuing possibility of constructing new solidarities *through* the intimate.

The 'continuing negotiations' proposed in this Introduction resist closure and project their multiple and shifting dynamics across the following four chapters of this volume. That the structure of each of the four chapters is led by the identification of an individual director must be seen as a further pragmatic negotiation – that between the series and the volume, the Introduction and the chapters. The construction of *auteurism* posits a critical overview of the work of a director that suggests the support of critical statement by both coverage and selection, yet, as I write, these four directors are all still working. The configuration of different historical and cultural discourses will further shift around the nexus of their authorial identities as but one element of their oeuvre and therefore the proposed readings in the volume, free of unassailable retrospection, are presented without a general conclusion and wilfully open to further negotiation.

References

Altman, Rick (1999), *Film / Genre*, London, BFI.

Audé, Françoise (2002), *Cinéma d'elles 1981–2001*, Lausanne, L'Age d'homme.

Audé, Françoise and Garbarz, Franck (1998), 'Interview avec Laetitia Masson: On n'est pas neuf devant l'amour", *positif*, 451, 27–32.

Baqué, Dominique (2004), *Pour un nouvel art politique. De l'art contemporain au documentaire*, Paris, Flammarion.

Battersby, Christine (1989), *Gender and Genius: Towards a Feminist Aesthetics*, London, The Women's Press.

Becker, Howard (1982), *Art Worlds*, Berkeley, University of California Press.

Blewitt, John (1993), 'Film, Ideology and Bourdieu's Critique of Public Taste', *British Journal of Aesthetics*, 33 (4), 367–72.

Bourdieu, Pierre (1979), *La Distinction: critique sociale du jugement*, Paris, Editions de minuit.

Bourdieu, Pierre (1992), *Les Règles de l'art*, Paris, Seuil.

Brassart, Alain (2006), 'Qu'est-ce que l'auteurisme 30 ans après la Nouvelle Vague? Un exemple: Arnaud Desplechin' (Juillet–Août) www.cadrage.net/dossier/desplechin.html (accessed 10 October 2007).

Chauville, Christophe (2000), *Le Dictionnaire du jeune cinéma français*, Paris, Scope.

Ciment, Michel (2010), 'Editorial: une question de crédibilité', *positif*, 587, 1.

---

23 'to shed light on the dysfunctional nature of a sick society, to raise awareness and to bear witness'.

Creton, Laurent (1997), *Cinéma et marché*, Paris, Armand Colin.

Darre, Yann (1986), 'Les créateurs dans la division du travail, le cas du cinéma d'auteur', in R. Moulin (ed.), *Sociologie de l'art*, Paris, La documentation française (2nd edition 1999, L'Harmattan).

De Baecque, Antoine (1997), 'Aux aguets: que reste-t-il de la politique des auteurs?' *Cahiers du cinéma*, 518 (November), 22–5.

De Bruyn, Olivier (2000), '"Love Me": Les fantômes de la liberté' *positif*, 469, 21–2.

Denzin, Norman (1991), *Images of Postmodern Society. Social Theory and Contemporary Cinema*, London, Sage.

Dobson, Julia (2008), 'Jacques Audiard: Contesting Filiations' in Kate Ince (ed.), *Five Directors: Auteurism from Assayas to Ozon*, Manchester, Manchester University Press, 38–58.

Ezra, Elisabeth and Beugnet Martine (2010), 'Traces of the Modern: An Alternative History of French Cinema', *Studies in French Cinema*, 10 (1), 11–38.

Ferran, Pascale (2008), *Le milieu n'est plus un pont mais une faille, Le Club des 13: rapport de synthèse*, Paris, Stock.

Forbes, Jill and Kelly, Michael (eds) (1992), *Cinema in France after the New Wave*, Basingstoke, Palgrave Macmillan.

Frodon, Jean-Michel (2005), 'Famille politique', *Cahiers du cinéma* (September), 72–6.

Grant, Barry Keith (2008), 'The Action Films of Kathryn Bigelow' in Barry Keith Grant (ed), *Auteurs and Authorship: A Film Reader*, Oxford, Blackwell, 280–91.

Grassin, Sophie and Medioni, Gilles (2005), 'Spécial Cannes: la nouvelle nouvelle vague', *L'Express*, 2228 (May), 5–7.

Ince, Kate (ed.) (2008), *Five Directors: Auteurism from Assayas to Ozon*, Manchester, Manchester University Press.

Jeancolas, Jean-Pierre, Meusy, Jean-Jacques and Pinel, Vincent (1996), *L'Auteur du film: description d'un combat*, Arles, Actes sud and Institut Lumière.

Lamberbourg, Adeline (2010), 'Parcours croisés de Dominique Cabrera, cinéaste, et de ses proches collaborateurs', *Temporalités* (November), http://temporalites.revues.org/index1218.html

Lebovic, Elisabeth (ed.) (2004), *L'Intime*, Paris, Ecole nationale supérieure des beaux arts.

Marie, Michel (1998), *Le jeune cinéma français*, Paris, Nathan.

Martin, Alison (2003), 'Refocusing Authorship in Women's Filmmaking' in Jacqueline Levitin, Judith Plessis and Valérie Raoul (eds), *Women Filmmakers. Refocusing*, London and New York, Routledge, 29–38.

Maule, Rosanna (2008), *Beyond Auteurism: New Directions in Authorial Film Practices in France, Italy and Spain since the 1980s*, Bristol and Chicago, Intellect.

Mayne, Judith (1990), *The Woman at the Keyhole. Feminism and Women's Cinema*, Bloomington, Indiana University Press.

Moine, Raphaelle (2002), *Les Genres du cinéma*, Paris, Nathan.

Moine, Raphaelle (2005), 'Reconfigurations génériques de la comédie dans le cinéma français contemporain: l'émergence des 'comédies d'auteur', in

Raphaelle Moine (ed.), *Le Cinéma français face aux genres*, Paris, Association Française de recherches sur l'histoire du cinéma, 223–32.

Nacache, Jacqueline (2005), 'Nouvelle vague et jeune cinéma: les "opérateurs génériques" à la genrification du cinéma français' in Raphaelle Moine (ed.), *Le Cinéma français face aux genres*, Paris, Association Française de Recherches sur l'Histoire du Cinéma, 57–66.

Osganian, Patricia (2003), 'D' "Amerika rapports de classe" à "Rosetta". Sortie du naturalisme et subjectivation du réel', *Mouvements*, 3, 51–7.

O'Shaughnessy, Martin (2007), *The New Face of Political Cinema. Commitment in French Film since 1995*, New York and Oxford, Berghahn Books.

Prédal, Réné (2001), *Le cinéma d'auteur, une vielle lune?*, Paris, Editions du Cerf.

Prédal, Réné (2002), *Le Jeune Cinéma français*, Paris, Nathan.

Prédal, Réné (2008), *Le Cinéma français depuis 2000*, Paris, Armand Colin.

Puaux, Françoise (2001), 'Entretien avec Dominique Cabrera', *Cinémaction*, 99, 173–80.

Rabinovitz, Lauren (2005), 'Past Imperfect: Feminism and Social Histories of Silent Film', in Rosanna Maul (ed.), *Femmes et cinéma muet: nouvelles problématqiues, nouvelles méthodologies*, special issue of *Cinémas*, 16 (1), 21–34.

Rancière, Jacques (2000), 'Il est arrivé quelque chose au réel', *Cahiers du cinéma*, 545, 62–4.

Rollet, Brigitte (2003), 'Women Directors and Genre Films in France', in Jaqueline Levitin, Judith Plessis and Valérie Raoul (eds). *Women Filmmakers: Refocusing*, London and New York, Routledge, 127–37.

Sarris, Andrew (1968), *The American Cinema: Directors and Directions 1929–1968*, New York, Dutton.

Scott, Joan and Keates, Debra (eds) (2004), *Going Public: Feminism and the Shifting Boundaries of the Private Sphere*, Chicago, University of Illinois Press.

Sellier, Geneviève (2003), 'French Women Making Films in the 1990s' in R. Célestin, Eliane Dalmolin and Isabelle de Courtivron (eds), *Beyond French Feminisms: Debates on Women, Politics and Culture in France*, Basingstoke, Palgrave Macmillan.

Sherzer, Dina (2001), 'Gender and Sexuality in New New Wave Cinema', in Alex Hughes and James Williams (eds), *Gender and French Cinema*, Oxford and New York, Berg, 227– 40.

Stoll, Georges (2004), 'Donne-toi la peine, écoute-moi raconter des mythes' in Elisabeth Lebovic (ed.), *L'Intime*, Paris, Ecole nationale supérieure des beaux arts, 29–33.

Tarr, Carrie with Rollet, Brigitte (2001), *Cinema and the Second Sex: Women's Filmmaking in France in the 1980s and 1990s*, London, Continuum.

Tasker, Yvonne (2002), *50 Contemporary Filmmakers*, London and New York, Routledge.

Tasker, Yvonne (2002), *Fifty Contemporary Filmmakers*, London and New York, Routledge.

Trémois, Claude (1997), *Les Enfants de la liberté*, Paris, Seuil.

Vasse, David (2008), *Le nouvel âge du cinéma d'auteur français*, Paris, Klincksieck.

Vincendeau, Ginette (1989), 'Vu de Londres: mais où est passée la théorie

1

Dominique Cabrera: intimate constructions of a 'bonheur collectif'

Dominique Cabrera was born in 1957 in Relizane, Algeria, but left with her family for France in 1962 after the declaration of Algerian independence. She graduated from IDHEC (Institut des hautes études cinématographiques) in 1980, having specialised in directing and editing, and initially found work as an editor with FR3 television's regional services. Cabrera was a founding member of the Communist weekly *Marianne* and was directly involved in socialist party activism in the 1970s, serving as a local councillor. These party political commitments were combined with her filmmaking in the founding, with J. P. Thorn and G. Robard, of a production company, Ergonaut, which began by making short films that focused on situations of 'solidarité ouvrière' (working-class solidarity) commissioned by the major trade unions (Puaux 2001: 175). Through these links she met the writer and then editor of *Cahiers du cinéma* (1966–78), Jean-Louis Comolli, with whom she has written and edited documentary projects, produced by Iskra.

Although rejecting any deterministic notion that her cinematic output is determined by her sex, asserting frankly that 'je n'ai pas le sentiment que c'est seulement mon utérus qui pense quand je fais un film'[1] (ibid.: 179), Cabrera consistently posits the iconic female directors Agnès Varda and Marta Meszaros as the first and enduring influences on her career. Describing the ways in which her filmmaking is influenced by all aspects of her identity, including gender, Cabrera foregrounds her self-identification and sense of solidarity as a

[1] 'I don't get the feeling that it is just my uterus that does the thinking when I'm filming.'

feminist as vital to her engagement with politics and with cinema, an engagement counterbalanced by the power of creativity to construct a space of liberation from the self (ibid.: 179). Assertion of her own position is mitigated however by a clear awareness of the contextualising discourses and structures of the film industry which 'se nourrit sans cesse de la chair fraîche, notamment du côté des femmes. Les femmes de la jeune génération ont-elles vraiment fait leur place? Et les femmes qui tournaient des films dans les années 80, sont-elles toujours là?'[2] (ibid.: 178).

Starting with the conventional first productions of short films, she then moved in the mid-1990s to focus on documentary, a form whose influence has an enduring presence in her feature films. Identifying herself as a maker of mid-budget films (*Nadia et les hippopotames* had a budget of €1.2 million, *Folle embellie* €2.9 million), she maintains the importance of accessibility and narrative to political engagement. Her oeuvre presents a persistent exploration and consistent focus on the relationship between the individual and the collective, between the private and the public across a breadth of subjects that include the continuing legacy of France's colonial past (*L'Autre Côté de la mer* (1997)), contemporary class identities (*Nadia et les hippopotames* (1999)) and the status of the mother in contemporary social discourse and family structure (*Le Lait de la tendresse humaine* (2001)). Her engagement with the complex articulation of social identity extends in her work to an exploration of her own speaking and filming position, through the intensely intimate first-person documentary *Demain et encore demain (journal 1995)* (1997) which involves the filming of herself in an explicitly autobiographical context. Starting with a discussion of an early short film, this chapter will bring together discussion of her fiction and documentary work to reveal the central engagement with a renegotiation of cinematic convention and an intrinsic assertion of the therapeutic power of the moving image.

Obvious imperatives would invite this chapter to begin with a discussion of Cabrera's first short film *L'Air d'aimer*, made in 1985. Yet the film serves as a useful introduction in ways that exceed its chronological importance, as many of the central engagements of Cabrera's oeuvre that I will discuss are evident in this intriguing 13

2 'has an unceasing appetite for fresh flesh, particularly that of women. Have the new generation of women really made a place for themselves? And the women who were making films in the 80s, are they still here?'

minute film. The personal and social imperative of witnessing stories, the inherent link between the individual and society, between private and public, the therapeutic nature of the moving image and the possibility of transformation through art towards reconciliation, both with the social and with the self, are all present here. *L'Air d'aimer* centres on a series of meetings between an office worker, Raymond (Michael Lonsdale), and a young photographer, Frédéric. Lonsdale's melancholic nostalgia infuses the first half of the film, exploiting the almost uncanny presence constructed by his 'étrangeté douce, sa quiètude impressionnante, sa voix singulièrement susurrée' (de Baecque 2005: 18) (gentle strangeness, impressive calmness and unique whispering voice). After a first chance encounter the two men meet regularly at lunchtimes in the Jardin des Tuileries. The solitary Raymond confides in Frédéric that his wife has left him and spins a melancholy tale, revealing his background (his childhood in Algeria) and the double loss of Algeria and his wife, losses which are explicitly enmeshed in his telling of a love story about an old man whose love had left Algeria for France. To mark every day of her absence the old man put new leaves under her door as a measure of his devotion and of time passing, the time of their separation. When the woman returned the new and old leaves blew around her in the wind – a creative and dramatic demonstration of enduring love. The old man, however, was now confined to hospital and did not live to see her again. The evocative and moving narrative that Raymond shares inspires him to construct a parallel ritual as he substitutes photographs for the leaves and asks Frédéric to take his portrait every day until his wife, Isabelle, comes back to him. However, whilst this exercise begins as a documenting of Raymond's suspended state of waiting, with the polaroids functioning as a portraiture which both captures the present moment and bears witness to time passing, this documentation is revealed gradually, not as the monument to a love ultimately lost as in the story of the leaves but as a therapeutic process that will enable him to recover. The changing representations of Raymond allow the audience to perceive the evolutions in his state of mind and the ultimate impact of this process is represented through a telling juxtaposition of the still and the moving image.

The first photographs of Raymond convey a sense of awkward stasis and isolation, a reading supported by the frequent juxtaposition of careful compositions of the Maillol statues scattered in the gardens.

However, these statues assume an increasingly sensual presence as, following the example of a blind man, Raymond approaches and touches them. This sensual reawakening is represented as insufficient in itself however through Cabrera's recurring juxtaposition (through editing rather than spatial proximity) of Raymond with women lying immobile in the gardens next to the statues. An explicit intertextual marker follows as a lengthy close-up of a woman sleeping on the grass reveals her makeshift pillow to be a copy of Kawabata's *House of the Sleeping Beauties*, a text characterised by a sense of melancholy stasis, displaced eroticism and mortality.[3] The central character's frequenting of a brothel in which he pays to sleep next to (sedated) young women in order to gain 'chi' from their youth functions as an indication to the spectator of the foolhardiness of Raymond substituting art for life in an attempt to deny mortality and the passing of time. Raymond's return to the social and the sensual is achieved, not through a sensualised response to the statues but through the impact of the moving image. The pivotal narrative moment occurs as he gathers the series of portrait polaroids together and flicks through them to create a sense of animation, change and movement to his own identity. The sense of reanimation and a return to life is immediately supported by Raymond's behaviour as he begins to interact with those around him, becomes agent and observer as he takes pictures himself and invites another woman to pose for pictures with them. The narrative voiceover further emphasises the therapeutic charge of movement: 'Puisque les statues pouvaient marcher, Raymond se dit que les amants perdus s'oublieraient.'[4]

The use of direct sound, including birdsong, police sirens and a downpour, contrasts with the melancholy music which underpinned the first sequences and adds to the sensual immediacy of the later sequences as the carefully framed static compositions of the statues fade to accommodate the multiple tracking shots of Raymond's final trajectories. This move also represents the relationship between documentary technique and fiction film in Cabrera's oeuvre and the continual dynamic which functions between the forms and genres associated with both. This chapter will return to the proposal of the

3 Yasanuri Kawabata (1899–1972) was associated with the Japanese Neo-sensualists.
4 'As statues could now walk, Raymond told himself that lost loves could also be forgotten.'

therapeutic charge of the moving image in its discussion of Cabrera's moving account of her own relocation in the social through the intimate first-person documentary *Demain et encore demain*. The choice of a public park, whilst recalling the formal Nouvelle Vague traits of Varda's *Cléo de 5 à 7*, serves as a location in which conventional constructions of the public and the private, the personal and the social can be challenged. This use is repeated in the later fiction short, *Traverser le jardin* (*Crossing the garden*), which is set in the equally recognisable Parisian location of the Jardin des plantes. The narrative focuses on a meeting arranged by the central character, Hélène, with her lover's estranged son, Marc, in order to pass on the bad news of his father's serious illness. The film maintains a documentary feel constructed through the use of direct sound, the predominantly static camera and use of long shots, yet remains playfully aware of its own constructed and fictional status as witnessed in the inclusion of a self-reflexive set piece featuring a conversation between two women who are making a documentary about the gardens. The use of static camera allows Cabrera to construct an extended formal exercise in framing and positioning as the two central protagonists begin awkwardly seated on extreme ends of a bench and, after a series of dramatic departures by the son, negotiate shared confidences and space. The angry estrangement of the son and his refusal to be reconciled with his absent 'melodramatic' father is underscored as painful conversations invoking guilt, fidelity and loss are contrasted with the footage of the surrounding park life; idyllic scenes of family outings and lovers' meetings. Such life-affirming elements are represented via tracking shots in marked juxtaposition to the static camera used to film Hélène's conversations with Marc. Their conversation remains haunted by the absent father, and faltering communication is further highlighted by the intervention of direct sound and the almost musical accompaniment of their meeting by the sounds and conversations generated by other occupants of the park and characterised predominantly by a sense of blissful intimacy. Marc and Héléne are finally reconciled, united in their mutual horror of death which is repudiated by the surrounding images of natural abundance and *joie de vivre* epitomised in the lengthy, sensual close-up of the huge pink lollipops eagerly devoured by children. Cabrera again employs a technological device, in parallel to the use of the photographer's camera in *Un Air d'aimer*, to perform a *mise en abyme* of the role of her own film. As Marc relaxes in Hélène's company he embarks upon a passionate discussion of his work and the scientific equipment, that he has with him, which is used to measure air currents. This device functions clearly as a metaphor for the measurement of breath and the subsequent evidence of life, but also as an indicator of the parallel role of the camera as a technological witness to elements of life represented both through the narrative and through the sensual impact of the gardens.

Documentary evidence: the Val Fourré films

The presence of the documentary is evident in both short films discussed above, and the conventional role of the form in bearing witness to stories and giving access to locations and people not normally seen or heard in film remains central to the development of Cabrera's documentary oeuvre. The elements of documentary style identified in the discussion of a selection of Cabrera's short films discussed above continue to be evident in her full-length fiction features, yet one of the central aims of this chapter is to assert Cabrera's status as one of the most engaged and successful documentary filmmakers working in France today. A series of films that she made on the impact of changes to the physical urban environment provide further evidence of the centrality in all her work of an insistence upon the recognition of the social as personal to all and the importance of a projected *bonheur collectif* or collective happiness. These films also demonstrate Cabrera's engagement with the structures of documentary-making itself, with its dominant modes and genealogies and the ethical questions that cannot be sidestepped either when filming others or when filming the self. Michael Renov sets out the ethical challenge facing the creation and reception of contemporary documentary:

> The pitting of ethics against epistemology is highly pertinent for documentary studies. When we talk about the prospects for documentary representation, we are most likely asking about knowledge ... The ethical view refuses this appropriative stance, choosing instead receptivity and responsibility, justice over freedom. (Renov 2004: 161)

Cabrera's documentary output addresses the ethics of appropriation and represents an ongoing exploration of the relationship between filmmaker, documentary subject and spectator. In 1993, Cabrera made a series of films that bear witness to the changes wrought on a community by the demolition of tower blocks on an estate in Val Fourré, Mantes la Jolie. The area, 50 kilometres to the west of Paris, underwent intense urbanisation in the 1960s to house workers for the car industry and, in the 1990s was characterised by a high immigrant population and unemployment running at 27 per cent. These films serve as an explicit intervention in a public and filmic discourse that defines such locations, and their resident communities, as problematic sites of social and economic failure (of 'fracture sociale'), tension, exclusion and alienation. One of the first films, *Une Poste à la Courneuve* is the most traditional of her documentary works – fulfilling the function of documentary as visible evidence, recording everyday hardships of the local community,[5] whilst invoking a wider picture of the relationship between the public services and the individual citizen in need. Cabrera remarks that she made this film because 'cette idée de service public, d'égalité, d'un espace commun, qui est celui de la nation, de la République, me tient à coeur'[6] (Mathieu 2003: 71). She researched the project for a year, working with the sociologist Suzanne Rosenberg on the evaluation of public services in deprived areas, and showed the final edit to post office workers before permitting any public screenings.

Cabrera's main concern for her longer film on the same issues, *Chronique d'une banlieue ordinaire*,[7] was to produce a film that would serve as a counter to the dominant media coverage of events, which would draw a parallel between the built environment of the towers and the perceived failure of such communities, thus positing the demolition as a marker of a new start in which the past communities and abandoned built environment have no positive values. Such coverage thus severed the link between community and place, suggesting that material regeneration, the reduction of the towers to rubble, is an uncontested marker of social progress and normalisation. Cabrera's interest was in going beyond such reductive constructs of the relation-

---

5 The subject matter and use of framing devices in the film recalls Kieslowski's documentary *The Office* (1966).

6 'this idea of public services, of equality, of a shared space which is that of the nation, of the Republic, is dear to my heart'.

7 The term *banlieue* remains hard to translate into English as its topographical equivalent is the suburbs, yet its socio-economic equivalent is the inner city.

ship between an individual and their spatial environment in order to assert the role of the condemned and vilified towers in providing community and a positive sense of place to their tenants. In pursuit of the past life of the towers, rather than investment in their projected replacements, Cabrera contacted former tenants and invited them to revisit their old apartments, now empty and ready for demolition. The film is made up of a series of moving encounters between ex-tenants and the rooms in which they once lived and it is their personal recollections, stories and memories that construct the narrative of the towers rather than the impersonal public discourse of urban renewal and economic regeneration.

Giving a voice and assuring the socio-cultural representation of the tenants' experiences constitutes a central element of Cabrera's project and is indicated explicitly in her choice of title which immediately recalls Jean Rouch's seminal documentary *Chronique d'un été* (1961) in which ordinary Parisians were asked about their dreams and desires, a process which ultimately incorporated their own responses to the edited rushes of the film. Rouch's foregrounding of the ethical and formal challenges of filming others forms a political and aesthetic response to the 'dominance of the victim as the realist documentary subject' (Winston 1995: 230) which permeates the history of the documentary form. Rouch's film asserts the position of those filmed as subjects of the documentary, subject *to* the consequences of being filmed and creative subjects who engage with questions of self-representation. This assertion of the voices and emotional responses of the ex-tenants affirms the subjective, lived experience of place – an experience that prevails long after the physical destruction of the towers and their replacement by the next utopian model. Rather than celebrating 'la mise à mort d'une forme architecturale dans laquelle le "mal des banlieues" est localisé',[8] Cabrera's film celebrates the ties of community, the solidarity of neighbours and the emphatic emotional engagement with these lived spaces delivered through the memories of these tenants. The nostalgic narratives shared by the tenants provide evidence enough of their positive experiences of such spaces, yet the power of many of these sequences is located in their physical and sensual engagement with the apartments. Different tenants recreate their sensual experiences living in the flats; a woman crouches on a

---

8 'the condemnation of an architectural form seen as harbouring the "problems of the banlieue"'.

balcony to recreate her visual perspective as a child, a man peels back layers of wallpaper in search of his child's drawings, a woman retraces the position of her prayer mat.

The demonised towers, labelled in public discourse as redundant and removed from all indicators of aesthetic value or sensual pleasure, are thus reinstated as spaces of beauty. The tenants' personal, sensual responses are reinforced by Cabrera's stylised filming of the empty interiors of the building which punctuate the tenants' stories. The use of extreme close-ups of the exotic blooms on wallpaper prints, the careful Mondrianesque compositions of doorways and the slow melancholic tracking shots along balconies and corridors construct a sense of texture and haptic visuality which foregrounds an intimate, multi-sensory perception of these spaces rather than a distanced consideration of them in terms of realist or symbolic representation.[9] Whilst the recurring, sweeping tracking shots provide a clear inter-textual link to Godard's *2 ou 3 choses que je sais d'elle*, and the latter's exposition of the alienating impact of such tower blocks and estates on the working populations, Cabrera's independently mobile camera performs an explicit reclaiming of the iconic architectural imagery. The film language thus constructs the built environment as a lived space, inseparable from its inhabitants and performing a positive role in their constructions of identity.

Cabrera's film thus works to undermine distinctions between the personal and the social and to disrupt dominant representations of these spaces, yet the structure of the film pursues these subversions further through an explicit *mise en abyme* of the conventional role of the documentary format. The film is punctuated by both documen-tary footage of the now derelict towers and utopian public informa-tion films that were made to mark the opening of the towers and which, through their utopian and positive narration, reflect ironically on the dominant discourse in which the towers are now represented. Eschewing the use of additional commentary, Cabrera distances her own film from past documentaries through the use of classic oppositional editing. Cabrera's assertion of the inseparability of environment and identity constructed through the filmic integration of past memory into present space is distinguished from the public information films which focus on discourses of modernity, progress

9 For further discussion of the haptic see Marks 2002.

and the commodification of a homogenised 'lifestyle' which forms an ironic contrast to the ex-tenants' diversity. Yet, if the narrative content of *Chronique d'une banlieue ordinaire* can be read as overly and simplistically nostalgic, it remains clear that the formal strategies of the film, and their engagement with the representation of time, subvert the dominance of linear narratives of progress and substitution. The structure of *Chronique d'une banlieue ordinaire* goes further in challenging the dominant social and filmic tropes of degeneration and regeneration that address such places and their tenants by insisting upon the coexistence of past and present, the centrality of memory and experience in constructing identity and the enduring quality of sensual experience.

In a rare discussion of the film, Jean-Louis Comolli suggests that Cabrera's strategy of asserting the past life of the building by interviewing ex-tenants fails as 'C'est ce retour des vivants qui reveille les fantômes, et fait du même coup apparaître les traces anciennes comme telles, comme traces'[10] (Comolli 1994: 42). Yet this account overlooks the subversion of cinematic convention that works to prevent the temporal redundancy of such traces. Deleuze's analysis of the rise of *cinéma vérité* as constructing a representation of the real that is ultimately reliant upon the accepted norms of cinematographic fiction (Deleuze 1985: 149) is relevant here as Cabrera's insistent disruptions of linear time and space in the film reveal a reflexive recognition of the pervasive role of the cinematographic conventions of fiction film in spectatorial expectations of the documentary. A striking example of such disruption is achieved through Cabrera's play with film stock and the audience expectations that accompany it. The conventional opposition between the 1992 colour footage of the flats and the black-and-white sequences provided by the public information films of 45 years ago mutates into a more ludic pattern as nostalgic, colour, home movie footage from the 1960s is intercut with formal, black-and-white compositions of present day groups. As Cabrera's camera shifts between tracking from left to right and from right to left in the melancholic sequences of the deserted buildings, conventions of camera movement and the accompanying narrative connotations of progression or flashback are upset. Such formal, temporal disorientations contest the public discourses of regenera-

10 'It is the return of the living that awakens the ghosts and, in the same way, reveals the old traces for what they are, mere traces.'

tion through an assertion of the continuities of time and space, and a sense of social habitus, the cherished *bonheur collectif* remembered by the tenants, is projected beyond the destruction of the physical environment.[11]

Despite its challenges to conventional narrative, *Chronique d'une banlieue ordinaire* fulfils conventional functions championed by *cinéma vérité* such as the rhetorical use of documentary to provide visible evidence for a social thesis. A problematic that remains awkwardly evident in the film remains however the position of the filmmaker in relation to those she films as the technique of Cabrera's repeated (but largely unheard) questions to the tenants linger as traces of the filmmaker's unacknowledged interventions. Such technique draws on a particular heritage in French documentary including Varda's *Daguerrotypes* and Marker's *Le joli mai*, films which both assert the importance of giving voice to the fears and hopes of the population[12] and so challenge the 'Griersonian victim tradition' (Winston 1995: 200) of the subjects of traditional documentary. In her film on the Val Fourré demolitions, *Rêves de ville*, Cabrera chooses to engage explicitly with this problematic through the use of two main elements. Firstly, she introduces a clear distancing device between her film and the motivations of the media crews covering the events. Even as she includes footage of local politicians delivering their pre-demolition speeches she positions her camera in such a way as to include the attentive media in her frame – thus acknowledging her own position as witness whilst simultaneously positioning herself within the crowd and distancing herself from the dominant political discourse of sanctioned regeneration. The question of the degree of participation of the subjects of the documentary in the process of filmmaking is also addressed here as the film contains video footage[13] shot by a local resident, Badou, alongside his own comments on the filming and editing process. Badou's humour and creativity are foregrounded as he misses the detonations but selects alternative poetic images

---

11 It remains equally important that the demolition is not shown in this film, thus removing its role as anticipated narrative climax.

12 Marker's question to Parisians as to whether they were happy was politically charged in the contemporary context of the Algerian war, whilst Varda asked the inhabitants of her street about their dreams.

13 These sequences are clearly distinguishable through their video format (including the date and time of filming left on the screen) and filmed discussions of the editing process.

that mark a subjective experience that remains distinct from the media coverage of events. His discussion of Aimé Césaire and the importance of cultural empowerment through representation reflect emphatically on the parallel motivations of Cabrera's film.

A further intervention in the debate on the ethics of filming others is presented in a short film made by Cabrera in the same location, focusing on a scheme to help the long-term unemployed return to work. *Réjane dans la tour* is an incredibly powerful 15-minute film which follows the eponymous local woman as she shows Cabrera the routine of her work as a cleaner in the tower blocks. As Cabrera and hand-held camera start at the top of the block and follow her down as she cleans the landings and stairwells on each indistinguishable floor, Réjane begins to recount her life story including her recurring depression, grief at the loss of her parents, suicide attempts, hospitalisation and her imminent abandonment by partner and son. The contrast between the bland, deserted landings, the repetitive nature of her work and the quiet despair of Réjane's heartrending story are striking and trigger a further evolution in Cabrera's ongoing strategies for implicating the self (director and spectator) in the filming of urban space to create both personal and social intimacy. Moved by Réjane's frankness and seeming resignation, the viewer senses Cabrera's acute sensitivity to her own position as her hesitation over the appropriate physical distance from which she should film her subject denotes her anxiety over the unexpectedly personal nature of the material that is emerging. As Cabrera and her camera hesitate at the physical thresholds of another doorway or another landing so the director enacts a haunting physical representation of the dynamics of the ethical relationship between (documentary) filmmaker and filmed subject across the more blurred and problematic thresholds of the public and private, caught between the drive to validate and politicise subjective experience and the dangers of constructing the documentary subject as victim or, indeed, as spectacle of suffering.

Demain et encore demain: filming (in) the first person

The central cumulative elements of Cabrera's documentary film making reach a self-reflexive peak in her autobiographical film made in 1997. *Demain et encore demain* continues a search for a notion of collective happiness, interrogates the links between the personal and the political and explores further the ethics of the documentary process through the adoption of the first-person form. Since the late 1990s there has been a marked increase in the production of first-person documentary that transcends configurations of national cinemas and, whilst it should be examined in the context of the huge increase in production and distribution of documentary film in the same period,[14] is becoming a prominent mode.

Examples of the first-person mode in French documentary present a diverse range of approaches and styles including: *No Sex Last Night* (Calle, 1996), *Leçons de ténèbres* (Dieutre, 1999) and *Le Filmeur* (Cavalier, 2004). This phenomenon is clearly indicative of a broader contemporary socio-cultural tendency towards the increasing mediatisation of personal experience and, in its more pernicious forms, builds upon the rampant individualism proposed through the dominant cultural models of the public confessional and reality television. The emergence of the first-person documentary itself is a symptom of such developments as: 'the very subjectivity of these documentaries makes an implicit social comment on the erosion between public and private spheres in daily life and on the rise of identity formation as an active, self-directed process' (Aufderheide 1997: 43). This cultural shift has been supported and reinforced by advances in the technological realm as the accessibility of digital video and the potential of sharing film via multi-platform web-based systems have precipitated a real and metaphorical turning of the camera on the self to offer 'historically grounded, newly-democratized rhetorics of realness, tokens of immediacy' (Arthur 2005: 19) which fulfil Astruc's vision of the *caméra stylo* (camera-pen). However, as Prédal notes, the technology does not offer an inherent solipsism as 'si la petite caméra (DV) favorise l'observation de soi-même (intimisme), elle facilite aussi les contacts, donc l'approche de l'autre'[15] (Prédal 2002: 62). Cabrera's move to a documenting of the self may also reflect her ethical hesitation during the filming of *Réjane dans la tour*, supported

14 Over fifty documentaries received a theatrical release in France in 2004. Since 2000 there have been striking commercial successes including *Les Glaneurs et la glaneuse* (Varda, 2000), *Etre et avoir* (Philibert, 2002) and *La Marche de l'empereur* (Luc Jacquet, 2005).
15 'If the small digital video camera favours the observation of the self, it also enables contact with, and an approach to, the other.'

by a more general perception of a crisis in the traditional documentary's assumed relationship with objectivity and the real (articulated through conventions of photographic indexicality). Perhaps the most legitimate realm for contemporary documentary has indeed become that of an assertively subjective experience.

Whilst the contemporary tendencies of the documentary form provide relevant contexts, it remains clear that the single most important motivation behind the making of this film was Cabrera's personal need to address her own severe depression which continued for nine months of 1995. The filming is thus undertaken as an explicitly therapeutic activity and introduced in a first voiceover as such: 'Je fais ce film pour reprendre contact avec le monde extérieur, avec autre chose que ma peur' (I'm making this film in order to regain contact with the outside world, with something other than my fear).

The film offers a brutally frank portrayal of Cabrera's central concerns (her relationship with her son, a new lover and the impact of her depression on her family) and the major symptoms of her depression (loss of self-esteem, insomnia and a latent bulimia). Yet these personal concerns are consistently set within clear social and political frameworks; the political and social problematic of a choice of school, the socially constructed nature of mother-daughter relationships and the impact of changing economic landscapes on personal and political allegiances. The film thus escapes the narcissistic limitations of a 'fétichisme du soi...cette utopie existentielle d'une insularité du moi valant pour l'universel'[16] (Grat 2000: 2), and continues the insistence, established in her Val Fourré documentaries, of the unbreakable ties between the personal and the political, the individual and the social. Cabrera recognises this in her later description of the work as 'un film documentaire où je voulais m'exposer dans mes choix, mais c'est quand même les autres qui sont sur le devant de la scène'[17] (Cabrera 2000: 39). This sense of the social self is complemented in the film by the therapeutic insistence upon the self as creative instrument asserting: 'the extraordinary pliancy of the first person: not simply that it *has* a story, but that it can *tell* one. The self is not a source or a subject; it is an instrument' (Hampl 1996: 57).

16 'a fetishism of the self ... an existential utopia in which the insularity of the self is equated with the universal'.
17 'a documentary film in which I wanted to expose myself through the choices I make, but nonetheless it is often other people who remain in the foreground'.

The film, as its subtitle (*journal 1995*) suggests, proffers an under-lying chronology, yet Cabrera's central tropes of a ludic approach to conventions of time and the inherently therapeutic function of the moving image dominate its narrative structures. Questions of performance, editing, motivation and constructed readership that beset the construction of any journal form are addressed through the reflexivity of the filmed material, culminating in 'cette vision du réel conjuguée au goût de la représentation (tout cela est à la fois en vie et en représentation, capté et mise en scène)[18] (Binh 2004). Indeed the film's 'artful construction' (Tarr with Rollet 2004: 155), presents the practice of filmmaking as a more successfully therapeutic practice than the writing of a rarely seen journal. Cabrera's insistence upon the process of self-representation challenges classical definitions of documentary which suggest that:

> Appropriating its photographic genealogy, the documentary form is able to offer itself as a metaphysical guarantee, offering presence and coherence through the possibility of knowledge ... [taking] on a manage-able form and substance, providing the spectator with the position of mastery over a potentially threatening world. (Scheibler 1993: 138)

In *Demain et encore demain*, such omniscient positions are rendered impossible for both filmmaker and spectator, replaced by a blurring of boundaries between (visible) evidence and the ongoing act of narration. The film eschews the narrative progression that one might expect from a diary (or indeed from therapy), yet progression remains present in Cabrera's exploration of the filming of the self. *Demain et encore demain* is punctuated by haunting sequences in which Cabrera films herself filming and during which time seems to be suspended. The dual reflective and reflexive nature of these sequences is empha-sised by the choice of windows as reflective surfaces, so rejecting the narcissistic, hermetic model of the mirror for a trope that invokes the framing qualities of the camera lens. These assertions of the physical presence of the filmmaker can be read as markers of documentary authenticity, yet the stillness and composition of the self-images suggest rather a transgressive intimacy as they insist on the 'represen-tation of experience and, therefore, the body itself as witness' (Nichols 1993: 127). Cabrera counters her sense of social and personal failure

---

18 'This vision of the real combined with a sense of representation (all of this is simultaneously lived and represented, captured and staged)'.

in the relationships filmed with an assertion of her own position as creative agent, as object *and* subject of the documentary process. A significant feature of these sequences is the intrusion of the bulky Hi8 camera that obscures Cabrera's face,[19] thus invoking the sinister science-fiction hybrids of human and machine that frequently serve as metaphors of cinema. Cabrera's construction of the monstrous self seems overplayed yet remains interesting in its suggestion of the limitations of human self-representation – the experience of our own death.[20] Cabrera's faith in the therapeutic function of the moving image as one that counters an oppressive sense of mortality is central to the film.

The conventions of documentary film posit a genealogical link with photography and invoke the latter's association with mortality established through several seminal theoretical engagements with the photographic form.[21] Bazin described the power of cinema as subverting such deathly trajectories to reveal life (Bazin 1985: 87) and it is this function that Cabrera adopts in *Demain*. The title of this film originates from Lady Macbeth's infamous speech that continues 'and all our yesterdays have lighted fools, the way to dusty death'[22] and Cabrera has commented that her films indeed constitute 'une lutte contre une sorte de pulsion de mort' (Cabrera 2000: 38) (a struggle against some kind of death drive). In the early sequences of the film, Cabrera's self-portraits are marked by her static position in contrast to the ceaseless movement of the world around her, creating parallels with the framed portraits of her lover's mother and his long-term partner that dominate her nervous exploration of his apartment. An anxious fascination with the power of framing and fixity pervades these sequences, representing both the comforting and suffocating power of a stilled, embalming image. Her stillness as creative subject invites comparison with recurring long takes of inanimate objects, a process that Cabrera refers to as an initial reassurance: 'J'étais heureuse de filmer la lumière sur les objets. Je rassemblais mes

---

19 *Demain et encore demain* was filmed in Hi8 and then transferred to 35mm.

20 For examples of such models see *La Cité des enfants perdus* (Jeunet and Caro) and *Strange Days* (Bigelow), both also released in 1995.

21 See Barthes's discussion of the punctum in *La Chambre claire* (Paris, Editions du Seuil, 1980) and Sontag's association of the photograph with imperial subjectivities and sublimated murder in Susan Sontag, *On Photography* (New York and London, Picador, 1977).

22 Shakespeare, *Macbeth*, 5.5.18–28.

forces sur quelques éléments pour essayer de comprendre ce qui comptait' (Cabrera 2000: 39).[23] However these objects resist stasis: as water boils and evaporates, raw materials are transformed into named dishes in cooking and plants grow, blossom and change with the seasons.

As discussed earlier in relation to *L'Air d'aimer*, it is the relationship between the still and the moving image that, for Cabrera, signals recovery and embrace of the social. The pivotal sequence of the film constructs explicit parallels between her own state and that of a framed still life before responding with an image of therapeutic movement which emphatically includes both personal and political discourse. Cabrera films her reflection in a shop window, a still figure amidst a busy street environment. A series of reframings compels us to compare her image with that of the painting displayed in the window and the message beneath it that invites the spectatorial consumer to 'offrez ces fleurs qui ne se fanent jamais' (give flowers that will never wilt). The painting is a still life, a *nature morte*, and, whilst this pictorial representation is trumpeted as everlasting, it is its lack of life that is important here in its sinister echo of Cabrera's self quotation from a session with her psychoanalyst: 'Je ne vis pas, comme ça je ne suis pas tuée' (I don't live, that way I can't be killed). This verbal and visual acknowledgement of her paralysing fear of change is challenged as the shot cuts carefully from the painted flowers to a real bouquet and Cabrera's inserted footage of Mitterrand greeting a group of (female) award winners. The strikingly mobile camera follows him around the room as Cabrera's voiceover recalls her admiration of the way in which all those present were both spectators and active participants in a politically and personally therapeutic scene founded on the acknowledgement of transformation and change. This recognition of the power of the moving image – the same power felt by the heartbroken protagonist of *L'Air d'aimer* as he flicks through the portrait polaroids – expands through *Demain* as Cabrera relinquishes a static relationship with the camera, allowing herself to film others and others to film her as the film opens up to social time and space. The recurring shots of the dark, deserted street from Cabrera's window and solitary kitchen scenes that represent the cyclical time and closed spaces dictated by her insomnia and bulimia become less frequent. A variety of social

23 'I was happy to film light falling on objects. I was focusing my energies on a few things in order to understand what was important.'

and political spaces, from the intimacy of her mother's kitchen to a pre-*présidentielles* rally for the Front national, increasingly situate her crisis within specific socio-historical structures and discourses, including the position of the Left faced with the hard choices of the final round of the Presidential elections of 1995. The reinsertion into social time is accompanied by an acceptance of the present that is articulated in Cabrera's voiceover but also through formal filmic devices. The film's title evokes a written journal yet does not present such a document as a supporting commentary on visual sequences. It is the relationship between the processes of filming and writing that is foregrounded (rather than the relationship between events and the moment of writing); a shifting relationship underscored by the employment of both voiceovers made in direct sound which suggest immediacy and those that are identifiable with the constructed and retrospective tropes of autobiography. The cathartic nature of the final sequences unites the two *journals* (written and filmic) as Cabrera films herself writing in her journal. The ongoing process of filming thus becomes an explicit performance of the sentence that she writes: 'J'accepte que la vie s'est remise en marche et j'accepte qu'elle me transforme' (I accept that life has started up again and I accept that it will change me). Cabrera's self-portrait now unites both creative agent and observed, documentary subject to constitute a creative and positive response to the conventional photographic portraits and paintings of women discussed earlier and to her own static shots of herself in reflective surfaces that articulated her petrified anxiety. This dual affirmation of the power of the filmic image and the strengths of creative subjectivity create a positive trajectory that evokes the political aesthetics of the Deleuzian subject-as-image – always becoming, still moving.

Cabrera's documentary work across the Val Fourré films and *Demain* persists in a *mise en abyme* of the conventions and the processes of documentary filmmaking. These films represent considered interventions in mediatised constructions of identity, challenging both the politically expedient homogenisation of the inhabitants of Val Fourré and the conventions of self-portraiture. They foreground the inherent links between forms of documentary and fiction and the inextricable relationship between what happens to the self and what happens to others.

L'Autre Côté de la mer: the politics of belonging

Documentary aesthetics and a continuing interest in the relationship between place and identity inform Cabrera's first feature-length fiction film *L'Autre côté de la mer*, which was made in 1997 and presented at the Cannes festival. The use of direct sound and hand-held camera imbue the confrontations and reconciliations that structure the film with a sense of proximity and authenticity. Indeed, Cabrera first addressed the displacements of her own *pied-noir* family in documentary form in two short films that she made a decade earlier. *Ici là-bas* is a 13-minute documentary in which she questions her parents about their attitudes to their displacement and loss of Algeria and provides personal commentary to images of their lives there. Inspired by the story of her uncle who, having been tortured and imprisoned for harbouring an Algerian suspect, took Algerian nationality, she made *Rester là-bas*. This film, made for television, contains interviews with a group of *pieds-noirs* thirty years after their decisions to stay on in post-independence Algeria. The film is accompanied by a book of the same title, in which Cabrera reflects upon the filmmaking process. The book includes interviews with people who refused to be filmed and provides a wider range of characters and frank responses to the events of the war. In the book, Cabrera recognises the personal therapeutic motivation behind the project as she 'cherche un sens au tableau, cherche à guérir le chagrin, cherche à brûler le passé' (Cabrera 1992: 74) (seeks to find meaning in the scene, seeks to heal the sorrow, seeks to burn the past), whilst attempting to articulate a more general message of tolerance and integration. Yet her reactions to the final rushes were mixed as she acknowledged that during the process of filming they had 'masqué, brouillé, annulé avec constance. Il n'y avait pas les Algériens dans le film'[24] (ibid.: 117).

The tension Cabrera expresses between making the documentary and the draw of fictional structures and the difficulty of foregrounding others' experience of the painful questions of belonging and loss that saturate her own life, led her to undertake a fictional exploration of these same issues in her first feature film. The choices made by those who leave or stay, the multilayered denials inherent in different discourses of belonging and the haunting nature of exile are at the

---

24 'Consistently masked, blurred, and cancelled out. The Algerians were not in the film.'

heart of *L'Autre Côté de la mer*. Such complex constructions are articulated through the developing relationship between a *pied-noir* and a second-generation immigrant. The central character Georges Montero (Claude Brasseur) stayed in Algeria after independence but has now returned to France for the first time to undergo eye surgery. His surgeon, Tarek Timsert (Roschdy Zem), has family who originate from the same region of Algeria in which Georges lives. The film engages with both the immediate consequences of the Algerian war and contemporary constructions of identity through a focus on a central, evolving relationship between Georges and the young *beur* doctor, Tarek, who performs his cataract operation. Indeed, the metaphor of sight, or rather of the prevention of blindness, is clearly evoked throughout the film as Georges and Tarek both have their eyes opened to the different perspectives and blindspots that both construct and disturb their respective senses of identity. Georges's recurrent self-examination in mirrors charts the progress of his improved vision but also an increasingly problematic interrogation of identity. Devices of perception and framing are further highlighted as Georges's sense of anxious displacement is rendered through the recurring trope of him watching or being watched through windows – from the car journey that follows his arrival and journey through central Paris, to the repeated scenes of him seated in café windows. These multiple framings articulate the complexity of his position in the Parisian environment and dispel all projections of this as a narrative of resolution or homecoming. After leaving the hospital in bright sunshine, his brief stroll beside the iconic monument of Notre Dame is accompanied by Arabic music again foregrounding his perception as an outsider rather than the revelation of an inherent affinity with traditional representations of France that would suggest a homecoming.

Yet the structure of the narrative does not rely on unfolding changes in perception but is rather underpinned by a series of confrontations between the central and secondary characters, confrontations that explore the dynamics of loss, guilt and blame at play in their different narratives of displacement and alienation. Georges must face family and friends who exert emotional and financial pressures in their attempts to convince him not to return to Oran, but whose suggestions he angrily rejects. Tarek's successful middle-class profile masks his anxious denial of his own background and the resulting sense of alienation and inferiority for which he compensates through an economic over-consumption and aggressive individualism that threaten to wreck his marriage. Georges defends his life in Algeria against his sister Marinette's (Marthe Villalonga) vision of a site of vengeance in which all traces of their past lives have been erased or defaced. Georges's angry open question 'Pourquoi tu crois que tout est difficile en Algérie?' (Why do you believe that everything is difficult in Algeria?) is, however, placed in quietly ironic contrast to his regular anxious phone calls to his foreman, Ali, to ensure that all is secure in his absence. Yet Georges's bitter contestation of his sister's image of a violent Algeria and her refusal to accept the past pales besides his sense of outrageous betrayal at secret negotiations that have arranged a fiscal amnesty for him in return for the uncontested sale of his estate to the local tax inspector when he leaves. His identification with the land that he farms, and with Algeria, is reflected in the markedly slower pace and inclusive framing that characterises an idyllic visit to an olive farm with Tarek.

The central relationship between Georges and Tarek is established succinctly through the mismatch between the physical proximity necessary for the eye examination and the clear antagonism between the two; a tension aggravated by Georges's unwelcome attempts at communication in Arabic. His sullen acknowledgement of the reversal of historical power relationships, his being looked after by 'a kid from the "bled"', is met by Tarek's rejection of any attempt to create a shared cultural or linguistic heritage. However, when Georges suffers a panic attack, Tarek quickly acknowledges the possibility of communication and speaks to him in Arabic to calm his fears. Tarek strives to distance himself from the role Algeria must play in his identity, complaining that Algerians address him as 'brother' when he perceives himself as French, yet, paradoxically, engages in an argument with Georges that involves the competitive recounting of tales of suffering from both sides of the colonial divide. The inextricable link between their experiences is underlined as the heavies sent to scare Georges into agreeing to the sale of his business break into Tarek's house and threaten his family, bringing with them a violent reminder of the unresolved conflicts of Algerian political and economic identity. Even such violent conflict is mediated, however, as the intruders return later with compensation for the damage done and confound Tarek's assumptions about their cultural and financial otherness.

The central protagonists' shifting sense of identity is played out against a series of different spatial contexts. Whilst Georges's evident sense of displacement is shown in his lack of local contacts and his discomfort in the makeshift bedroom in Tarek's garage, spaces of sanctuary and communication are represented. In the first half of the film Georges can find no escape from the demands of others that he should redefine his identity through permanent relocation; family spaces are represented as claustrophobic and conflictual, public space is riddled with unwelcome encounters and he has no private space. Even in the sanctuary sought in a romantic reunion with his lost love, Maria, her private, domestic space is disrupted by memories of the atrocities that she witnessed before leaving Algeria thirty years ago. As the film progresses and both Georges and Tarek work through the hostile positioning of their respective identities, the communal space of the café becomes increasingly important, acting simultaneously as a site which enables Tarek to engage with his own cultural heritage and as a conduit for news from Algeria as the unceasing commentary of the television delivers news of further atrocities and fulfils a central choric function. The increased focus on the common spaces inhabited by the two central protagonists is complemented by use of the cinematic frame to suggest a growing emotional proximity as the camera emphatically abandons shot-counter-shot to privilege more inclusive framings of the pair together in mid-shot and then close-up.

The narrative resolution sees both protagonists reaching a clearer understanding of their relationship to Algeria. Georges decides to return to Algeria yet has made peace with the exiled community in France. Tarek's announcement that he made a journey and his recognition that he lost some baggage on the way signal a more successful integration of his cultural inheritance into his present identity. These acceptances are reflected in the film's markedly upbeat final sequences as the party scene in the café is dominated by the joyous sound of the trumpet and the mobile camera that, immersed in the dancing crowd, communicates a sense of liberty and life that contrasts markedly with the prominent use of a static camera and the mournful music that dominate the rest of the film.

Benjamin Stora has argued that representations of Algeria in print and films in France in the 1990s exploited references to contemporary atrocities in order to revisit the reductively generalised trauma of the Algerian war and so failed ultimately to engage with the historical specificities of either set of events (Stora 2001). *L'Autre Côté* does not foreground specific historical events[25] preferring to focalise the consequences of war through its engagement with the serial denials at the heart of both Georges's and Tarek's sense of self. The film's lack of wider political engagement and its positing of a largely sentimental closure may be criticised, yet its insistence on the evolving nature of (post)colonial identities and the importance of addressing their impact on and through interrogations of personal identity across generations remains both forceful and nuanced.

Nadia et les hippopotames: the community of politics

The search for community across different lines is at the heart of Cabrera's next feature film, *Nadia et les hippopotames*, which focuses on the railway workers' strike of winter 1995/6. The divisions in this film include not only those between strikers and those continuing to work, between the salaried and those with more precarious incomes, but also amongst union representatives themselves and the different motivations for their political activism. A shorter version of the film, entitled *Retiens la nuit*[26] was originally released as part of the series *Droite/gauche* commissioned by Arte and screened in 2000. Co-written with the sociologist Philippe Corcuff, the script, based on documents from the 1995 railway workers' strike, and the casting of railway workers who were encouraged to improvise dialogue creates a 'sensibilité quasi ethnologique' (Chevandier 2000: 161).

Although the late 1990s and early 2000s saw a marked resurgence within French cinema of depictions of the world of work and the problems caused by unemployment (see Cadé 2000), there remain few representations of the 1995 strikes that caused major economic and logistical disruption to most major French cities.[27] Indeed many films represent a marked absence of collective representation in the workplace and foreground rather the social value of work through

25 An exception to this is the news report of the 1994 assassination of the Raï star Cheb Hasni.

26 The title is taken from a sentimental ballad sung in a picket-line sequence. The song, written by Charles Aznavour in 1962, was further popularised by Johnny Hallyday in the 1980s.

27 *Vendredi soir* (Denis, 2002) uses the gridlock caused by the public transport strikes as a narrative device to bring the central couple together.

the alienation of central protagonists from both economic and social structures.[28] It should be noted that in many of these films made in the 1990s (including those discussed in other chapters of this volume) it is central female protagonists who represent those directly affected by changes in working conditions. In her search for community Cabrera continues to emphasise the deconstruction of conventional binaries of the individual and the collective, the personal and the political and indeed personal stories and the grand narratives of History, to propose a more organic and holistic model of these interrelated spheres. She insists, that in *Nadia* she wanted to 'faire sentir comment la vie privée, la vie sentimentale sont traversées par les idées; et puis, comment les idées aussi proviennent de l'histoire vivante, de ce qui s'est passé la nuit avant'.[29] Audé states that *Nadia*

> n'est pas un film de lutte de classe, pas de patrons, peu d'affrontements et un "tous ensemble" soudé à la chaleur humaine plutôt qu'à l'idéologie. C'est une chronique lyrique qui réussit en douceur à exprimer le "possible" du terrain.[30] (Audé 2002: 152)

The film features neither revolutionary heroes nor (melo)dramatic denouements of political justice, yet it does explore the necessary desire, and consequent melancholy, of attempting to sustain a bridge between reality and utopia and the importance of this both to the individual and to the community. The hippopotami in the title reflects a term used by Corcuff to describe the unwieldy 'weight of tradition, critical thinking associated with modernity and cynicism of postmodernity' (Corcuff 1999: 47) attributed to the activists in the face of the insubstantiality of the modern world which the character Jean-Paul characterises as valuing 'sucre sans sucre, beurre sans beurre, histoires sans histoires' (sugarless sugar, butterless butter, stories without stories / without trouble).

Nadia et les hippopotames focuses on three trade unionists: Claire (Marilyne Canto), Serge (Thierry Frémont) and Jean-Paul (Philippe

28 See for example, *La Vie revée des anges* (Zonca, 1998), *Rosetta* (Dardennes, 1999) and *L'Humanité* (Dumont, 1999). *Ressources humaines* (Cantet, 1999) features a caricatured union representative.

29 'make us realise how our private lives, our emotional lives ... are traversed by ideas; and then, to show how ideas also come from living history, from what happened the previous night'.

30 'is not a film about the class struggle, there are no bosses, few confrontations and a solidarity held together by human warmth rather than ideology. It's a lyrical tale which succeeds in gently showing what is possible.'

Fretun) who drive around Paris supporting those on the picket lines during the SNCF strike. They take Nadia (Ariane Ascaride), a single mother on the minimum wage, and her baby, to find the baby's father who had been spotted by Nadia on the television news amongst strikers at the Gare d'Austerlitz. As the group's relationships develop in the social warmth of the strikers' braziers and the increasingly intimate spaces of the van, more complex questions of personal and political affiliation and representation arise. O'Shaughnessy rightly identifies the context for this search for a renewed solidarity as 'the decline of the institutional left and the deliberate and systematic dismantling of the organised working class' (O'Shaughnessy 2004: 220). He asserts further that a reaction to this lack of collective representation is found in the new realism and concomitant focus on embodied suffering found in post-1995 French cinema. The hardline attitude of the union representatives is disturbed by the presence of Nadia who has no collective support and criticises the strike as a luxury enjoyed by civil servants whose livelihoods are not implicated in a job market charac-terised by precarity and exploitation. Nadia remains mostly silent and it is indeed her physical presence (the bulky pram, the crying baby, her frank expression of both hostility and desire) that disrupts the dominant, stagnant collective discourse that initially excluded her. Cabrera's interest in a renewal of a collective politics of the left is articulated through a political solidarity in which it is possible to remain individual subjects and played out across a narrative struc-ture in which scenes of political meetings and collective struggle are alternated with scenes of an ostensibly more intimate nature that address the personal anxieties and desires of the central protagonists. A stop to buy provisions in a hypermarket sees Serge questioning Claire's personal investment in political activism, Jean-Paul declaring undying love for Nadia and Nadia attempting to counter her exclu-sion from the overwhelming choices of consumerism through theft. In a lengthy sequence, which Cabrera describes as a metaphor for the whole film (Audé and Tobin 2000: 36), Claire establishes an unexpected intimacy, emphatic in its combination of the personal and the political, with a non-striker who drives her home, and the pastoral interlude that ensues when the van is stranded in silence, snow and moonlight opens a space within the collective for individual desires, through Nadia's assertion of sexual agency. The personal is also foregrounded through the potentially melodramatic subplot of

Claire's realisation that her husband is the missing father of Nadia's baby. Spectatorial expectations of generic denouement are, however, thwarted as the long-awaited appearance of the father takes place in a collective space, which results in Nadia leaving the room to allow him time with the baby but denies any recognition of his identity. This denial may be an act of personal solidarity to save Claire's marriage, but also constitutes a refusal of an individualised romantic closure, enabling the new configuration of the personal and the political to endure in the closing sequences of the film.

The spaces governed by an institutionalised collective politics are punctuated with scenes set in the transitory, yet intimate, spaces of the van. It is within this space that a new collectivity emerges and is expressed in terms of bodily proximity as the central characters are compelled to huddle together to keep warm, even breathing in unison as if part of one (social) body. The exhilarating sequence in which, after failing to rouse anyone to help them after they have run out of petrol, Nadia, Serge and Jean-Paul race down deserted streets chanting an appropriated slogan of the 1995 strikes, 'tous ensemble' (all together), has an energy that contrasts with the warmly lit but static tableaux of the pickets. After this, they huddle together to keep warm in a basic reassertion of the need for solidarity across class divides and political discourses enacting an 'effective reconnection of a leftist language with embodied struggle' (O'Shaughnessy 2007: 127). In the final sequences, as Serge addresses the strikers and draws on his own personal experience to make an impassioned plea for social justice, this energy brings about a new collectivity marked by its engagement and the inclusion of Nadia's situation. The initial solidarities and the evolution of personal relationships are articulated through careful framing, the alternation of mid-shots and close-ups and a predominantly static camera which uses an inclusive frame, rather than the convention of shot-counter-shot, to foreground the personal negotiation of political debate and to underscore the documentary feel of many of the central sequences of the film. Following the running sequence described above, the final sequences are characterised by a more mobile roving camera which communicates a sense of integration and inclusion and stands alongside Nadia, asserting her position as part of the crowd, as she listens attentively to Serge's final speech. The mood has also changed from one of confrontation, fear and anxiety to one of possibility and change, of characters having moved beyond their everyday experiences to create new connections and to express openly their desires. The project's original title was indeed 'Peut être' ('Could be').

Le Lait de la tendresse humaine: proximity and otherness

Cabrera's next feature film was written before *Nadia* and can be seen as inherently connected both to that film and to *Demain et encore demain*. *Le Lait de la tendresse humaine* centres on Christelle (Marilyne Canto) who, after the birth of her third child, a daughter, suffers depression and leaves her family to seek refuge with a neighbour, Claire (Dominique Blanc). As her husband (Patrick Bruel) searches for her and questions friends and family, the repercussions of her disappearance lead them all to re-evaluate their own relationships. The narrative thus combines an exploration of the paralysing force of depression, as represented so movingly in *Demain*, with a recognition of the potential for love, tenderness and intimacy that defines humanity and is capable of overcoming such crises. The film shares with *Nadia* a non-judgemental exploration of complex emotional needs and relationships and foregrounds striking representations of friendship, intimacy and parenthood. A clear intertextual marker to these earlier films is provided as Claire turns on the radio and we hear a musical adaptation of Lady Macbeth's famous speech 'Tomorrow and tomorrow and tomorrow...', the speech that provided the title for Cabrera's documentary self-portrait. An exceptional cast sees the continuation of Cabrera's collaboration with a group of actors, with Marilyne Canto in the lead role, Olivier Gourmet as Jean-Claude and Marthe Villalonga and Claude Brasseur in more minor roles. However, it is the notable casting of the mainstream star Patrick Bruel as husband, Laurent, that did much to widen the film's box office appeal.

Christelle's disappearance triggers revelations from both family and friends as Laurent doubts their closeness, her sister denounces such selfish behaviour and Christelle's father reveals that her mother also suffered from (post-natal) depression. Other characters re-evaluate their loves and lives in the light of Christelle's disappearance and their subsequent realisation of the importance of seeking and valuing intimacy. The only character with no positive experience of the rediscovery of loves current and past is Josiane (Valeria Bruni-Tedeschi), as her husband Jean-Claude's chance encounter with a former lover, Babette (Yolande Moreau), signals the end of their marriage. Indeed Josiane's despairing speech, in which she describes herself in the third person as someone defined by loss, remains hauntingly incongruous in the context of the generally restorative narrative closure. The narrative structure is fragmented, forgoing a focus on plot development in linear time and space (the quest for the missing mother) to follow the central metaphor provided by the ripples radiating out from pebbles tossed into a lake by Christelle's son. The idea of the transpositional linking of several stories is central to Cabrera's parallel engagement with the idea to 'superposer au film fait le labyrinthe du film rêvé, du film raté, du film secret, du film qui m'a échappé'.[31] This narrative layering finds its formal articulation in a central visual motif of the film provided by the device of filming through windows, resulting in the superimposition of interior and exterior spaces. This is most striking in the establishing sequence as the image of blocks of flats under construction is placed, almost like a filter, on top of our first images of Christelle in her kitchen and they becoming indistinguishable from the shapes of the furniture and interior borders. The same technique recurs throughout the film, notably through projections on the car window as Laurent takes his family with him in a search for Christelle. Such layering insists upon the interconnectedness of interior and exterior, of the personal and the social; a connection central to the narrative structure and plot development of the film as intimacy and tenderness transcend recognised social structures (such as marriage) to create more fluid and inclusive relationships.

The setting of the film, the Jura, presents a striking contrast between the ongoing construction of tower blocks and the imposing natural landscape of surrounding mountains and lush forest. The two environments are not set in simplistic opposition to each other – indeed many of the scenes shot outside insist on the close framing of groups and use of close-up but rather their juxtaposition serves to articulate the convergence in the film of the everyday and the banal with the timeless almost mythical aspect of narratives of loves lost

---

31 'super-imposing on to the finished film the labyrinth of the dreamt film, the failed film, the secret film, the film that got away'. Dominique Cabrera, DVD cover notes.

and found. Contrast is maintained however in the tones and lighting of the external landscapes and the interior decors. In an interview included in the DVD release, Cabrera describes the visual influences on the film as encompassing a range that includes her own family photographs and the paintings of Vermeer. From the former she takes the framings of intimacy and awkwardness that constitute family groups and from the latter the range of sombre colours and warm light that characterises the film's interior sequences. These muted, intimate spaces are thrown into relief by the dazzling, overexposed light of several of the initial outdoors sequences in which Christelle runs from the building in confusion and panic, trying to seek contact and shelter in a telephone kiosk before returning to the building.

Christelle's depression renders her almost mute for much of the film, yet this absence of verbal agency is countered by her physical presence which, from recurring shots of her passive, immobile form slumped on beds and sofas to the bowls of breast milk that begin to encroach upon the spaces of her neighbour's flat and fridge, is both awkward and imposing. Questions of intimacy and the transgression of private space are articulated through an emphasis on the changes wrought by forced cohabitation as Christelle is framed crossing the multiple internal boundaries and frames of Claire's apartment. In return, both Claire and her lover, Serge (Sergi Lopez), watch Christelle sleeping. It is her physical presence, rather than complex verbal exchanges, that carry the themes of solidarity and responsibility which are foregrounded from her initial fainting into Claire's arms, to her childish, physical refusal to move when Serge demands that she leaves the flat.

Indeed much of the intimacy represented in the film is created through touch and communication that exceeds the logocentrism of conventionally represented dialogue. Christelle's depression means that for much of the film she has no desires to express, yet the comfortable silences of others represent non-verbalised intimacy. Claire and Serge communicate through looks and through singing with and to each other whilst the chance meeting and subsequent rekindled passion between Jean-Claude and Babette (Yolande Moreau) allows little time for conversation. It is equally suggested that the characters who talk a lot (Christelle's sister, Sandrine, and Jean-Claude's wife, Josiane) are those least at ease with themselves and most invested in the displacement or denial of their own needs.[32] The emotional impact of the narrative resolution, as Christelle finally returns to her flat to find Laurent and the three children having breakfast, owes much of its overwhelming force to the muted, still nature of the scene which focuses on her sons' silent tears and her quietly hypnotic incantation of their names.

An emphasis on physicality, the senses and bodily responses connects the film to the horror genre and, indeed, the first fifteen minutes of the film construct just such a generic mood. After a brief telephone conversation, Christelle returns to the hall of her flat to witness water flooding out from under the bathroom door.[33] The point of view shots that isolate the vulnerability of her feet near the water, her inability to open the bathroom door and her immediate panicked exit from the building create mystery and apprehension as to the nature of her escalating fears. This unease is further compounded by the lack of dialogue, the increasing volume of a haunting soundtrack and the jerkiness of the hand-held camera, which follows her at speed as she runs out into the harshly lit, inhospitable hard landscape of the car park. Informed by the employment of these seemingly distant generic conventions to construct meaning, Cabrera extends them to provide an important element of the central protagonist's characterisation and a motif which functions throughout the film. Reduced to animalistic reactions to her fear, Claire's identity in the first half of the film is characterised by her heavy breathing, a sound that, in the numerous wordless telephone calls that she makes to her family, undertakes the complex signalling that she is alive but in some distress. In one of the few clues provided to the trigger for her depression Christelle mentions her difficult labour, criticising the midwives' instruction to 'soufflez, soufflez' (breathe out, breathe out) in response to her pleas for pain relief. This motif is emphatically present towards the end of the film in the scene in which she decides to return home. Serge's unsuccessful attempts to oust her from the apartment come to a close as she informs him that today is her birthday and we cut to a low-lit, close-framed scene in which Claire and Serge present her with a cake

32 We could interpret their anxieties as linked to maternity through Sandrine's impending motherhood and Josiane's increased awareness of her desire to have a child.

33 Liquids are ever-present in the film and represent the unrestrainable energies of life.

and sing 'Happy Birthday'. The following entreaty on their part for her to blow out the candles, to 'soufflez, souffles', is marked by its tenderness (emphasised by the linguistic shift from the formal 'vous' to the 'tu' form) and, in its celebration of *her* birth, can be understood to extend to a rehabilitation of that of her daughter. This marked reference to breath as a positive witness of life recalls the measuring device featured in *Traverser le jardin* that serves as a metaphor for the central characters' acceptance of both life and mortality.

Cabrera thus reframes a deeply personal, and culturally neglected, narrative of post-natal depression to articulate wider concerns about the central human need for proximity and intimacy. This is achieved through a refusal of the gendered clichés of domestic melodrama in favour of references to horror and myth and an insistence upon the impact of such crises not simply on the maternal body and mind but on the community as a whole. The interrogation of group identities and mutual dependencies continues in Cabrera's next feature film, *Folle embellie*.

Folle embellie: freedom and inclusion

An evident, but ultimately superficial, link between *Le Lait de la tendresse humaine* and *Folle embellie* can be made through the disturbances in the main protagonists' identity and behaviour caused by mental illness. There are, however, more engaging thematic and formal continuities present which include Cabrera's increasing interest in the filming of natural landscapes, an investigation of the function of dialogue and the search for a relationship between the individual and the collective which allows for both liberty and solidarity.

The film is set in June 1940 when, under bombardment by Nazi forces, great swathes of the French population abandoned their homes to seek safety elsewhere. The ensuing chaos enables a group of patients in a large psychiatric institution to leave the hospital unsupervised, and the film's episodic structure maps their shifting relationships, with each other and with wider society, as they travel through abandoned villages eventually finding stability through work and refuge on a farm. The central characters experience a range of reactions to the potential of social integration and each comes to different resolutions of their needs for both support and freedom.

The origins of the project lay in Cabrera's own experience of working in a psychiatric institution over two summers in the early 1970s, and a story recounted to her of patients who had joined the exodus, some of them achieving successful and independent reintegration into family and society. This material also provided the basis for her entrance presentation to IDHEC, 25 years before *Folle embellie* was made.

The impact of psychiatric illness on an individual's ability to form social relationships constitutes a clear continuation of questions broached in both *Demain et encore demain* and *Le Lait de la tendresse humaine*. Cinematic representations of those affected by mental illness have been notoriously reductive and stigmatising, relying on a series of transnational and pangeneric stereotypes that include the homicidal maniac, unstable seductress, zoo specimen and narcissistic parasite (Wedding, Boyd and Niemic 1999: 32). The central characters of *Folle embellie*, however, retain roots in normality, construct social relationships with others and remain largely undefined by constructions of either traumatic etiology or harmless eccentricity. Indeed the specific historical setting provides further contextualisation as the patients' reactions and behaviour seem acceptable within those of the general population suffering from shock and trauma during this period. Cabrera had, however, initially resisted the original historical setting of the narrative:

> Pour simplifier le tournage, j'avais pensé ... transposer l'histoire au présent, dans un pays, soit en proie à la guerre, soit à une catastrophe naturelle, ou pourquoi pas dans un avenir indéfinissable ... mais la débâcle de juin 1940 est, en soi, l'exemple parfait de l'intrusion de la folie dans l'Histoire.[34] (Cabrera 2004).

This broader notion of the disruption of normality, a disturbance that provides a historical echo of that suffered by the patients, is effective, but the choice to maintain historical specificity may also be informed by other factual considerations, namely that of the controversial treatment of patients in mental institutions under the Vichy regime in occupied France. In the period 1940–45 more than fifty-thousand patients starved to death, leading to accusations of 'neglect' of those

---

34 'To simplify the filming, I had planned ... to transpose the story into the present, to a country affected by war or by natural disaster, or why not to an undefined future ... But the debacle of June 1940 is, in itself, the perfect example of the intrusion of madness into History.'

who were classified by the Vichy regime's as being 'of no social value' (von Bueltzingsloewen 2002: 104). The film's staging of the patients' inclusion in the exodus of 1940 bears witness to such neglect whilst also imagining a more positive trajectory.

Heritage cinema dominated French national production from the mid-1980s to the early 1990s and is commonly interpreted as concerned primarily with the construction of nostalgia and conservative values. Such films were characterised by high production values (with concomitantly vast budgets), attention to authentic detail (realised through reconstruction of costume and decor), the adaptation of literary classics, star casts, spectacular set pieces and sumptuous rural settings that evoke 'la France profonde' (an essential France). *Folle embellie* evidently contains several of these traits; however, more fruitful comparisons can be made with heritage productions that also function to provide allegories for contemporary events, such as Chéreau's *La Reine Margot* (1994) which performs a visceral evocation of the Bosnian conflict. This generic capacity for 'playing out contemporary anxieties and fantasies of national identity' (Higson 1993: 118) is demonstrated in *Folle embellie*, as the long sequences of the exodus of June 1940 explicitly recall contemporary news footage of refugees and displaced populations fleeing ever-present global conflicts. Whilst allegorical associations between refugees or *sans papiers* and those suffering from mental illness would be ill conceived, the encounters between the group and wider society evoke problematic negotiations of contemporary cultural differences. Whilst Julien jokes knowingly with a fellow farm-labourer that some of the group's unusual behaviour can be attributed to the fact that they are Swiss, the farmer's reaction to the revelation of the group's true origins and her crushing advice that they should return to the asylum for their own safety serve as a marker of dominant discourses that impede tolerance and integration.

The film does not engage with the details of war – the armistice is reported to Julien and shots of both Nazi officers and returning wounded troops maintain the general historical context. The presence of a series of lingering shots of the corpses of black French soldiers goes beyond generic assurances of authenticity to assert the contemporary political and cultural importance of representing all those who fought. The film does contain documentary elements, as early scenes set in the hospital feature a mixture of professional actors and psychiatric patients from a hospital in Angers, yet these would remain arguably unnoticed by spectators and thus provide little disruption of generic codes. Indeed, this documentary element would seem to contrast sharply with the choice of a cast of central protagonists that, in keeping with the heritage genre, includes some of the most prominent stars of French cinema. The central couple, Alida and Fernand, are played by Miou-Miou and Jean-Pierre Léaud, and their son, Julien, by the star of the Dardennes' *Le Fils*, Morgan Marinne, whilst Marilyne Canto (Colette), Julie-Marie Parmentier (Lucie) and Yolande Moreau (Hélène) excel in supporting roles. The inclusion of such figures assures a wide box office appeal, yet their extra-textual prominence may detract from the credibility of their roles here. Exceptionally, the characterisation of the intellectual, poetic and unpredictable Fernand evidently draws on Léaud's star persona as a troubled and enigmatic figure who combines historic associations with histrionic expectations.[35] This association is reinforced by Fernand's recurring interest in his own performance, his rehearsed lines, extravagant gestures and theatrical manner suggesting a carefully constructed identity. Having left the hospital, Fernand stumbles across an alfresco dinner at a German officers' camp and insists on serving them dessert and coffee. Recognised by an officer as a former Parisian *maître d'hôtel*, he joins in their ironic toast to 'la belle France' before reciting Ronsard and disappearing as enigmatically as he arrived, shedding his costume and his role as he leaves the stage. Indeed this and other episodes of virtuoso performance recall the iconic physical appearance and declamatory, hallucinatory rhetoric of Antonin Artaud as the theatre of cruelty is echoed in the 'theatre' of war.

The angry retort of Fernand's exasperated doctor – 'Je m'en fous de vos symptômes – vous auriez encore plus mal si vous ne sentiez plus rien'[36] becomes Fernand's personal mantra in his sustained defence against social normalisation and his rationale for choosing to enter another asylum. Whilst he is unable, or unwilling, to abandon identificatory reliance upon his 'symptoms' and proves ultimately indifferent to social integration, the group do not follow his lead. The search for

---

35 Léaud became an iconic figure of the Nouvelle Vague through his roles in Truffaut's Antoine Doinel films, but has since been associated with an unfulfilled, radical persona in both filmic and extra-filmic constructions of his star identity.
36 'I don't give a damn about your symptoms – you'd be in even more pain if you felt nothing.'

constructions of social utopias that underwrites the closing scenes of *Nadia et les hippopotames* is rendered more emphatically in *Folle embellie*. Cabrera described the narrative as 'une matrice idéale pour raconter une utopie, une transformation sociale' (Audé 2004: 128) (an ideal matrix through which to talk about utopia, about social transformation) and focus remains predominantly on the positive impact of social interaction. We return here to Cabrera's persistent engagement in the search for formations and discourses of community and the social in which the individual remains a subjective force. It could be suggested that the characters chosen in *Folle embellie* represent an exaggerated individualism and nonconformity that proves, nevertheless, inherently capable of social function. This thematic strand is also articulated through film language as Cabrera's rhythmic alternation of long shots from above, which frame the characters together and integrate them with the natural environment, and close-ups from below which frame them in heroic profile against the sky, enables a construction of the protagonists both as part of a unit and as separate entities.

Fernand's self-appointed leadership reflects social prerogatives as he polices the group (triggering the punishment and consequent suicide of Hélène), accesses economic systems (ensuring proper payment for their work on the farm) and attempts to integrate others (entreating Lucie to speak). However, his paternalistic adoption of this role is disrupted by extreme episodes as he attempts to provide food by killing a cow with a sledgehammer as his behaviour shifts from that of benevolent hunter-gatherer to sadistic executioner. Seemingly incapable of wider social integration himself, his solitary return to institutionalisation frees both Alida and Julien from any further responsibility for him. The rest of the group encounter therapeutic contact with others. Alida's brief stay with Moïse, and the socialisation of life on his boat, enables her to express desire and to calm her panic attacks without medication. Lucie recovers her speech and, when she finally opens the tiny, mysterious suitcase that she has defended throughout the film, is able to leave behind the dress that represented her life before institutionalisation, a life that she can now accept as irretrievable. The healing nature of social contact is accompanied in the narrative by rehabilitation through paid work. The actual money that the group receive provides a clear marker of their integration into social and economic systems, in contrast to the tokens of notional value that Alida took from the hospital. The nostalgic and picturesque nature of this work, gathering in the harvest by hand, constructs a utopian pastoral idyll, yet not a delimited interlude as it offers both Julien and Lucie tangible futures through economic independence and emotional stability.

The overwhelming presence in *Folle embellie* of the beauty of the chosen locations of the Maine et Loire region was presaged by the sweeping shots of the lush Jura landscape that punctuated *Lait de la tendresse humaine*. This shift in perspective and sense of scale is clearly linked to the central themes of liberty and escape: 'il s'agit là de la libération, de liberté, de fuite, d'horizon qui s'ouvre, au sens propre comme au sens figuré. Tout cela donne un sentiment de bonheur, d'exploit presque'[37] (Cabrera 2004). The inclusion of new and broader horizons is complemented by the constant presence of the Loire as lengthy aerial shots of its banks, bridges and the shifting sands of its estuaries provide a central metaphor for the flux of life and the inevitable interconnectedness of social relations. Many such sequences in the film provide visual support to its utopian narrative trajectory, drawing on the lush natural setting and blurring boundaries between reality and hallucination to create a calm, oneiric quality that is further enhanced by Milan Kymlicka's haunting music. As Moïse leaves and his white-sailed boat sails silently into the misty distance as if it were a ghost ship, a close up of its name, L'Angelus, suggests its unearthly nature. The presence of an overabundant magical landscape, in which owls and deer witness Fernand's walk across the treetops, and the scene in which Florent, having eaten poisonous mushrooms, instructs Julien to catch his fiery floating soul in a jam jar, are reminiscent of the riotous magical realism of Kusturica's cinema and work to disrupt the narrative codes and iconography of the heritage genre through their privileging of the subjective and the imaginary. The otherworldly impact of the landscape and music is complemented further by the marked lack of dialogue in the film, a lack which signifies neither incomprehension nor isolation but rather a privileging of the sensual.

After a period of unfulfilled projects, 2009 saw the appearance of two films by Cabrera, one, *Ranger les photos*, a short, intimate documentary, the other, *Quand la ville mord*, a violent thriller made for

---

37 'It's about liberation, about liberty, about escape, about a horizon opening up, both literally and figuratively. All of this gives a sense of happiness, almost of adventure'.

television. Markedly different in provenance, genre and budget, the films nevertheless sustain a complementary interest in the role of creativity in enabling the survival of an assertive subjectivity. *Ranger les photos* is a 'film à quatre mains' (two-person film) which Cabrera made with the documentary film maker Laurent Roth in 1998 as she was moving into a new house (and finishing work on *Demain et encore demain*). The film arose as a challenge in which Roth wanted to try out the fade button on his new camera and Cabrera wanted to explore the relationship between environment and memory. The film's rigid formal constraints (they allowed themselves 12 shots, two fades and no further editing) are countered by a ludic inventiveness in which they fashion the credits from Scrabble tiles. A largely static camera alternates between shots of Cabrera's family photographs and her discussion of the role of photography and provokes a meditation on the relationship between the still and the moving image and between the image and the construction of memory that shift the epic, seminal obsessions of *La Jetée* (Marker, 1962) into an understated domestic setting. Indeed Cabrera's comments on photography's ability to encompass lightness and gravity (engraving) describe the former as a 'flutter of the eyelids' that paradoxically recalls the impact of the only moving image in Marker's film (Cabrera 2010). The film forms an elegiac bridge between the past and present gift of happy memories and the unknown potential for the creation and recording of present and future memories in the new home. The film lay forgotten between 1998 and 2009 and its release is accompanied by further layers of reflection on memory and the image as it followed the death of Cabrera's father, himself a photographer, whose image closes the film.

Cabrera's other 2009 release, *Quand la ville mord*, was also made to a set of constraints; the generic conventions of the thriller, a limited choice of texts to adapt, a €1.5 million budget and a 60 minute length prescribed by its commissioning as part of a series of adaptations, 'Suite noire' for France 2.[38] Cabrera chose to adapt the Marc Villard novel, *Quand la ville mord*, in which a young Congolese woman, Sara, is forced into prostitution by the trafficking gang that brought her and her cousin Zina to Paris. She sustains her desire, inspired by the figure of Basquiat, to become a painter but also becomes a killer, first

38 Other directors involved in this series include Claire Devers, Orso Miret and Laurent Bouhnik.

on impulse when she avenges the killing of her cousin by their pimps and then, through careful planning, when she targets others involved in the exploitation of trafficked women. Cabrera's film makes great use of the physical and aesthetic parallels between Sara's (Aïssa Maïga) assertion of creative agency through her painting and the increasingly structured nature of her killings as the film's dominant palette of red and black reflects both its genre-driven aesthetics and the emerging visual tropes of Sara's work. Cabrera's scrupulous research into contemporary trafficking networks and her clear articulation of the 'vrai enjeu de solidarité' (Cailletet 2009: 58) (the real issues of solidarity) see documentary and thriller elements interwoven in a fable-like narrative in which the dynamic heroine asserts both violent and creative agencies to posit an empowering mood shared by the spectator. Indeed Cabrera changes the ending of the novel to assert a more positive closure.

Social intimacy: 'Etre avec'

In a wide-ranging text that challenges dominant perceptions of the relationship between contemporary art and politics, and which engages throughout with constructions of intimacy, Dominique Baqué identifies contemporary documentary film as one of the few forms which harbours the potential to articulate individual and political consciousness. The hope expressed is that documentary could:

> Passer le témoin: pour libérer la parole et la faire circuler ... pour mettre au jour les dysfonctionnements d'une société malade, éveiller les consciences et construire le témoignage. Construire peut-être, dans ces moments de grâce, de l'être-avec. (Baqué 2004: 281)[39]

This detailed engagement with Cabrera's oeuvre reveals this potential as realised in her work across documentary and fiction. A brief review of *Folle embellie* picks out the evident empathy of the director for her central protagonists, stating that 'Dominique Cabrera est avec tous ceux qu'elle filme' (Strauss 2004: 23) (Dominique Cabrera stands with all the people that she films), and it is this notion of 'être avec'

39 '"Provide a witness": to liberate expression and to help it to circulate ... to shed light on the dysfunctional nature of a sick society, to raise awareness and to bear witness. To build perhaps, in these moments of grace, a "being with".'

or 'being with', in its suggestion of intimacy, proximity and solidarity, that permeates her oeuvre. An insistence upon the importance of the simultaneous recognition of individuality (desire, creative expression) and the need for a sense of collectivity (solidarity, inclusion) is present throughout Cabrera's films, its expression ranging from the sensitive responses of the post office workers in Courneuve to their clients' distress to the personal message written on the hand of Cabrera's lover in *Demain et encore demain*: 'être avec toi c'est une joie et un énigme' (being with you is a joy and an enigma). Such persistent constructions of intimacy transcend the narrative and iconographic conventions of romantic love or sexual desire, and eschew the solipsistic withdrawal from the social and the political with which the intimate in art is often associated, to construct a wider social intimacy,[40] or 'bonheur collectif' (collective happiness). It is this pursuit of the representation of social intimacy, whether through documentary, realism or utopian fiction, which counters the reductive consequences of confining (and thus commodifying) all constructions of the public and private, the political and personal to binary (and hierarchical) oppositions, with a representational politics of inclusion, generosity and tenderness.

References

Althabe, Gérard (1994), 'La Ville rompue', in Jean-Louis Comolli and Gérard Althabe, *Regards sur la ville*, Paris, Editions du Centre Pompidou, 65–104.

Arthur, Paul (2005), 'Extreme Makeover: The Changing Face of Documentary', *Cineaste*, 30 (3), 24–6.

Audé, Françoise (2002), *Cinéma d'elles 1981–2001*, Lausanne, L'Age d'homme.

Audé, Françoise (2004), 'Folle embellie: aperçu sur un décrochage heureux', *positif*, 521, 127–8.

Audé, Françoise and Tobin, Yann (2000), 'Dominique Cabrera: On a raison de se révolter', *positif*, 470, 35–9.

Aufderheide, Patricia (1997), 'Public Intimacy: The Development of First Person Documentary', *Afterimage* (August), 42–53.

Baecque, Antoine de (2005), 'J'en ai assez de la cravate: entretien avec Michael Lonsdale', *Libération* (15 June), 18.

Baqué, Dominique (2004), *Pour un nouvel art politique*, Paris, Flammarion.

Barthes, Roland (1980), *La Chambre claire*, Paris, Editions du Seuil.

Bazin, André (1985), 'Ontologie de la photographie', in *Qu'est ce que le cinéma?*, Paris, Cerf.

40 I am not invoking the specific quantitative indicators of social intimacy used in clinical and psychological research.

Binh, N. T. (2004), 'Dominique Cabrera' www.festivallarochelle.ord.fr/categorie.asp?id=115 (accessed 11 November Faber 2004).

Bueltzingsloewen, I. von (2002), 'Les "Aliénés" morts de faim dans les hôpitaux psychiatriques français sous l'Occupation' *Vingtième siècle. Revue d'Histoire*, 76, 99–115.

Cabrera, Dominique (1992), *Rester là-bas. Pieds noirs et Algériens, trente ans après*, Paris, Editions du Félin.

Cabrera, Dominique (2000), 'Entretien', *positif*, 470, 39–41.

Cabrera, Dominique (2001), 'Les Idées sont vivantes et la vie est politique', www.peripheries.net/g-cabr.htm.

Cabrera, Dominique (2004), 'Déjeuners du film français', www.lefilmfrançais.com/270804/dejeuners1.htm.

Cabrera, Dominique (2010), Interview with Zoe Chantre in *Réel*, www.cinemadureel.org/article4327.html.

Cadé, Michel (2000), *L'Ecran bleu, la représentation des ouvriers dans le cinéma-français*, Perpignan, Presses universitaires de Perpignan.

Cailletet, Marie (2009), 'De peinture et de sang', *Télérama*, 3103 (July 2009), 58.

Chevandier, Christian (2000), 'Nadia et les hippopotames', *Vingtième siècle. Revue d'Histoire*, 67, 161–3.

Comolli, Jean-Louis (1994), 'La vie filmée', in Jean-Louis Comolli and Gérard Althabe, *Regards sur la ville*, Paris, Editions du Centre Pompidou, 13–64.

Corcuff, Pierre (1999), 'Soyons fiers de notre côté hippopotame', *Les Inrockuptibles* (12 May), 47.

Deleuze, Gilles (1985), *Cinema 2, L'Image-temps*, Paris, Editions de minuit.

Grat, Alain (2000), 'Retour du mémoire', in *Rencontres cinématographiques de la Seine Saint Denis*, Paris, 2–4.

Hampl, Patricia (1996), 'Memory's Movies', in Charles Warren (ed.), *Beyond Document: Essays on Nonfiction Film*, Hanover, Wesleyan University Press, 52–63.

Higson, Andrew (1993), 'Re-presenting the National Past: Nostalgia and Pastiche in the Heritage Film', in L. Friedman (ed.), *British Cinema and Thatcherism: Fires Were Started*, London, UCL Press, 109–29.

Lamberbourg, Adeline (2010), 'Parcours croisés de Dominique Cabrera, cinéaste, et de ses proches collaborateurs', *Temporalités* (November 2010) http://temporalites.revues.org/index1218.html.

Marks, Laura U. (2002), *Touch: Sensuous Theory and Multisensory Media*, Minneapolis, University of Minneapolis Press.

Mathieu, Lilian (2003), 'La Solidarité, ça ce n'est pas si facile', *Mouvements*, 27/28, 65–72.

Nichols, Bill (1993), 'Getting to know you … Knowledge, Power and the Body', in Michael Renov, (ed.), *Theorizing Documentary*, London and New York, Routledge, 174–91.

O'Shaughnessy, Martin (2004), 'Suffering in Silence: Bodily Politics in Post-1995 French Film', *French Cultural Studies*, 15, 219–33.

O'Shaughnessy, Martin (2007), *The New Face of Political Cinema: Commitment in French Film since 1995*, New York and Oxford, Bergahn Books.

Powrie, Phil (1997), *French Cinema in the 1980s: Nostalgia and the Crisis of Masculinity*, Oxford, Oxford University Press.

Prédal, Réné (2002), *Le Jeune Cinéma français*, Paris, Nathan.

Puaux, Françoise (2001), 'Entretien avec Dominique Cabrera', *Cinémaction*, 99, 173–80.

Renov, Michael (2004) *The Subject of Documentary*, Minneapolis, University of Minnesota Press.

Scheibler, Susan (1993), 'Constantly Performing the Documentary', in M. Renov (ed.), *Theorizing Documentary*, London and New York, Routledge, 135–50.

Sontag, Susan (1977), *On Photography*, New York and London, Picador.

Stora, Benjamin (2001), 'L'Algérie d'une guerre à l'autre. Enseigner la guerre d'Algérie et le Maghreb contemporain', actes de la DESCO, www.eduscol. education.fr.

Strauss, Frédéric (2004), 'Folle embellie', *Télérama*, 2843, 12–13.

Tarr, Carrie with Rollet, Brigitte (2004) *Cinema and the Second Sex*, London, Continuum.

Villard, Marc (2006), *Quand la ville mord*, Paris, La Branche.

Wedding, Danny, Boyd, Mary Ann and Niemic, Ryan (1999), *Movies and Mental Illness: Using Film to Understand Psychopathology*, London, McGraw-Hill.

Winston, Bill (1995), *Claiming the Real: The Documentary Film Revisited*, London, BFI.

2

Noémie Lvovsky: rupture and transmission

The career path of Noémie Lvovsky remains distinctive from that of other directors discussed in this volume as, despite a conventional start with a degree in Humanities followed by membership of the first cohort of FEMIS graduates (scriptwriting, 1990), she now sustains multiple profiles as director, writer and actor. The opportunity to pursue these divergent roles was triggered largely by her collaborative presence within a group of filmmakers, writers and actors who started their careers in the early 1990s and formed a strong network that, whilst also receiving formal funding, was able to use social connections to bypass some of the conventional functions of agent, contractual obligation and lengthy forward planning.[1] Lvovsky worked with Desplechin on *La Sentinelle* (1992), co-wrote *Clubbed to Death* (Zauberman, 1997) and served as co-writer and producer on Valeria Bruni Tedeschi's directorial debut *Il est plus facile pour un chameau ...* and the later *Actrices* (2007). In addition to mainstream success as a writer and director she has acted in 24 films and now enjoys wide public recognition primarily as an actress. Lvovsky received critical acclaim early in her career for her two first short films, *Dis-moi oui, dis-moi non* (1989) and *Embrasse-moi* (1990). She continues to enjoy widespread recognition in France – her films regularly achieve both multiple César nominations and box office success – but they have yet to receive significant attention or distribution beyond France. Her films focus on individuals faced with situations of rupture and change

1 Indeed Emmanuelle Devos credits a meeting with Lvovsky (and consequent introductions to Valeria Bruni Tedeschi, Arnaud Desplechin and Eric Rochant) as enabling her to pursue a career in acting via 'friends not agents' (Devos 2009).

who struggle to channel their palpable energy into the construction of viable identities. This chapter will also suggest that although Lvovsky's films seem to develop from early social engagement to a focus on mainstream comedy these later films should, nonetheless, be read in relation to wider socio-political discourses.

Borderlines: *Oublie-moi* (1994)

The main characteristics of Lvovsky's first feature film are clearly anticipated in her short *Dis-moi oui, dis-moi non*, which formed part of her FEMIS graduation work and was released, to critical success, in 1989.[2] This very-low-budget work, filmed in Nanterre University buildings and at a house party, boasts a cast which includes Valeria Bruni Tedeschi, Emmanuelle Devos, Olivier Py and Emmanuel Salinger, who all went on to become key actors of their generation. The use of long sequences, tight framing, direct sound and natural light constructs an intimate portrait of the inability of the central character Cécile (Valeria Bruni Tedeschi) and others to make decisions over romantic commitments and future plans. As she hides from her best friend that 'her Frédéric' and 'my Frédéric' are indeed one and the same person, the group remains stuck in option paralysis, unable to accept responsibility for moving their narrative(s) onwards. The use of shooting through glass creates serial reflected profiles that present the characters' fragmented identities and construct a Kieslowskian formal tension between seeing and knowing.

Lvovsky's first feature film, *Oublie-moi* returns to these central preoccupations, in which the paralysing fear of decision articulated in *Dis-moi oui, dis-moi non* through the static camera, long takes and close framing continues. *Oublie-moi*'s elliptical narrative escapes domestic interiors however to feature sequences in which the central protagonist, Nathalie (Bruni Tedeschi again), undertakes exhausting journeys across city spaces. Apparently driven by an obsessive quest to identify 'real' love, she harasses ex-lover Eric (Laurent Grévill) at home and in his workplace, leaves current partner Antoine (Emmanuel Salinger) and alienates best friend Christelle (Emmanuelle Devos) by starting a relationship with the latter's depressed partner, Fabrice

2 The short was nominated for many awards and won the Jury Award at the Munich International Festival of Film Schools in 1990.

(Philippe Torreton). Nathalie's increasingly unpredictable behaviour serves to increase her social isolation yet her demands for romantic love seem increasingly to serve as a substitute for any sense of social belonging. The circular narrative and open ending suggest a problematic attempt at *réinsertion sociale* (social rehabilitation) via the re-establishment of the romantic couple. I will explore the film through the trope of the borderline – both that of the 'borderline' character and that of the borderlines conventionally drawn between public and private space (and thus between the intimate and the social). Such divisions, and the subversion thereof, must be considered here in the context of a dynamic that informs Lvovsky's oeuvre, the tensions between melodrama and realism, between authenticity and performance, which permeate her films.

In clinical discourse, those suffering from borderline personality disorder experience instability in moods, repetitive and compulsive behaviour, and will undertake extreme measures to avoid being alone (including physical aggression and self-harm). Some research has claimed that this 'disorder of emotion regulation' affects a quarter of young adults, predominantly women (Swartz, Blazer et al., 1990: 262). A film that adopts this very term as title, *Border Line* (Dubroux, 1992), features a woman whose grief-stricken behaviour exposes the fine margins between socially accepted response and perceived psychological disturbance. The figure of the 'borderline' heroine recurs in films of the mid-1990s (discussed here in relation to *Oublie-moi* but also relevant to Masson's Kiberlain trilogy) and it is interesting to note that the emergence of their male equivalents[3] comes almost a decade later. The borderline character is presented as an alienated and solitary figure who, unable to articulate personal fears and desires, becomes locked into an obsessive mode that threatens to separate them from the social. In *Oublie-moi*, Nathalie's need for intimacy and to share another's space becomes almost pathological as she pursues defunct relationships, embarks upon ill-considered actions simply to remain in company and reacts with increasing violence to any challenge. The apparently paradoxical mixture of her denial of change (rupture with Eric) with her inability to communicate except through conflict creates a fragmented and claustrophobic mood in which she runs, in

---

3 Primary examples include the characters of Ismael (Mathieu Amalric) in *Rois et reine* (Desplechin, 2004) and Paul (Romain Duris) in *Dans Paris* (Honoré, 2006).

ever decreasing circles, from one failing relationship to another. The 'borderline' heroine presents a negative version of the unruly woman of screwball comedy (discussed further in Chapter 4) displaying not opportunism but compulsion and replacing a spontaneous, unconventional *joie de vivre* with a performative *mal de vivre*.

Although terminologies change, such 'borderline' fictional characters are not a solely contemporary phenomenon and have, across national film histories, been constructed and represented largely within the generic templates of the melodrama, a genre associated with anxious responses to perceived shifts in social hierarchy. The status of melodrama in film history was perceived as a 'feminised' and therefore inferior genre until re-evaluations of its construction of spectatorship and use of *mise en scène* by feminist critics in the 1990s also identified the western and gangster film as containing inherently melodramatic features (Kaplan 1983). O'Shaughnessy identifies the use of generic codes of melodrama in forming contemporary filmic articulations of the political and argues that, in response to the loss of conventional political discourse and class solidarities, such forms can, paradoxically, provide a powerful critique of individualism (O'Shaughnessy 2007: 180). The very isolation of such 'borderline' protagonists may be seen as a barrier to any representation of the socio-political, yet their presence and the accompanying dramatisation of the narrow margins that separate tolerated behaviour from exclusion bring into relief the unstable and often arbitrary nature of the social order. Lvovsky's first films contain elements of melodramatic convention including the highly charged emotive focus on an individual character, the attempt to define relationships through serial, compulsive confrontations and a displacement of the verbal articulation of anxiety and repressed desire onto communication through the gestural and the body. This mode is challenged, however, by the rejection of other melodramatic characteristics, notably through the absence of confinement and domestic space in *Oublie-moi* and an insistence on group relationships, which reject the melodramatic primacy of both the isolated individual and the escapist romantic, in *La Vie ne me fait pas peur* (1999).

I have written elsewhere (Dobson 2001) on the striking parallels in the representation of the female subject in crisis in the city in the contemporaneous releases which both star Bruni Tedeschi, *Oublie-moi* and *Les Gens normaux n'ont rien d'exceptionnel* (Ferreira Barbosa

1994). While it is clear that the female protagonists of contemporary French film are no longer divided simply between the serial spatial confinements of romance or melodrama and the transgressive but fated (and fatal) inscriptions of the *femme fatale* in the cityscape, there remain startlingly few positive representations of a female protagonist's presence in urban space. Indeed although the *cinéma du look*'s domination of the previous decade provided its male protagonists with stylised new quest trajectories across (and often underneath) the cityscape, French films of the 1990s are notable for their displacement of the crisis of the female subject from the domestic to the urban outdoors. Yet the normalising narrative closure, which legitimises female visibility in the city through the establishment of the romantic couple, retains its power over even the most outwardly modern heroines (see *Chacun cherche son chat* (Klapisch, 1996)) and there is perhaps little cause for celebration in the realisation that one of the few assertively mobile female subjects in the city of recent years should be the eponymous heroine of *Le Fabuleux Destin d'Amélie Poulain* (Jeunet, 2001), contained as she is within a reductively conservative, nostalgic vision of Paris and its inhabitants.

Although it remains impossible to bypass the 'connotative chain of associated meanings ... informed themselves by the ideologies and aesthetics of gendered place' (Mulvey 1992: 56), *Oublie-moi* adopts a particular strategy of spatial trajectories. The film does not contain the crisis of its central female character in the traditionally suffocating, domestic interiors of melodrama, yet neither does it present a superficially unproblematic access to the traditionally masculine, public spaces of the city. Indeed the rare shots of domestic interiors share the same sombre palette and sparse decoration of the workplaces or public spaces seen in the film and offer neither sanctuary nor structure. Nathalie is located primarily in what Marc Augé describes as the *non-lieux* or 'non-places' of contemporary 'supermodernity', sites which lack the social functions of place and thus privilege 'un monde promis à l'individualité solitaire, au passage, au provisoire' (Augé 1992: 101) (a world promised to solitary individuality, the transitory and the provisional). Augé's non-differentiation between occupants of the *non-lieux* who, regardless of race, class or gender, enjoy an apparently equal access to such sites remains a persistently problematic context yet Lvovsky's film foregrounds rather the unliveable nature of such 'solitary individuality'. Nathalie's serial exclusions from domestic spaces (including the maternal home) are highlighted through her repeated struggles to cross domestic thresholds, whilst her lack of purchase on public space is constructed through the rare long shots that isolate her panicked movement within a static and indifferent setting. Her occupation of non-places (including metro platforms, bus shelters, shared landings and hospital corridors) thus supplies both a construction and reinforcement of her fragile, shifting identity, forms an effective spatial limbo to match the elliptical temporal mode of the film and suggests an ironic mapping of the very lack of social connections that paralyses and alienates the central characters.

Viewing the corporeal as 'un autre symptôme "parlant" du désarroi et du retrait du politique' (O'Shaughnessy 2005: 95) (another symptom which 'speaks' of the disarray and the withdrawal of the political) is not in itself problematic, yet important risks emerge when such narratives foreground the female body as the site of articulations of suffering. Melodrama has been identified as one of three generic modes (including pornography and horror) that posit the female body as site of excess and spectacle (Williams 1991), and this context must be considered in any evaluation of the role of the melodramatic as an articulation of the political. The assertion of communication via the corporeal as an articulation of suffering risks the evocation of familiar limiting discourses which threaten to define the (alienated) young female protagonist as modern hysteric, her agency and subjectivity sublimated into a spectacle of erotically framed bodily 'symptoms'[4] which, in turn, render her inherently incapable of engagement with the social. *Oublie-moi* was one of Bruni Tedeschi's first appearances in French film, and reviews were dominated by responses to her astonishing central performance. Whilst the dynamic between performance and authenticity is central to all constructions of star identity, this tension is particularly marked in Bruni Tedeschi's on- and off-screen reconciliation of the opposites of paralysing introspection and violent, ceaseless physicality.[5] Nathalie, the central protagonist of *Oublie-moi*, is characterised throughout the film not by a melodramatically excessive physical display but by her persis-

---

4 An association most famously evidenced in Charcot's (posed) photographs of female hysterics.
5 Her directorial debut (co-written with Lvovsky) *Il est plus facile pour un chameau ...* in which she also stars is punctuated by short bursts of acrobatics and dance that disrupt the narrative.

tently obstinate physical presence, as she refuses to move, to leave, to sit down or to stand up in different scenarios. Nathalie's verbal articulacy swings between dense outpourings and defiant silences, yet her block-like physicality remains consistent throughout and serves to counter frustrated spectatorial expectations of narrative coherence. As Nathalie's serial exclusions from the homes of others escalates, so does the violence of her physical responses to these rejections, progressing from the obstinate occupation of stairs and landings to banging her head against walls, kicking in doors and deliberately crashing her car. Even when her desperate attempts to provoke human contact through physical force prove futile, she does not become passive and, in her last confrontation with Eric as she refuses to sit down in the café, it is her lack of movement and obstinate mute glare that defeat all attempts at reconciliation or inclusion. Nathalie is also resolutely un-hysterical in her emphatic removal from the erotic, her body serving as a block to communication rather than the site of displaced (and eroticised) suffering. When a drunken Fabrice and Nathalie get into bed together any promise of escapism or narrative progression via the erotic (for protagonists or spectators) is quickly quashed by the marked absence of visual conventions of the eroticised body. This is further undercut by a dialogue of abjection in which a comparison of their respective failures to excel in sexual performances results, not in a construction of alternative models but in a further anti-climactic and mutual misunderstanding. The convention of the sexual encounter as bypassing social convention in order to reveal a more authentic (or at least alternative) mode of communication is thus rejected and then satirised further in a startling sequence in which Nathalie has sex with a stranger (Jacques Nolot) in a public toilet. The mood of this short scene shifts quickly from startled voyeurism to uneasy absurdity as Nathalie disrupts the primacy of the physical with a barrage of bitterly ironic enquiries as to the life-changing, romantic nature of their 'relationship'.[6]

Whilst no alternative mode of communication is provided by the physical intimacy of sex, it is dance, with its complex combinations of exhilarating physicality and narrative (social) patterning, that offers a freedom of self-expression central to Lvovsky's work, culminating

---

6 A tentative 'three in a bed' scene between Fabrice, Nathalie and Christelle ends in similar discord as Christelle ends her friendship with Nathalie and announces her pregnancy.

in the explicitly titled *Faut que ça danse*. Its importance is asserted in the opening sequence of *Oublie-moi*, which provides no conventional establishing functions, but rather immerses the audience in a closely framed sequence of Nathalie and Christelle dancing. The disconcerting lack of context, incongruously bright natural lighting and absence of dialogue oblige us to search the song ('Distant Fingers', Patti Smith, 1976) and the movements of the two women for narrative clues. The contrast between the lyrics' suggestion of a passive wait for love and Smith's inimitably assertive delivery provide a striking opening to the film and encapsulate the paradoxical nature of Nathalie's aggressively dependent stance. Her confident movements and physical proximity invite her friend's participation, yet Christelle is repeatedly wrong-footed and excluded as Nathalie's self-absorption fails to sustain shared choreographies. The carefully off-centre, partial framing of the two bodies in motion avoids any suggestion of fetishised display and provides rather a key to the narrative focus of the film as the characters' attempts to share space and to articulate identity remain emblematic of their pervasive disconnection with the social, and its consequent impact on the intimate.

This disconnection is also evident in verbal communication as all characters but Eric fail to engage in dialogue and remain absorbed in their own externalised monologues.[7] The lack of any access to an authentic subjectivity through language is heightened by the uncanny nature of Nathalie's confrontational speeches which do not take the form of the incoherent outpourings suggested by her erratic behaviour, but present scripted lines and compulsive deliveries of extreme versions of romantic discourse which switch between declarations of undying love and clichés of absolute rejection.[8] Her resistance to dialogue extends to her insistence that others repeat lines of her choosing and, whereas Eric can be seen to reject his role as mere prop for her performances, Antoine conspires in maintaining role plays that recall the ill-fated, tragicomic, reflexive constructions of coupledom in *Pierrot le fou* (Godard, 1965). In the closing sequence of the film Nathalie, driven by emotional regret or, implicitly, by financial desperation and homelessness, calls ex-partner Antoine from the telephone kiosk outside his flat. The frame of the kiosk evokes a podium or platform for performance and Nathalie, encouraged by

7 Eric's engagement with the social through work is also a notable distinction.
8 The choice of 'Télégraphe' as Nathalie's local metro station adds irony.

Antoine, engages in a scenario in which he pretends to be the new tenant who, undisturbed by her parodically extreme self-description as 'une vraie plaie, un poison, un calvaire' (a real pain, a poison, an ordeal), wants to meet her. Lvovsky maintains that the ending is positive in its signalling of Nathalie's recuperation (Audé 1995: 40), yet the continuing performativity of central relationships, the cyclical turn of the narrative (echoing an earlier phone call) and the ambiguity of the final freeze frame undermine this suggestion of redemptive narrative closure.

The explosion in contemporary culture of a focus and projection of the intimate to all public (and virtual) realms is commonly recognised and, in the context of political agency, the causes of 'ce repli sur l'intime' (Baqué 2009: 38) (this withdrawal into the intimate) have been identified as the loss of ideological metanarratives, a crisis in political engagement, the development of the society of the spectacle and the social alienations triggered by evolved capitalism. The central protagonist of *Oublie-moi* attempts to compensate for a lack of social intimacy (the support of microsociology through different types of collectivity) by resorting to solipsistic re-enactments of the conventional model of resolving individual or social alienation, that of the romantic couple. O'Shaughnessy similarly identifies the 'ideological risks' to political engagement invited through melodrama's privileging of an individual's psychological trajectory over wider determining factors in social alienation, such as class or the demands of late capitalist consumerism (O'Shaughnessy 2007: 3). Yet this can be countered by the conviction that discourses of the personal remain political, and that constructions, and representations, of individual subjectivity and the social cannot be disassociated. This inherent link is reflected in Osganian's claim that

> le décentrement progressif des conflits de la communauté ... vers la solitude de l'individu en proie à l'angoisse et à l'anomie laisse la subjectivité à la portée du social, nous rappelant que le social, précisément, ne va pas de soi.[9] (Osganian 2003: 51)

The apparently isolated and isolating struggle of the central characters to establish coherent identities thus does reflect the 'déliaison

---

9 'the gradual decentring of conflicts that affect a community ... towards the solitary individual plagued by anxiety and anomie leaves subjectivity within reach of the social, reminding us precisely that the social is not self-evident'.

sociale' or social disconnection that forms a central concern of the return to the political in 1990s French cinema.

Oublie-moi employs elements of the melodrama to support a central narrative that presents tensions between realism and melodrama, between constructions of authenticity and a reflexively performative mode. This formal dynamic creates a parallel articulation of the central characters' difficulties in sustaining a relationship with the real and with articulations of the social. The punctuation of the film by fades to black supports the elliptical narrative and this is reinforced further by a recurring melancholy motif that contrasts sharply with the energetic motivated music within the narrative. The short outdoor scenes are filmed with a jerky hand-held camera which reflects and constructs Nathalie's chaotic trajectories yet, whilst the interior spaces seem realistically dilapidated for the characters' lifestyles, this realist element is countered by the film's striking adherence to an artificially restricted colour palette of greys and white and the recurrence of beautifully composed frames that foreground their own *mise en scène*. Nathalie, Christelle and Fabrice are adults in their late twenties with no work, no routine, no plan and little sense of self, as is reflected in their repeated unsuccessful journeys, in which they possess neither literal nor metaphorical sense of direction or destination. Nathalie loses her flat and, whilst a series of shots of her waking in different apartments may suggest increased sexual promiscuity, it also reflects the material needs created by her homelessness. The absence of wider familial or social frameworks and the individualistic mantras of late capitalism have left her seemingly bereft of any solid foundations on which to build a self and her compulsive attempts to construct connection through conflict act as compensation for the lack of opportunities for wider social engagement or agency. Fabrice boasts of his inability to assume any responsibility and, whilst Nathalie's destructive pathologisation of romantic love is her chosen discourse of self-definition, he adopts a patchwork of literary quotations and music. His awkward prolonged translation of the lyrics of Lou Reed's 'There Is No Time' and his championing of it as a 'chanson révolutionnaire' retain a striking ironic function as the song's call to action (and rejection of 'endless thinking') will remain emphatically unanswered. Christelle's incapacity for decision is openly mocked yet she welcomes her pregnancy as an unavoidable catalyst for imminent change. Creating a mood that recalls the exhausting aimlessness of the central protagonists of Eustache and Garrel,[10] Lvovsky's characterisation provides little sense of the protagonists' formative pasts or futures as they cling resentfully to each other for self-definition. The economic and social *précarité* evident in the characters' interactions and environments permeates their sense of self as, inhabiting the spatial and temporal limbos of the film and of her social condition, Nathalie can only claim absurdly that 'le temps ne passe pas forcément' (time doesn't necessarily pass).

Coming of age: *La Vie ne me fait pas peur* (1999)

If the characters of *Oublie-moi* at times resemble strangely joyless teenagers, this representation is countered by the explosive and inventive portrayal of female adolescence in Lvovsky's next two films. *Petites* (1998) was made for television and can be seen as an unofficial addition to the series of nine films commissioned by Arte, *Tous les garçons et les filles de leur âge* in which a group of emerging directors were given the same brief – to make a film set in the period of their teenage years.[11] The identification of the series as a significant marker in the emergence of a new generation of directors, new relationships between film and television in France (Austin 1996: 171, Mayne 2005: 207) and the re-emergence of the *auteur* figure (Powrie 1999: 1, Wilson 1999: 34), have accorded a high profile to the 'coming of age' narratives produced in this period. After the success of *Petites*, Lvovsky made a feature film using 50 minutes of its original 90 minutes and expanding the narrative to include events that catch up with the central characters three years later. The resulting film, *La Vie ne me fait pas peur* (1999), remains one of the most striking films on adolescence, and it is this version that I will discuss here.

La Vie ne me fait pas peur constitutes a visceral, celebratory picture of four girls' journey from adolescence into adulthood which manages to avoid both nostalgic sentimentality and the classic narrative features of 'teenploitation' – witnessed in films which present voyeuristic constructions of teenage sexuality as a displaced locus of

---

10 Lvovsky co-wrote *Coeur fantôme* (Garrel, 1996).

11 The series included films by Téchiné (*Les Roseaux sauvages*), Assayas (*L'Eau froide*) and Denis (*US Go Home*) that went on to garner awards at international festivals.

monstrosity and excess.[12] Films on adolescence are dominated by rites of passage narratives which focus on an individual (and usually male) protagonist who works through revolt against the adult world towards a narrative resolution that invokes either socialisation or utopian escape as represented seminally in *Les quatre cent coups* (Truffaut, 1959). Yet, following the significant success of *Diabolomenthe* (*Peppermint soda*) (Kurys, 1977), French women directors have established a lineage of women-centred narratives of adolescence to form 'a persistent focus of French women's filmmaking since the 1970s' (Tarr with Rollet 2001: 25). The popularity of such narratives could be explained through the seductiveness of nostalgia and the established model of auteurist autofictions, but this does not exclude the stronger political imperative to counter the dominant voyeuristic representation of adolescent girls and to foreground the 'problematic rites of passage towards adult femininity' (Tarr with Rollet 2001: 25) encountered in patriarchal societies. *La Vie ne me fait pas peur* is described by Tarr as 'an exuberant post-feminist reworking of the themes of "Diabolomenthe" in its foregrounding of schoolgirls, female friendships and dysfunctional families' (Tarr with Rollet 2001: 28), yet, whilst the thematic convergences are clear, its boisterous mood and non-realist elements remain strikingly different to those of Kurys's work. The film can also be read as a female friendship film yet it cannot be categorised as sentimental melodrama (Hollinger 1998: 4) and maintains a radically different aesthetic from the tenderness, patience and understatement identified as characteristic of French cinematic articulations of this genre (Wilson 2001: 266–7). The main influence, cited by writers Lvovsky and Seyros, is that of Jane Campion's adaptation of Janet Frame's extraordinary autobiography, *An Angel at My Table* (Campion, 1991) (Strauss 2000: 23), and evident shared elements include the privileging of the sensual over the narrative (supported by Agnès Godard's attention to rhythm and close, hand-held camerawork), a refusal of anticipated narrative climax and a celebration of the role of the imagination in building identity. The script for *La Vie ne me fait pas peur* was informed by interviews with Lvovsky and her

12 *Carrie* (de Palma, 1976) and its articulations of anxiety around emerging (female) sexuality provide the prime example of such tropes, yet more recent examples, such as *American Beauty* (Mendes, 1999) or *Heavenly Creatures* (Jackson, 1994), repeat scenarios in which the projected sexual agency of female adolescent characters triggers destruction.

own teenage friends (Strauss 2000: 9), casting took six months and none of those chosen for the lead roles had significant prior acting experience. The film follows its four central characters Emilie (Magali Woch), Stella (Julie-Marie Parmentier), Inès (Ingrid Molinier) and Marion (Camille Rousselet) from their negotiation of new schools and serial crushes on classmates to their crossing of the different thresholds of sexual initiation and the *baccalaureat* (refreshingly, the latter is shown to be more problematic). The last scene is a fantasy musical sequence in which they provide mutual support for the projection of their individual ideal future identities.

Loss of virginity remains a recognised narrative trope in films on adolescence (Kaveney 2006: 4) and is commonly reconfigured through tragic or even comic moods (Tarr with Rollet 2001: 38). The characters' active seeking out of sexual experiences in the second part of the film and their view of virginity as a burden is common to other contemporary filmic representations of female adolescence including *36 fillette* (Breillat, 1988) and *Naissance des pieuvres* (Sciamma, 2007). The conventional narrative trope of sexual initiation by an older man is ironically undercut by Emilie's drama teacher's abuse of trust, Marion's joking provocation to her arrogant boyfriend to rape her is taken too far and Inès suffers an Italian boy's clumsy penetration. The matter of fact visual representation of these scenarios is reinforced by the subsequent lack of narrative privileging of the events and a refusal of their conventional status as life-defining or traumatic sites of gendered, personal and narrative development. If the trope of sexual initiation serves here rather as narrative anticlimax, this brings into relief the film's insistence on the un-eroticised physicality of the central protagonists. The sequence that immediately precedes their sexual experiences ends with another conventional marker of adolescent identity more commonly used in narratives of male adolescence; the forming of a blood pact to assert a group identity. The sequence ends with a striking and lengthy close-up of the girls' entwined and bloody fingers, and such insistence on the materiality of the body and the mess of life provides an anticipatory counter to any potential romanticisation of sex. The physical presence of the body as obstacle or stubborn matter that punctuates *Oublie-moi* shifts in *La Vie* to a celebration of the energy, rage and joy of the group as they run, fight and dance. In direct contrast to the suggestion that female friendship films reveal identification to be dependent on loss and illusion (Wilson

2001: 265), their relationships depend on proximity, physicality and creative fantasy. From an early extreme close-up of Emilie and Stella screaming into the camera to the final sequence of exuberant dancing the girls are rarely still and never passive. Physical interaction enables them to reassert both joyful and violent group identity as Stella and Marion resolve an argument by mimicking apes together, Stella gets the studious Inès's attention by assaulting her and, after visiting Inès in hospital, the others throw drinks over each other to reassert physical proximity, group dynamics and life in the face of serious illness. From Marion's and Emilie's riotous bedroom performance to 'Ballroom Blitz' (which turns into a fight) to the group's collective invasion of the dance floor when on holiday in Italy, scenes of dancing punctuate the film. This presents both a sanctioned outlet for physical exuberance and a space in which they rehearse the tensions between their private selves and the social constructions of (gendered) adulthood that await them. Such physicality is emphasised further by the extended use of loud, fast music, the urgency of Agnès Godard's use of extreme close-up and hand-held camera and the energy of partly improvised scenes.[13]

Whilst the characters remain distinctive from one another, it is their activity and identity as a group that dominate the first half of the film and, although we see them in isolation from each other in later sequences, the editing retains strong parallels between their experiences. Unlike the female friendships presented in *La Vie rêvée des anges* (Zonca, 1998) or *Mina Tannenbaum* (Dugowson, 1994) in which the dualistic pairings of female friends trigger melodramatically tragic endings, Lvovsky's group does not fragment. Whilst the tropes of classical melodrama haunt the film through the marginal character of Emilie's troubled mother (played by Bruni Tedeschi as a problematic vision of the central protagonist of *Oublie-moi*'s older self), the elliptical narrative and fast pace of the film allow little pause for broader, spectatorial reflection on the emotional or psychological impact of events. Melodramatic scenarios loom (a serious illness, a suicide attempt and a betrayal of trust), yet their dramatic portent and anticipated narrative trajectories are undermined and displaced through generic and formal disruption. Emilie's apparent suicide attempt is

13 In the only sequence in which physicality evokes danger, the contrast is constructed through the rare use of long shot and shot-counter-shot as the girls escape from drunken Italian boy racers.

undercut by humour as the medics recoil in disgust at the contents of her vomit, and Inès' victory over her illness is represented in the form of an early video game as an animated avatar blasts abnormal cells with a cartoon AK47. Physical articulation takes precedent over verbal communication in the first half of the film, yet a growing realisation of the importance of accessing alternative channels of communication becomes increasingly evident (Inès writes, Emilie acts, Stella tries music before training to work in radio). Verbal communication does not, however, form the anticipated rational counter to the excessive physicality of the film as it is linked primarily to negotiations between personal fantasies and external realities, between constructions of self and external discourses and environments. The film's exploration of the mechanisms of representation is stated clearly at the outset in a sequence which forms a striking parallel to the opening sequence of *Mina Tannenbaum*, in which an imaginative response to an optician's eye test (a different *way* of seeing) is discounted as failure. In the opening sequence of *La Vie ne me fait pas peur*, a young Emilie poses patiently as her father draws her only to discover that he has produced a picture of an apple (as she is his 'petite pomme') rather than a realist likeness. The blurring or reordering of distinctions between reality and perception are explored further in the girls' creation of alternative scenarios and improvisation throughout the film. The film language matches these constructions as the mock interviews in which they pose as older women recounting their numerous marriages are filmed in conventional documentary mode using a mid talking head shot with a fixed camera, and the ceremony in which they present material fetishes (doormat, discarded chewing gum, a tape recording) of the object of their schoolgirl adoration shifts from the realist to the fantastic through music, swirling camera movement and a densely stylised use of colour.

Lvovsky thus undermines generic expectations by exceeding the representation of their position through the point of view shot integral to filmic realism to create subjective distortions of time and sound, thus challenging a naturalism which stumbles 'sans cesse sur sa propre impossibilité et se retourne comme un gant' (Chauvin 2010) (incessantly over its own impossibility and is turned completely inside out). The recurrence of such episodes can be read as the protagonists' responses to events that are worked through not via the intrusive, involuntary and deferred modes of traumatic discourse but as controlled, creative projections that counter loss, fear and repression with playful and empowering resolutions. Fantasy dominates the film's closure as the protagonists, located in an explicitly set-like space, both celebrate their continuing solidarity and challenge the limitations of socio-cultural discourse as to what their gendered future may hold. When dressed in iconic and exaggerated costumes (Emilie as white-gowned pregnant bride, Stella as Marilyn Monroe, Marion as androgynous ringmaster) the group's adoption of stereotypes is clearly ironic and continues the playful challenges made by the film both to realism and to the conventional representation of female identity. The ending has been read as a replacement of the angry contestation of earlier scenes with 'feel-good, postmodern irony' (Tarr with Rollet 2001: 35), yet the restless energy behind the knowing manipulation of such representations exceeds this and supports the rejection of conventional closures that offer the limited options of sanctioned social integration or melodramatic tragedy. The choice of song in the final sequence further supports this as the first verse of Dassin's 'A toï' (To You) provides a parodic undercutting of the groom's serenade to his pregnant bride, and the later verses, which accompany the friends' final joyful dance, insist upon the projection of the 'nous' (we) as an alternative collective identity which here remains unbroken by the conventions of the coming of age narrative and supported by both shared memory and sustained community.

Chorus and discord: *Les Sentiments* (2003)

The box office success of *Les Sentiments* (the only film by the four directors in this volume to cross the million entry threshold) triggered a marked change in Lvovsky's profile that can be linked to the film's clear generic framework (dramatic comedy), an (over)familiar narrative (mid-life crisis triggering relationship breakdown) and stellar ensemble cast. The film also received critical acclaim, winning the prix Louis Delluc in 2003 and garnering widespread praise for its script, acting and cinematography. These familiar contexts of affluent Parisian suburb and bourgeois mid-life crisis also serve to offer a new generational context for the continuation of Lvovsky's focus on moments of transition and personal crisis which, although featuring no explicit engagement with wider social and political discourses, presents the spectator with unexpected devices of identification and *distanciation* which undermine spectatorial expectations. Such devices include the engagement with filmic intertexts, the unexpected physical exuberance of the central characters in set pieces which disrupt narrative flow, the hyper-real use of colour and music which challenges generic, realist conventions and the quietly tragic understated ending.

Middle-aged doctor Jacques (Jean-Pierre Bacri) and his wife Carole (Nathalie Baye) welcome their new neighbours, a younger couple François (Melvil Poupaud) and Edith (Isabelle Carré). François will take over Jacques's medical practice and early parallel sequences assert conventional divisions of space and time as the two men bond at work and the two women share long lunches at home. Early divisions blur as the neighbours socialise more frequently as a group and Jacques is seduced by Edith's different vision of his identity. He falls in love with her and, after she unexpectedly kisses him, their relationship develops into a sexual affair. Jacques's behaviour changes, yet, as he expounds upon his 'new personality', François and Carole remain unaware of their respective betrayals. The situation continues without conflict until Carole discovers the pair kissing in the wine cellar, at this point the tone escalates dramatically until Jacques pushes Carole against a window causing serious head injury. Edith rejects Jacques and, reconciled with François, they leave, whilst Carole recovers and returns home. A final silent sequence focuses on Jacques's distraught and isolated situation.

Lvovsky cites *On ne badine pas avec l'amour* (Musset, 1834) as one of the central influences on the film and credits her visit to a 1993 production of the play (starring Isabelle Carré who plays Edith) as triggering this project (Lvovsky 2003). Elements of Musset's play indeed speak to several of Lvovsky's recurring concerns in *Les Sentiments*, including the challenge to generic expectations of dramatic comedy and of tragedy, the difficulties of transition from a childlike state to the adult world and the unconventional use of a chorus. However, whilst Musset's romanticism provides these general concerns, the cinematic intertexts are much more specific as evidenced in Lvovsky's description of her divided filmic heritage:

> Ce sont les films de François Truffaut qui m'ont fait aimer le cinéma ... puis j'ai découvert ceux de Maurice Pialat. Depuis, je me sens tiraillée entre leurs deux familles. Le mélancolique qui aime le spectacle plus

que la vie, qui fait des films pour raconter une vie plus belle, plus drôle ou plus romanesque, et l'enragé qui arrache à la vie des bouts de vie tout crus[14] (Lvovsky 2003).

Despite Lvovsky's expressed admiration for Truffaut, *Les Sentiments* maintains an ambivalent relationship with its core Truffauldian intertext, *La Femme d'à côté* (Truffaut 1981).[15] The choice and filming of the setting (two low buildings around a courtyard and shared garden, initially seen from a plane), the punctuation of the narrative by repeated shots of characters framed at windows looking across to their neighbour's house and the use of a shared plot (a love affair between married neighbours) construct a set of explicit references to Truffaut's film, yet *Les Sentiments* contests many of its central premises. This change of approach to a well-worn narrative was welcomed as Lvovsky was seen to free the narrative of adultery from its 'oripeaux puritains' (Guerin 2002: 84) (puritanical trappings) and the associated genres of farce or bourgeois tragedy.

The explicit evocation of *La Femme d'à côté* serves to better underline the interventions made by Lvovsky and thus construct not a simple homage to Truffaut's work but an assertion of a different engagement with realism and with gender politics. Truffaut's narrative and filmic construction of the younger woman, Mathilde, which draws heavily on the conventions of the *femme fatale* (presenting female sexual agency as transgressive and punishable by death) and the reductive narrative closure of a woman driven to mental instability, self–destruction and murder by sexual passion, is resolutely rejected in *Les Sentiments*. Lvovsky's Edith is not characterised (or caricatured) by a sense of fatal seduction, dangerous sensuality or feminised nature (in opposition to a masculine culture), rather she exhibits a childlike exuberance for life and a naive belief in her own unique invulnerability to misfortune, which displaces a focus on sexual difference to posit a generational opposition between the two couples. This opposition is reflected in the contrasted interior decoration of their

14 'It's the films of Truffaut which made me fall in love with cinema ... then I discovered Pialat's work. Since then I feel as if I'm torn between their two families. The melancholic who prefers spectacle to real life, who makes films in order to recount a life that is more beautiful, more comic or more like fiction, and the fanatic who tears off raw bits of life.'
15 Baye's stardom was established in films by these two directors in *La Nuit américaine* (Truffaut, 1973) and *La Gueule ouverte* (Pialat, 1974).

two houses (pseudo-bohemian clutter versus clean empty spaces) and articulated in both Jacques's irritation at the quiet confidence of his younger 'remplaçant' and Carole's bemused responses to Edith's idealistic statements on the transcendent nature of love. The age difference between the new lovers provides comic incongruity as the presence of a portrait of General de Gaulle in a hotel room prompts Jacques to defer seduction in favour of a digression on his childhood. The question of a generational rupture is also represented in a striking sequence in which Carole and Jacques's two children perform a sketch to celebrate their father's birthday – the finale of which is their incongruous rendition of Brel's scathing 'Les Bourgeois' (Brel, 1961).[16] Whilst the prominence given to the song in the film's trailer suggests a social critique largely absent from the film, the suggestion of generational friction is clear. The children's performance suggests permitted familial self-derision, yet the focus on François and Edith's alienated reaction posits a disjuncture of reception and a rejection of the older couple.

Escalating rivalry between the two men is maintained in comic bicycle races and the knowing off-loading of the trappings of Jacques's abandoned sporting aspirations on to François. It is notable that the two women are not configured as rivals as criticism of Carole's domestic inadequacies is undermined through comic framing and further contested when she abandons the housework to dance confidently around the house to a disco classic. In a welcome reversal of gendered discourses of ageing, it is Jacques who takes a long hard look in the mirror and declares himself to be a 'gros, vieux con moche' ('fat, ugly old prick').

Whereas *La Femme d'à côté* privileges violent, melodramatic set pieces in order to suggest a disruption of the social order by a repressed primal physicality, notably associated with the feminine in Truffaut, this is supplanted in *Les Sentiments* by the materialisation of the emotional through physical gags. As Jacques makes a first nervous phone call to Edith from work he unknowingly wipes ink all over his face, creating an absurdly indelible trace of what he seeks to hide. The

---

16 The lyrics repeat: 'Les bourgeois c'est comme les cochons, Plus ça devient vieux plus ça devient bête. Les bourgeois c'est comme les cochons, Plus ça devient vieux plus ça devient con' (The bourgeois are like pigs. The more they get old the more they get stupid. The bourgeois are like pigs. The more they get old the more they become pricks).

suggestion in *La Femme d'à côté* of the adulterous passion or indeed of a monstrously maternal, female sexual agency as an animalistic force (see Gillain 1991) is reinforced by the recurrence of the presence and sounds of dogs barking and cats squealing. Lvovsky ironises these specific references, and the wider suggestion of a contrast between natural sexual passion and cerebral romantic love, by using nature in *Les Sentiments* to provide humorous commentary on the narrative. As Jacques indulges his new passion for photography (driven by the need for an excuse to visit Edith in her new job) his comically significant failure to move fast enough to capture a cockerel on film forces him to settle for the portrait of a tortoise instead. As the pair face each other in extreme close-up, the composition suggests Jacques's reflection on his ageing masculinity which is acknowledged in turn by the tortoise's apparently complicit wink to camera. *Les Sentiments* posits an anticlimactic closure in which melodramatic finality, involving punitive closure for the female protagonist, is replaced by an understated, ongoing tragedy located firmly with the central male protagonist.

In addition to the intertextual markers of the narrative discussed above, other formal elements signal a self-reflexive *distanciation* from the conventions of both realism and the romantic intrigue, to find 'les archétypes de la comédie de moeurs à la française, dynamités autant que dynamisés,' (Prédal 2008b: 261) (the archetypes of the French comedy of manners are exploded as much as they are expanded). Truffaut's *La Femme d'à côté* features the striking use of a narrative voice, that of Madame Jouve who is herself struggling with the emotions triggered by the return of an ex-lover. In contrast to the melodramatic layering of this involved, intradiegetic narrator, *Les Sentiments* takes its identity as a 'film choral' (ensemble piece) literally and inserts a chorus, sung by a choir, which provides musical interlude and narrative commentary.[17] The choir performs multiple functions: acting as a classical dramatic chorus in providing information in fuller knowledge of the denouement, it represents a 'fifth character' (Lvovsky 2003) whilst its emphatic visibility and heightened performances create spectatorial distanciation through the songs' amplification of the characters' feelings. The disruption of realist conventions represented in the formal and aesthetic functions

17 Note Jean-Pierre Bacri's involvement, as co-writer and actor, in Resnais's hit *On connaît la chanson* (Resnais, 1997), the success of which Lvovsky recognised as having initially inhibited her writing of this film (Lvovsky 2003).

of the choir are supported by other elements that introduce a stylised choreography to the film. The emphatic use of bright colours draws attention to itself through its visual domination of the establishing sequence as Carole speeds along in her red convertible, passing red lorries, greeting her husband's arrival in a red plane and even dumping red branded supermarket carrier bags on the kitchen table. Vibrant, hyper-real colours permeate the early scenes, and Edith's wardrobe of simply shaped dresses, covered with oversized simple geometric shapes, recalls the kitsch aesthetic of Jacques Tati rather than the anticipated realist frameworks of bourgeois drama.

Tension in *Les Sentiments* is created by a conflict not between social order and repressed drives, between associated conventional projections of masculine and feminine, but between generational perspectives on the familiarity of the affair narrative and the desire for imagination and reinvention that is triggered both within the central characters and through the film's formal innovations. The lovers' meetings are characterised by a childlike exuberance and creative energy rather than sexual fulfilment or guilt-ridden complexity, indeed their capacity for burlesque (self)invention recalls the powers of adolescent imagination in *La Vie ne me fait pas peur*. Their passions are inscribed not by erotic cliché but by the exaggerated vision of comic animation as Jacques's gaze transforms Edith's bottom into a colourful hot air balloon and Edith's drawing pictures the couple sailing away on a steamboat cheerfully powered by his erection. The lovers find no easy reconciliation with wider realities as the ending departs from the film's unpredictable, episodic structure to assert a much darker mood. A lengthy final close-up shows Jacques, rejected by Edith and isolated from his family, break down in tears before the screen fades to black. The credits' emphatic reprise of the cheesy disco soundtrack to which Carole danced ('You're Just Too Good To Be True' (Boys Town Gang, 1982)) provides a bleakly ironic conclusion as camera position and use of close-up invites a hesitant identification with Jacques's distress. Thus the 'feelings' delineated so simply in the title are revealed as neither absolute nor authentic but a complex, shifting network of relative desires which are both triggered by proximity and opportunity and supported by the ambiguous power of escapist invention.

The weight of (his)story: *Faut que ça danse!* (2007)

In what could be read as the third element of an informal trilogy, Lvovsky's most recent film, *Faut que ça danse!*, extends her engagement with the shifting identities of adolescence, then middle age to explore the 'third age' through a central protagonist set in stubborn denial of his advancing years. The three films share preoccupations with the importance of physical energy and movement in the face of constraining discourses of identity, the power of the imagination in constructing the self and the problematic transmission of identity from one generation to another. *Faut que ça danse!* articulates these concerns and adds a reflection on the transmission particular to the context of Jewish identity which are addressed both within the narrative and through the intertextual referencing of Jewish filmmakers.

Whilst there is not space here for a detailed discussion of the historical representation of Jewish identity in film, we can establish some useful wider contexts. Itzkowitz argues that the 'proliferation of new Hollywood Jews' (Itzkowitz 2006: 243) in contemporary American cinema, which echo the 1960s 'Jewish fool' in their representations of an abject Jewish masculinity, employ the defiant elusiveness of secular Jewish identity as the quintessential fragmented, postmodern identity. There has been no parallel proliferation of representation in contemporary French cinema and, whilst recent studies have addressed the perpetuation of tropes of heroism and otherness in representations of French Jewish identity in the Occupation (Hewitt 2010) and a discussion of the place of Jewishness in contemporary France in terms of its 'problematic relationship to (visible) ethnic authenticity' (Rose 2007: 478), these issues do not feature in Lvovsky's film. The most striking popular cinematic representation of Jewish identity is found in the huge commercial success of *La Vérité si je mens!* (Gilou, 1997) and its sequels which follow the adventures of a central protagonist who pretends to be Jewish. Yet their success lies as much in the comedic tropes of misrecognition, the odd couple and visual gags as in its engagement with yiddishisms or a specific cultural milieu – elements which remain absent in *Faut que ça danse!*

Implicit references to other Jewish filmmakers create a different mode of cultural transmission, and the description of Salomon as 'ce Juif plutôt Lubitsch-Chaplin que Levi-Lanzmann, du côté de la jouissance physique plutôt que de l'angoisse métaphysique"[18] (Kaganski 2007) reveals some of the heritages evoked in the film. The filmmakers evoked directly are Ernst Lubitsch and Woody Allen, yet the references go beyond their shared Jewishness to provide a projected comedic heritage for the film, supported by the involvement of all three directors in writing, directing and acting.[19] The famous 'Lubitsch touch' is evoked in the film's visual wit, oblique use of dialogue and the concomitant foregrounding of gesture and facial expression to express character psychology. The choice of the family name Bellinsky was taken from the central protagonist of Lubitsch's comedy *Cluny Brown* (Lubitsch, 1946) and Salomon retains his character trait of charming anti-conformity. The repeated use of clips from *Top Hat* (Sandrich, 1935) derives its narrative motivation from Salomon's obsession with Fred Astaire, yet also evokes the conventions of classic screwball comedy and forms a bridging reference to use of the same film in *The Purple Rose of Cairo* (Allen, 1985). A more explicit reference to Allen's work features in Salomon's negotiation of a first kiss with Violette, a scene which, through dialogue and framing, recalls a pivotal scene in *Annie Hall* (Allen, 1977). A prominent review of Lvovsky's film describes Sarah as the daughter that Woody Allen and Diane Keaton never had (Sotinel 2007), yet Salomon does not share the self-alienated intellectual preoccupations of Allen's leads and *Faut que ça danse!* can be read as asserting an oppositional stance to the anxious response to potential sensual pleasure that dominates *Annie Hall* and permeates Allen's oeuvre.

Suggestions that the film's dominant context should be that of a broad Jewish cultural heritage should be countered. Bauman's exploration of the ways in which allosemitism (the identification of Jewishness as a radical difference and of Jewishness as a perpetual and homogenised alterity) leads to reductive discourses that find their ultimate expression in persecution or romanticisation is pertinent here (Bauman 1998: 44). Indeed his assertion of the dangers inherent in isolating the study of (anti)Semitism from those of wider

---

18 'more of a Lubitsch-Chaplin than Levi-Lanzmann kind of Jewishness, aligned with physical pleasure rather than metaphysical anxiety'.

19 Salomon and Sarah watch *In the Soup* (Rockwell, 1992). The intertextual relevance is unclear and perhaps signals simply the production company as the film was Why Not Productions' first film. There is a similar nod to Berri's role as producer in *Les Sentiments*' inclusion of a clip from *Le Poulet* (Berri, 1963).

engagements with constructions of otherness is articulated through *Faut que ça danse!* as Salomon's belligerent claim that he is Jewish only *if* and *when* he wants to be, and his parallel refusals to be defined by age or family ties, counter discourses of allosemitism.[20] This challenge to definitions of identity is also present in Lvosky's first acting role in *Ma femme est une actrice* (Attal 2001), in which she plays a Jewish woman struggling to convince her non-Jewish partner of the need to circumcise their son.

Salomon Bellinsky (Jean-Pierre Marielle)[21] is devoted to the determined denial not only of his age and mortality but also of his Jewishness, his family responsibilities and the power of personal and collective memory. Salomon's defiance of his age includes the personal ad in which he exploits the difference between 'homme jeune' (youthful man) and 'jeune homme' (young man) and an attempt to donate his body to science that ends in flirtation with a young student. Sarah (Valeria Bruni Tedeschi)[22] idolises her egotistical, unpredictable father and struggles to communicate with her mother, Geneviève (Bulle Ogier), who, supported by her carer, Mr Mootoosamy (Bakary Sangaré), has retreated from the world. After a series of disastrous blind dates, Salomon meets Violette (Sabine Azéma) and their relationship triggers an acceptance of his own mortality. Having believed she was unable to have children, Sarah (a clear reference to her biblical namesake) greets news of her pregnancy with panicked incredulity. After a series of adventures in which Geneviève and Mr Mootoosamy seek lost wealth in a Swiss bank account, Salomon is locked in the War Museum overnight and Sarah gives birth while visiting her mother's psychiatric clinic, the narrative resolves the characters' respective predicaments to end with a joyful dance between new mother and daughter. *Faut que ça danse!* defies expectations on many levels. Whilst clearly recognisable as a mainstream comedy, it engages with Jewish identity, survivor guilt and collective memory through a comedic framework, to create a 'chronique mélancomique' (Kaganski 2007)

---

20 The opening documentary-style footage of celebration of the Hindu festival of Ganesh in Paris imposes a wider reflection on shifting identities.

21 Marielle plays a Jewish lead in Akerman's comedy *Demain on déménage* (2003) which also addresses the intergenerational transmission of identity.

22 Collaboration between Lvovsky and Bruni Tedeschi was particularly intense at this point as Lvovsky, having co-written the script for Bruni Tedeschi's second film *Actrices*, was preparing her role in it at the same time as directing Bruni Tedeschi in *Faut que ça danse!*

(melancomic chronicle). Rather than forming an evenly paced family saga, the film maintains a fragmented structure as sketch-like scenes interweave the ridiculous and the moving and destabilise narrative expectations in order to better assert the mutual intergenerational dependence of the central characters.

Kaganski describes this narrative structure as relying on the tension between 'le poids identitaire et l'envie de l'alléger' (ibid.) (between the burden of identity and the desire to lighten it) and tropes of burden and lightness permeate the film. Salomon's refusal to be defined by history is epitomised in his routine of immediately cashing and gambling away the pension he receives as an 'orphan of deportation', presented as heavy bags of coins. Sarah feels obliged to undertake his duties (representing him at a funeral, suggesting a visit to the Memorial to the Shoah) and, whilst Salomon travels light and alone, Sarah is seen repeatedly struggling with heavy bags and dreaming of a hurdles race whilst heavily pregnant. Salomon's visceral response to a past defined by the trauma of personal loss is to assert his vitality in the face of age discrimination and survivor guilt through his tap dance classes and obsession with Fred Astaire.[23] Yet Salomon's captivation by a freeze frame of Astaire in *Top Hat* (Sandrich, 1935), suspended in mid-air and apparently immune from age and all forms of gravity, a sublime moment suspended from the demands of narrative coherence and historical context, reveals the impossibility of maintaining such weightless transcendence and projected isolation. Astaire's function as canonical symbol of timeless Hollywood charm is underwritten here by another function as, born Frederick Austerlitz (Billman 1997: 14), Astaire remains a figure commonly discussed in terms of representations of Jewish identity.[24] The consequent collapse of an apparently oppositional identification renders the motivation for Salomon's choice of idol ambiguous and the transmission of Astaire's energy across time serves as a complex counterpoint to Salomon's rejection of an identification with the historical narratives of Jewish identity.

The film explores the power of history and story (both 'histoire' in French) by setting out different modes of storytelling and transmis-

---

23 This same obsession is shared by the Jewish father in Renée Blitz's *Berkeley's Green and Pleasant Land* (Berkeley, Regent Press, 2001).

24 Astaire was descended from a paternal lineage of Austrian Jews, although his father had converted to Catholicism.

sion. Salomon's rejection of determinant aspects of his identity (from familial to historical) is set in relief through the figure of his wife. Geneviève's unexplained condition constructs an awkward combination of the real symptoms of advancing dementia and a whimsical rejection of reality, yet her emotional disconnection and loss of memory serve both as an exaggeration of Salomon's state and a welcome prop for his own escapism. Free from the constraints of broader coherence, he speaks to her in the English of Astaire and plays the superhero in his apparent halting of traffic. Whilst Geneviève remains a troublingly passive recipient of other people's stories, Salomon's refusal to engage with (shared) history results in a disturbing displacement of stories. His refusal to dwell on the past, epitomised in the brutally succinct announcement that his family 'sont partis en fumée' (went up in smoke), leads to the transfer of such issues from the realist elements of the film to the realm of fantasy and nightmare. Sarah's childhood bedtime story in which Salomon recounted his heroic assassination of Hitler contains an unsettling visual combination of comic absurdity (Hitler's swastika-themed bedroom) and gory excess (the blood-saturated bed). The discourse and film language of the horror genre spreads from fantasy into the apparent realism of Salomon's environment as his visit to a neighbour, an ex-military doctor (Daniel Emilfork in his last role) creates a mood of claustrophobic grotesque. The insertion of these fantasy sequences signals escapism, but the displaced storytelling and unconventional mode of response also evoke the impossibility of representation in relation to accounts of the Holocaust. Whilst Sarah asserts that the revelation that this story was fictitious did not change her view of her father as a hero, her deeper response to this fantastical substitution is articulated in her own animated nightmare of a return of the repressed in which, her father's attempts to kill Hitler with an axe results in a cackling multitude of Hitlers that overwhelm them both. The blurring of boundaries between fantastic horror and the real reflects the difficulty in transmitting the horrors of the Holocaust and also occurs in relation to the future transmission between Sarah and her expected child. The comic disbelief and anger directed towards her doctor when Sarah is told that she is pregnant echo Salomon's confrontation with the insurance company manager's bureaucratic articulations of ageist exclusion. Similarly, her acceptance of her role as mother is constructed and resolved in parallel with Salomon's acceptance of his mortality.

As she progresses from the fearful spectatorship of an alien birth (an extract from *The Fly 2* (Walas, 1989)) to an awestruck response to the ultrasound image of her unborn child, Salomon moves from a refusal to consider death to the choice of a cemetery plot in which he and Violette could be buried together. This is not a simple opposition of death and birth or the banal evocation of a circle of life, but rather an insistence on the complexity of constructions of transmission as Lvovsky explains that 'pour les enfants de survivants, le simple fait d'être né ne va pas de soi' (for the children of survivors the simple fact of having been born is not straightforward) (Lvovsky 2007).

The discovery that Salomon's lover, Violette (Azéma), is a history teacher would suggest a narrative opposition between the alternative stories constructed by Salomon and Sarah and the conventional historical discourses. Such expectations are reinforced as he agrees to accompany her on a visit to the War Museum and, having clambered into a tank and fallen asleep, is locked in the museum overnight. The anticipation of a melodramatic return of the repressed through an encounter with the historical real is quashed however, as he reacts to his comically engineered imprisonment by wrapping himself in the French flag and saluting General de Gaulle rather than addressing images of deportation and genocide. This rejection of a fearful, institutionalised encounter is finally countered in an unannounced sequence towards the end of the film in which Sarah persuades Salomon to visit the Memorial of the Shoah with her and he silently points out the engraved names of his family members who were deported to Auschwitz. The fragmented narrative prevents discursive exposition of this event, yet this understated inclusion of a newly opened memorial, situated explicitly within the context of contemporary reality, inscribes both witness and creative transmission as functions of the film itself. The film thus asserts the importance of both historical witness and the subjective responses of storytelling in the transmission of Jewish heritage and wider identities. This correspondence is perhaps most evident in a striking anecdote from the making of the film, included in the DVD release. Lvovsky recounts how she had chosen the name Bellinsky as a tribute to the character of Adam Bellinsky, the Czech intellectual and refugee, in Lubitsch's comedy *Cluny Brown* (Lubitsch, 1946). At a later stage in filming, she approached the director of the Shoah memorial to deportees for permission to film, but this was initially blocked on the basis that the director could not permit the insertion of the fictional names of Salomon's family for the purpose of the film. This was overcome by Lvovsky's discovery of the existence of very real counterparts and the names of a whole Bellinsky family who were deported from Paris and already inscribed.

The film's episodic, parallel stories are brought together in a coherent set of final sequences. Whilst she is visiting her mother in a psychiatric clinic, Sarah's labour is triggered by her father's televised delivery of his philosophy for life, the title 'faut que ça danse!' straight to camera. The birth, attended by a psychiatrist and located in the library of a psychiatric hospital, suggests heavy-handed analogies of deliverance, yet its brutal surrealism, the knowing mockery of the representational conventions of unexpected births and its lack of status and narrative closure succeed in avoiding cliché. The parallel narrative resolutions and their respective closures are articulated via a switch from the hitherto dominant shot-counter-shot to a series of rare inclusive framings of different couples. Salomon's routine gamble with his orphan's pension hits the jackpot and, after desperate attempts to lose the money, he reconciles himself to a positive use of this tragic heritage by using it to provide care for Geneviève.[25] After their chaotically melodramatic rupture and reconciliation, Violette's romantic regret that nothing will remain of their 'histoire' is met by Salomon's agreement that they could share the same grave, thus reconciling his love of life with an acceptance of mortality that remains undetermined by his Jewish identity (they will not be buried in a Jewish cemetery). Their playful discussion of graveyard sites that echoes estate agent jargon immediately precedes a final set piece featuring a typical physical performance by Bruni Tedeschi as, following her father's example, but with heightened awkwardness and exuberance she dances around her apartment in joyous celebration of and with her baby daughter. Transmission is thus seen to be successful, not the transmission of a specifically Jewish past but the passing on of a recognition of universal mortality as an exhortation to live. The title's deliberate non-specificity of the dancer thus asserts the unrestricted and undefined nature of intergenerational transmission, foregrounds the importance of movement in relation to the other and

25 The sub-plot of the quest for lost wealth in Swiss bank accounts provides a whimsical parallel to the search for other forms of inheritance, yet only confirms Geneviève's dependence on others.

suggests the careful interdependence of joyful physical release and the careful choreographies of social existence.

Realisa(c)trices

The contemporary French filmgoer is more likely to be familiar with Lvovsky's work as an actor than a director and she has developed a profile as one of the most successful supporting actors as reflected in her recurring presence amongst the César nominations for best supporting actress, including nominations in 2002 (*Ma femme est une actrice*, Attal), 2005 (*Backstage*, Bercot), 2007 (*Actrices*, Bruni Tedeschi) and 2010 (*Les beaux gosses*, Sattouf). Indeed, since the release of *Faut que ça danse!* she has concentrated on her acting career, and has accumulated a series of roles that explore the functions and nature of performance itself. Lvovsky's long-term collaborator Bruni Tedeschi uses the term *'réalisactrices'* (diractor) to refer to her own move from acting into directing and her equal investment in both (Bruni Tedeschi 2008). Since 2000, French cinema has seen a marked trend for women actors to undertake this move[26] and many of their films adopt autofictional approaches including a narrative focus on acting and performance. Lvovsky's opposite direction of travel remains singular, and, although articulated in interviews as having accidental rather than aspirational origins, also involves a series of roles within the milieu of film and theatre. The different connections between her writing, directing and acting practices may reach their ultimate configuration in 2010 as she stated that she was planning to write and direct herself as the sole protagonist of her next film.

Conclusions

Attesting that her generation were primed to think of identity not in terms of class struggle but in terms of psychoanalysis and 'ce qui fait prison' (Baumann and Garbarz 2008: 22) (what imprisons us), Lvovsky responds to criticism that her films represent a 'cinéma

26 The list includes Valeria Bruni Tedeschi (*Il est plus facile pour in chameau …* 2003, and *Actrices*, 2007), Sophie Marceau (*Parlez-moi d'amour*, 2002), Julie Delpy (*Deux jours à Paris*, 2007), Agnès Jaoui (*Le goût des autres*, 2000).

bourgeois très parisien' (a very Parisian middle-class cinema) by asserting that setting alone defines neither a film's intent nor its audience (ibid.: 22). Lvovsky's cinema is dominated by the struggle of her protagonists to find a feasible channel through which energy can be projected outwards in order to forge connections between the individual and the world and, increasingly, to construct viable modes of transmission across generations. Her early films show the destructive nature of this energy as alienated subjectivities, whose search for connections is impeded by the *déliaisons* inherent in social and financial precarity, and the lack of coherent socio-political discourse or sense of viable community. In *Dis-moi oui, dis-moi non*, this results in a claustrophobic paralysis of will, whilst in *Oublie-moi* Nathalie's energies are turned inwards creating a cycle of compulsive and performative humiliations.

The possible coexistence of transmissions of cultural identity and free self-expression is glimpsed in these two films through brief sequences of dance and the positive potentiality of dance permeates Lvovsky's later films, from the riotous explosions of energy in *La vie ne me fait pas peur*, through the more subdued, secret moments of self-abandon in *Les Sentiments* to its culmination in the explicit exhortation to dance as a philosophy for life in *Faut que ça danse!* These dance scenes epitomise Lvovsky's assertion of the centrality to her films of the search for joy, which she describes not as a passive state but as an energetic exultation (Baumann and Garbarz 2008: 20). The suggestion of the singularity of dance as a state of transcendence is present in philosophical discourse from Nietzsche's vision of the dancer-philosopher (see Commengé 1988) to Nancy's assertion of the proximities of dancing and thinking (*danser* and *penser*) (Nancy, Monnier, Denis 2005). The director Claire Denis's collaborative role in the latter reinforces her engagement with both the filming of dance and the representation of filming as dance.[27] Despite the considerable differences evident in their aesthetic approaches and career profiles, parallels can be made between Lvovsky's use of dance and Denis's similar association of pivotal narrative moments with sequences of dance, from Galoup's (impossible) celebration of a liberated subjectivity at the end of *Beau travail* (Denis, 1999) to the tender renegotiation of loves in *35 rhums* (Denis, 2008). Dance in the work of Lvovsky

27 See Denis's work with choreographer Mathilde Monnier, *Vers Mathilde*, 2004

and Denis signifies an assertion of physicality, sensuality and the materiality of the body in response to overdetermining discourses of identity, but does not set these forces in binary opposition. Rather dance represents a form in which, through Bourdieusian constructions of body and habitus, links between the individual and collective, between the sublimely subversive moment of the dance and the historical context of social identities can be reconfigured. In *Faut que ça danse!* Salomon's tap dancing asserts an alternative heritage and collective memory inscribed through his body, whilst Sarah's final dance asserts the liberation triggered not by maternity as transcendence but as an acceptance of her active role in the transmission of personal and collective identities.

Lvovsky's current profile provides a rare example of the straddling of the perceived divide between popular cinema and *auteur* filmmaking. Her name features in a recent assertion of the richness of contemporary French filmmaking (Ciment 2010: 1) and in a list identifying contemporary *auteurs* (Vasse 2008). This latter status is further reinforced by the DVD reissue of *Oublie-moi* and *La vie ne me fait pas peur* in the highly selective *Cahiers du cinéma* series devoted to 'les films qui ont marqué leur époque' (films which had an impact on their time). Whilst close collaborative networks of directing, writing and acting locate her firmly within her generation of French filmmakers, wider comparisons with the profiles of a wider range of contemporary directors of accessible and self-reflexive tragicomedies including Nanni Moretti and Pedro Almodóvar are justified. Her films address the fragile construction of personal and social identities through the singular combination of multilayered intertextual construction and exuberant, idiosyncratic formal exploration of rupture and change.

References

Audé, Françoise (1995), 'Noémie Lvovsky, une belle personne', *positif* (February), 9–42.
Audé, Françoise (2002), *Cinéma d'elles 1981–2001* (Lausanne: L'Age d'homme).
Augé, Marc (1992), *Non-lieux. Introduction à une anthropologie de la surmodernité*, Paris, Seuil.
Austin, Guy (1996), *Contemporary French Cinema*, Manchester, Manchester University Press.
Baqué, Dominique (2009), *Pour un nouvel art politique. De l'art contemporain au documentaire*, Paris, Flammarion.

Bauman, Zygmunt (1998), 'Allosemitism: Premodern, Modern, Postmodern' in C. Bryan and L. Marks (eds), *Modernity, Culture and 'the Jew'*, Palo Alto, Stanford University Press, 143–56.

Baumann, Fabien and Garbarz, Franck (2008), 'Entretien avec Valeria Bruni Tedeschi et Noémie Lvovsky. Trouver sa méridienne', *positif*, 563, 15–24.

Billman, Larry (1997), *Fred Astaire: A Bio-bibliography*, Westport, Greenwood Press.

Bourdieu, Pierre (1979), *La Distinction*, Paris, Editions de minuit.

Bruni Tedeschi, Valeria (2008), Interview included in DVD release of *Actrices*.

Chauvin, Jean-Sébastien (2010), 'Eclats sauvages', DVD notes, *La Vie ne me fait pas peur*.

Ciment, Michel (2010), 'Editorial: une question de crédibilité', *positif*, 587, 1.

Commengé, Béatrice (1988), *La Danse de Nietzsche*, Paris, Gallimard.

Devos, Emmanuelle (2009), 'Les Rôles de ma vie', *Elle* (May 2009), www.elle. fr/elle/Loisirs/Cinema/Dossiers/Emanuelle-Devos-les-roles-de-sa-vie/ (gid)/888080.

Dobson, Julia (2001), 'Running Out of Place: Gender, Space and Crisis in Ferreira Barbosa's *Les Gens normaux n'ont rien d'exceptionnel* and Lvovsky's *Oublie-moi*', in Alex Hughes and James Williams (eds), *Gender and French Cinema*, Oxford and New York, Berg, 241–53.

Gillain, Anne (1991), *François Truffaut: Le secret perdu* Paris, Hatier.

Guerin, Marie-Anne (2002), '"Les Sentiments" de Noémie Lvovsky', *Cahiers du Cinéma*, 569, 84.

Guilbert, Laure (2000), *Danser avec le IIIe Reich: les danseurs modernes sous le nazisme*, Paris, Editions Complexe.

Hewitt, Leah D. (2010), 'Ethnicity and Nationality: Recent Representations of French Jews in Films on the Occupation' *L'Esprit créateur*, 50 (4), 111–21.

Hollinger, Karen (1998), *In the Company of Women: Contemporary Female-Friendship Films*, Minneapolis, University of Minnesota Press.

Itzkovitz, Daniel (2006), 'They Are All Jews', in V. Brook (ed.), *You Should See Yourself: Jewish Identity in Postmodern American Culture*, New Brunswick, NJ, Rutgers University Press, 230–52.

Jousse, Thierry and Strauss, Frédéric (1995), 'Entretien avec Noémie Lvovsky', *Cahiers du cinéma*, 448, 20–3.

Kaganski, Serge (2007), 'Une comédie sur le troisième âge pleine de fantasie et de vitalité, et subtilement filtré par la Shoah', *Les Inrockuptibles*, (14 November) www.lesinrocks.com/cine/cinema-article/t/37937/date/2009–05–01/article/faut-que-ca-danse/.

Kaplan, E. Anne (1983), 'Theories of Melodrama: A Feminist Perspective', *Women and Performance: A Journal of Feminist Theory*, 1 (1) 40–8.

Kaveney, Roz (2006), *Teen Dreams: Reading Teen Film and Television from 'Heathers' to 'Veronica Mars'* London, I. B. Tauris.

Lauretis, Teresa de (1988), 'Aesthetic and Feminist Theory: Rethinking Women's Cinema', in E. Pribram (ed.) *Female Spectators: Looking at Film and Television* London, Verso, 186–208.

Lebovic, Elisabeth (ed.) (2004), *L'Intime*, Paris: Ecole nationale supérieure des beaux arts.

Lvovsky, Noémie (2003), 'Entretien avec Noémie Lvovsky', www.allocine.fr/

film/anecdote_gen_cfilm=47139.html

Lvovsky, Noémie (2007), 'Entretien: Noémie Lvovsky', www.scenesmagazine. com/spipphp/article781

Mayne, Judith (2005), 'Tous les garçons et toutes les filles', *Studies in French Cinema*, 5 (3), 207–18.

Morice, Jacques (2007), 'Portrait Valeria Bruni Tedeschi', *Cahiers du cinéma*, 473, 40.

Mulvey, Laura (1992), 'Pandora: Topographies of the Mask and Curiosity', in Beatrice Colomina (ed.), *Sexuality and Space*, New York, Princeton Architectural Press, 52–71.

Nancy, Jean-Luc, Monnier, Mathilde, Denis, Claire (2005), *Allitérations: conversation sur la danse*, Paris, Galilée.

Osganian, Patricia (2003), 'D' "Amerika rapports de classe" à "Rosetta". Sortie du naturalisme et subjectivation du réel', *Mouvements*, 3, 51–7.

O'Shaughnessy, Martin (2005), '"Reprise" et les nouvelles formes du cinéma politique', in G. Hayes and M. O'Shaughnessy (eds), *Cinéma et engagement*, Paris, L'Harmattan, 83–98.

O'Shaughnessy, Martin (2007), *The New Face of Political Cinema. Commitment in French Film since 1995*, New York and Oxford, Berghahn Books.

Powrie, Phil (ed.) (1999), *French Cinema in the 1990s: Continuity and Difference*, Oxford, Oxford University Press.

Prédal, Réné (2008a), *Le Cinéma français des années 1990* (2nd edition), Paris, Armand Colin.

Prédal, Réné (2008b), *Le Cinéma français depuis 2000*, Paris, Armand Colin.

Rose, Sven-Erik (2007), 'Mathieu Kassowitz's "La Haine" and the Ambivalence of French-Jewish Identity', *French Studies*, 61 (4), 476–91.

Rouyer, Pierre and Vassé, Claire (2003), 'Valeria Bruni Tedeschi: la foi et la richesse', *positif*, 507, 28–32.

Sotinel, Thomas (2007), 'Faut que ça danse! – grossesse, névroses et quiproquos' *Le Monde* (14 November 2007), 26.

Strauss, Frédéric (2000), *Lvovsky: La Vie ne me fait pas peur: Lycéens au cinéma*, Paris, CNC / BIFI.

Swartz, Marvin, Blazer, Dan, George, Linda, Winfield, Idee (1990), 'Estimating the Prevalence of Borderline Personality Disorder in the Community', *Journal of Personality Disorders*, 4 (3), 257–72.

Tarr, Carrie with Rollet, Brigitte (2001), *Cinema and the Second Sex*, London, Continuum.

Trémois, Claude (1997), *Les Enfants de la liberté*, Paris, Seuil.

Vasse, David (2008), *Le Nouvel Âge du cinéma de l'auteur français*, Paris, Klincksieck.

Williams, Linda (1991), 'Film Bodies: Gender, Genre and Excess', *Film Quarterly*, 44 (4), 2–13.

Wilson, Emma (1999), *French Cinema since 1950. Personal Histories*, London, Duckworth Press.

Wilson, Emma (2001), 'Identification and Female Friendship', in Alex Hughes, and James Williams (eds), *Gender and French Cinema*, Oxford and New York, Berg, 255–67.

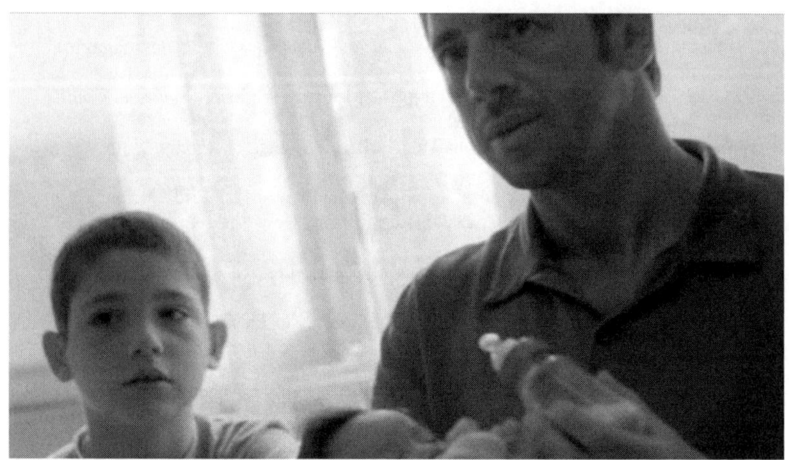

1 *Le Lait de la tendresse humaine* (Cabrera, 2001)

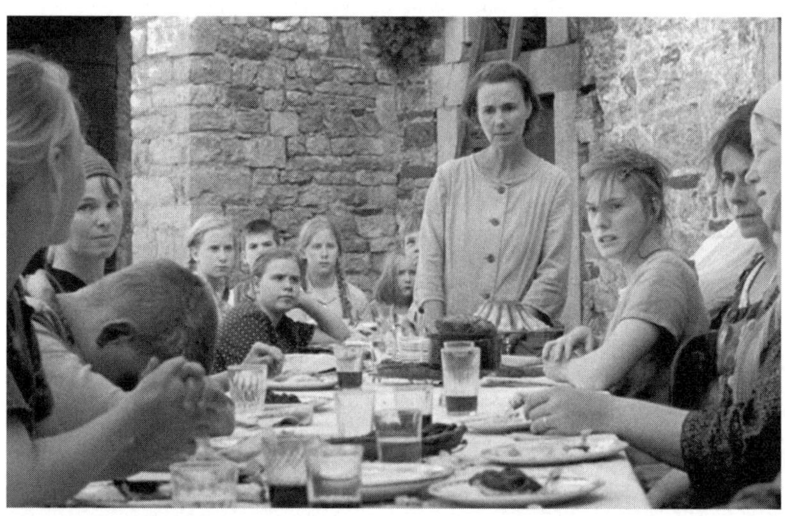

2 *Folle embellie* (Cabrera, 2004)

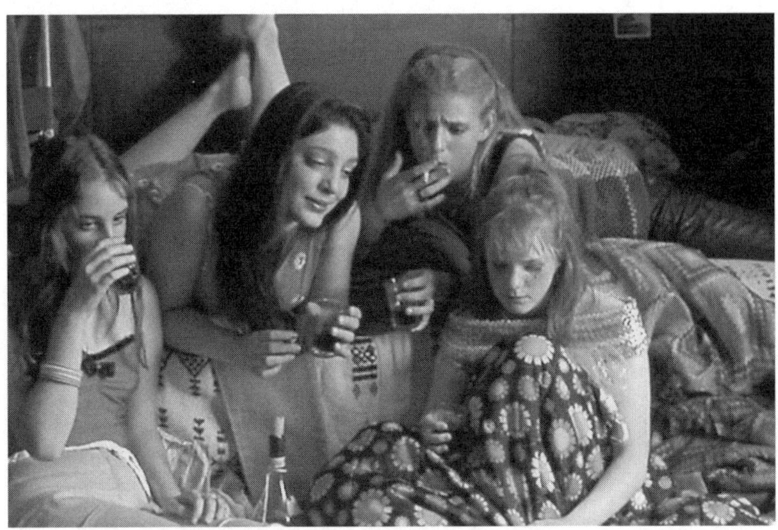

3 *La Vie ne me fait pas peur* (Lvovsky, 1999)

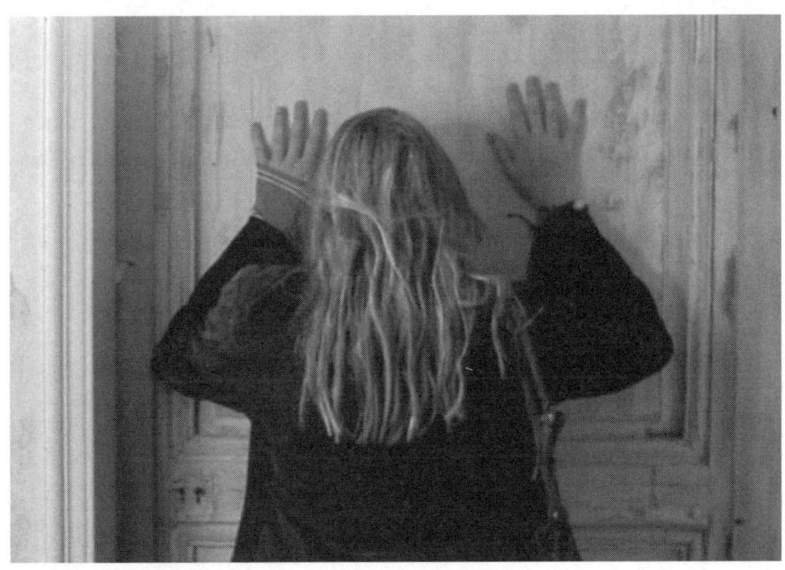

4 *Oublie-moi* (Lvovsky, 1994)

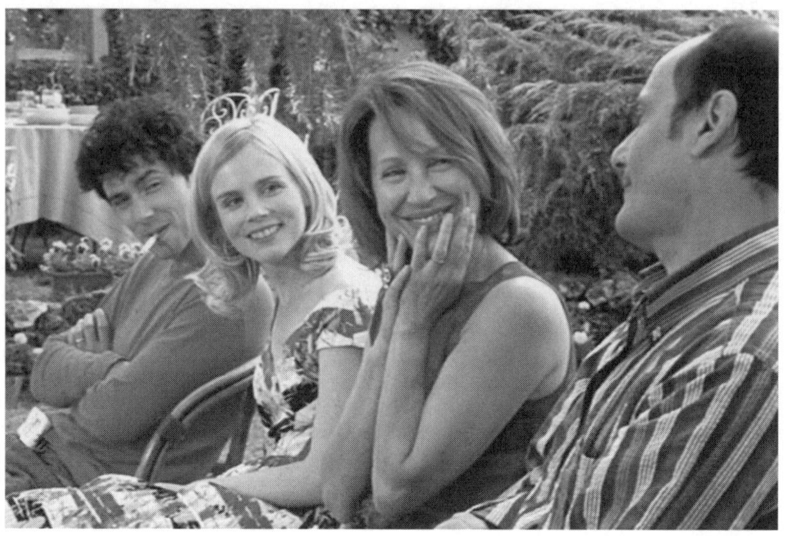

5 *Les Sentiments* (Lvovsky, 2003)

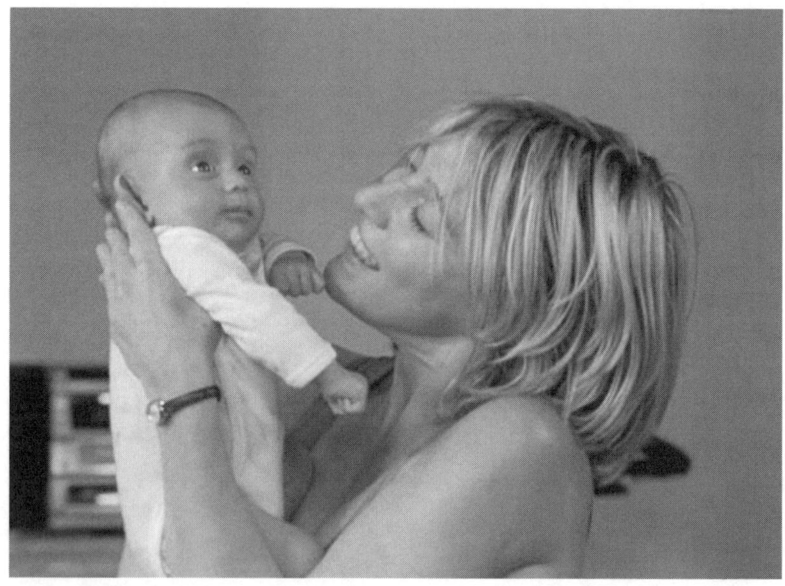

6 *Faut que ça danse!* (Lvovsky, 2007)

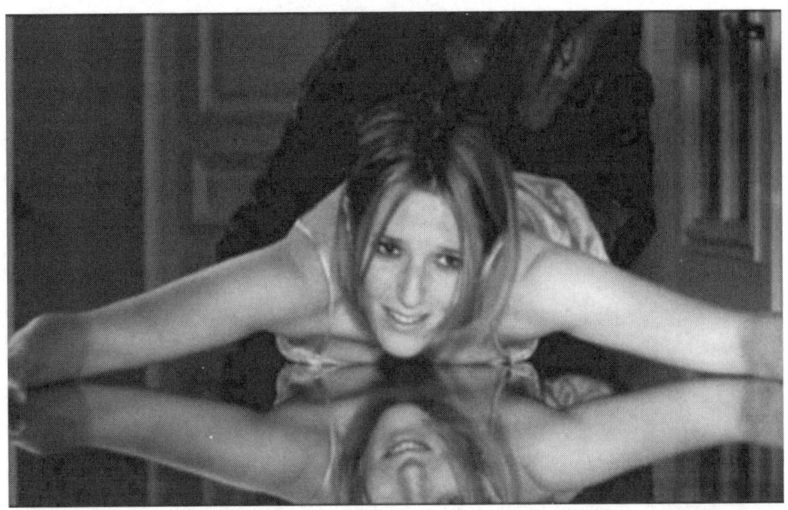

7 *A vendre* (Masson, 1998)

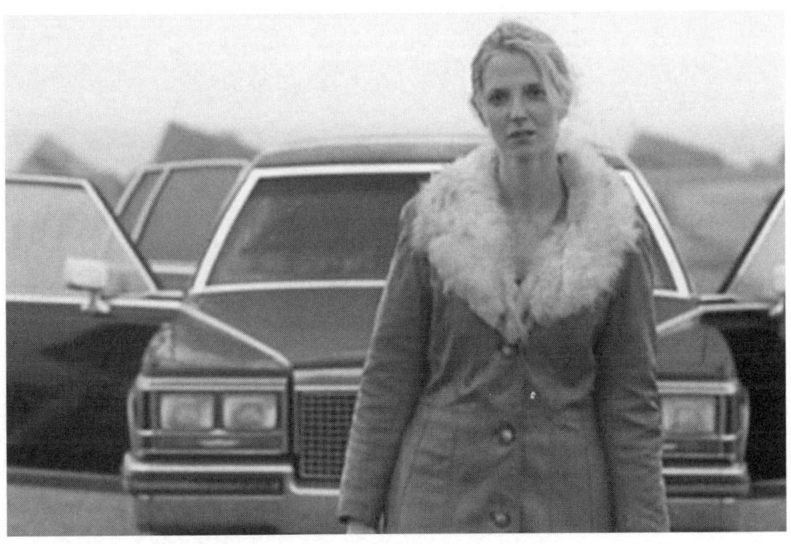

8 *Love me* (Masson, 2000)

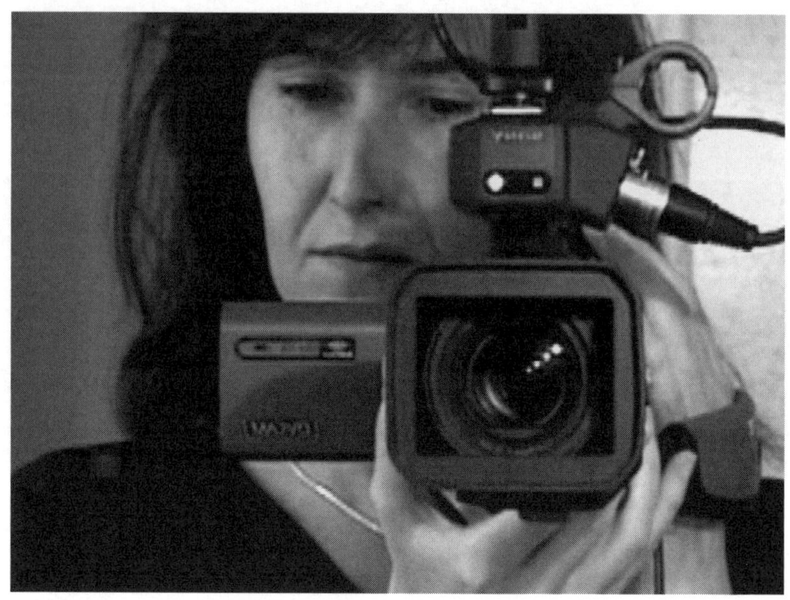

9 *Pourquoi (pas) le Brésil* (Masson, 2004)

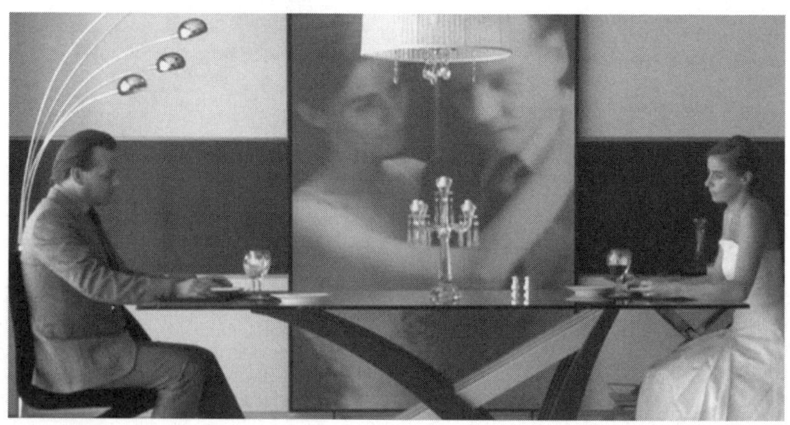

10 *Coupable* (Masson, 2008)

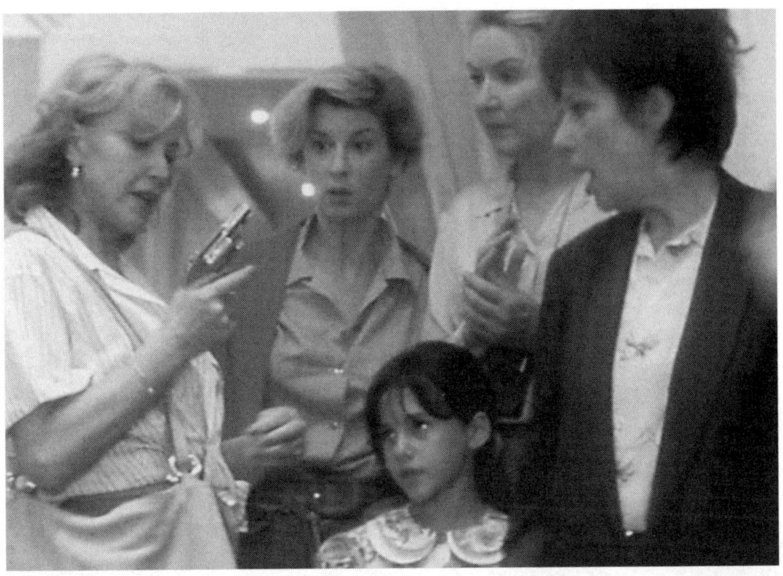

11 *Personne ne m'aime* (Vernoux, 1994)

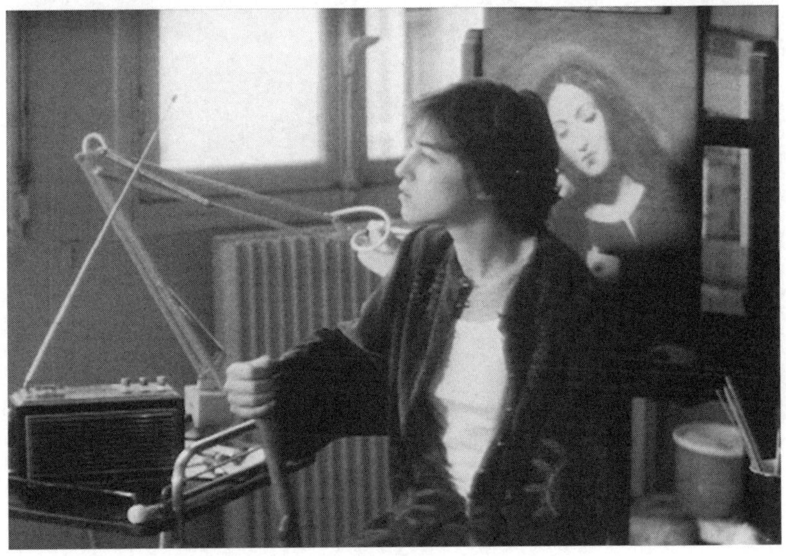

12 *Love etc.* (Vernoux, 1996)

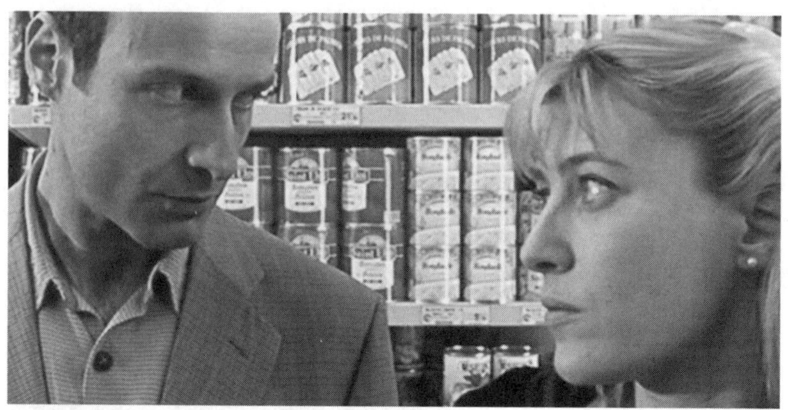

13 *Rien à faire* (Vernoux, 1999)

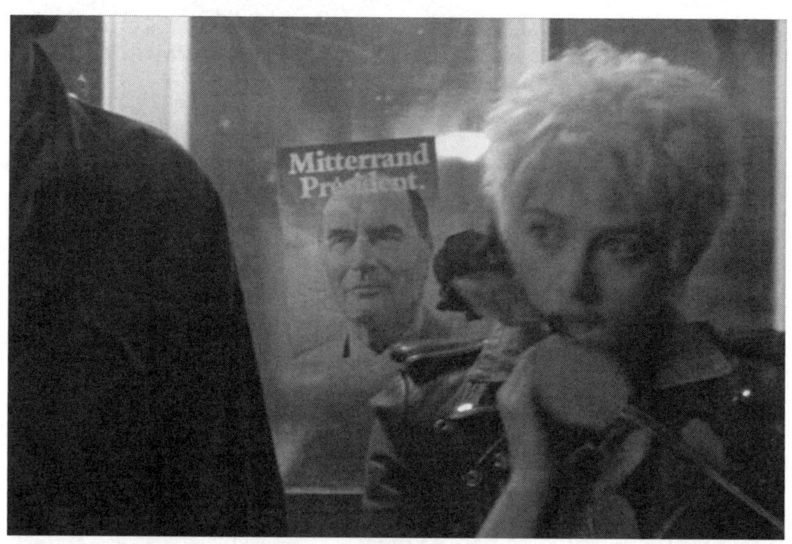

14 *Rien dans les poches* (Vernoux, 2008)

3

Laetitia Masson: suspect identities

A recent issue of *Sight and Sound*, tracing the trajectories of French cinema since 1968, includes a list of 'directors to watch' who remain largely unknown to UK audiences owing to the still limited practices of international distribution. Laetitia Masson is name-checked amongst these as 'an erratic but adventurous' figure (Romney, 2008: 44) and, whilst box-office success and critical reception of her films are equally uneven, her oeuvre remains singularly engaging both in its recurring concerns and in its challenge to generic and filmic categorisations. Having established its presence through a series of critically acclaimed short films, Laetitia Masson's work has been characterised by the complexity of its narratives and characters and the provision of outstanding roles for Sandrine Kiberlain in *En avoir (ou pas)* (1995), *A vendre* (1998) and *Love Me* (2000). The three films of this apparent, but unmarked, trilogy stage different connections between the conventions of romance narratives and the harsh realities of socio-economic disenfranchisement in contemporary France. Masson describes her central subject matter simply as 'the links between emotions, work and money' (Masson 2007). The narrative trajectory of *En avoir (ou pas)* suggests some salvation from reductive definition of the self as an economic object through the potential for agency in personal relationships and wider communities, yet *A vendre* counters this optimism with a narrative influenced by both classic film noir (the detective searching for an errant woman and her lover's money) and Godardian discourse on economic and sexual prostitution. *Love Me* would seem to suggest more conventional romantic tropes, yet these may be the delusory products of the central protagonist's unstable mind. The films' formal innovation coupled with their highly intertextual construction challenges the escapism and artifice of both Romance and realist narrative conventions.

Laetitia Masson was born in Nancy in 1966 and went on to study Arts and Cinema at the University of Paris III. She enrolled at FEMIS, in the section 'Image' and has, throughout her training and career, expressed explicit interest in the politics of aesthetics and formal innovation. Echoing Godard's insistence on the inherent political force of aesthetic choice, her interviews bear witness to her engagement with, and sensitivity to, the vocabulary of film language: 'le zoom m'intéresse par sa dimension subjective ... c'est une forme d'élan qui existe dans la vie. Les ralentis, c'est aussi une question de regard'[1] (Herpe and Kohn 1996: 22). She worked as an assistant to Cedric Kahn and with Anne-Marie Miéville[2] before embarking upon her own directorial career. Masson's early films *Nulle part* (1993) (a Bonnie and Clyde narrative) and *Chant de guerre parisien* (1991) (a reflection on militancy in the cinema in relation to the first Gulf War) provide evidence respectively of her interest in the struggle to sustain emotional commitment in a society characterised by multiple fragilities (of identity, employment, income) and the difficulty of mass political engagement in an era of allegedly post-ideological fragmentation. These films remain inaccessible and this chapter will focus primarily on the trilogy of films that established Masson as a major director and the subsequent development of her oeuvre. Despite clear political engagements, including the signing of the filmmakers' petition against the *loi Debré* in 1997 (far-reaching legislation which further eroded the rights of immigrants and obliged employers and landlords to report cases of irregularity), Masson has described her unease with militant action, preferring to withdraw from identification with traditional political discourses to express her views through her films and, citing Claire Denis as primary example, admires those whose films present a complex interweaving of the political with the personal and aesthetic innovation (Audé and Garbanz 1998: 32).

Masson's short film, *Vertige de l'amour* (1994), based on an original idea by Laetitia Carton, was part of a television series '30 Films Against a Virus', which commissioned emerging scriptwriters. The series's

1 'I'm interested in the zoom because of its subjective element ... it's a form of impulse that exists in life. Slow motion shots are also to do with a way of looking'.
2 Miéville's career in directing, editing and writing (including her serial collaborations with Godard) reveals a sustained engagement with the politics of film form.

thematic parameters prescribed the theme of the prevention of HIV and AIDS, and this narrative presents the recognisable scenario of teenagers negotiating their first sexual experience. The film, which contains straightforward dialogue, an everyday scenario and unknown actors, targets a teenage audience successfully. The linear narrative follows a conventional romance pattern as the two teenagers meet up at a party and plan to have sex for the first time. However, overcoming the challenge set by her boyfriend's self-interested preference for unprotected sex, the girl asserts her own (sexual) agency and leads him off to find a condom vending machine. This understated narrative is overlaid with a range of innovative cinematic techniques to build mood. Identification with the couple is constructed not through conventional point of view shots, or through inclusive close framing, but through the evocation of their sensual experiences. The sequences on the dance floor are marked by their insistence on the dominance of the music thus occluding the privileges of conventional realism in which the couple's conversation would remain audible (to us). Communication is asserted otherwise through a lengthy exchange of glances, close-ups of the slightest gestures and the (wordless) movements of their lips. Such emphasis asserts the sensual and intimate nature of the exchange rather than seeking its inadequate representation in conventional (filmic) language or as illustration of public policies of (sexual) health. The high lighting (which bleaches out the couple's features to emphasise the redness of their lips) and the use of blue and orange filters continues beyond the narrative motivation of the dance floor setting to disrupt the realist mode. Whilst access to the couple's conversation is often denied, the use of voiceover provides access to the girl's thoughts and her reflections further assert her status as equal, and then leading, participant in negotiations. Whilst the ending suggests the survival of the couple, the conventional denouement of romantic reconciliation through (glamourised) sexual activity is not shown, nor does conflict lead to melodramatic rejection. The short film provides a striking intervention, both familiar and stylised, in the sexual and social politics of safe sex, without recourse to narrative stereotypes based on gender stereotypes or moral absolutes.

Masson's directorial profile continues to be associated primarily with the three films that she made in the mid-to late 1990s which star Sandrine Kiberlain in narratives of women's quest to escape financial and social dependency within a climate of economic crisis and social alienation. The films reflect the contemporary focus on a renewed engagement with the interrelationship between economic status and personal identity and feature marginalised central protagonists who find themselves excluded from social, domestic or economic structures. As in one of the most critically successful films of this mode *La Vie rêvée des anges* (Zonc, 1998), Masson's films foreground such exclusion through the representation of explicitly working-class women, who struggle to express themselves both within and against the dominant narratives of (gendered) social conformity and economic dependency. Indeed Masson's work has been compared to that of Leigh, Loach and Zonca in its insistence upon 'une vision du réel en termes de rapports de classe' (Osganian 2003: 51) (a vision of the real in terms of class relations). Whilst the narratives of this trilogy centre on lone female protagonists, they all assert the impact of the social, of class structures and of economic necessity. Such narratives, which focus on the struggles of an individual rather than a group or community, can be seen, as Osganian argues, not to deny the importance of the social in favour of an all-consuming individualism but rather to emphasise the inherent link between social context and individual subjectivity (ibid.). Masson comments on the importance in her work of the relationship with the other:

> Je voulais aussi aborder le rapport aux autres, comme issue pour supporter ce tourbillon du monde. Le rapport suprême aux autres, finalement, c'est l'amour ... et ça m'intéressait de voir comment deux personnes, dans une situation pas facile au départ, pouvaient espérer vivre mieux en se rencontrant.[3] (Herpe and Kohn 1996: 25)

Thus it is an insistence on the interweaving of the personal and the social and the relationship between harsh socio-economic realities and the impact of personal mythologies and fictions that link these films. As Masson asserts: 'J'ai souvent l'impression qu'on parle soit des sentiments, et c'est presque abstrait, soit du social, et les personnages semblent prisonniers de leur destin'[4] (ibid.: 25). Indeed, these

---

3 'I wanted to approach the question of how we relate to others, as a way of getting through this whirlwind of a world. The supreme relation to the other is that of love ... I was interested to see how two people who start off in a difficult situation could hope, through meeting, to have a better life.'

4 'I often feel that either we talk about emotions and it's almost abstract, or we talk about the social and the characters become prisoners of their own destiny.'

three films, whilst containing complex engagements with the conventions of romance narratives, all posit the notion that a collective sense of social intimacy remains necessary to the successful construction of individual subjectivity. Masson's trilogy presents young women struggling to accede to adult relationships and responsibilities, 'rebellious, independent-minded characters whose hard, brittle surface belies an underlying vulnerability to what the world has to offer them' (Tarr with Rollet 2001: 79). The lack of conventional social structures and the dominance of fleeting encounters and unresolved relationships provide the context in which the central characters attempt to give meaning to their lives and are reflected in the narratives which 'are generally characterized by disconnected episodic structures and open endings' (ibid.: 79).

Serial exclusions: *En avoir (ou pas)*

Masson's first feature film received advance state funding, but had to rely further on the personal investment of its producers as it failed to attract bids from television companies. In common with many films of this period, the narrative locations eschew Paris and are split between the bleak industrial settings of Boulogne sur mer and Lyons, although the city spaces of the latter are barely represented on screen. Following a documentary sequence in which a series of women are interviewed for a mundane administrative post and tracking shots of a production line in a fish-processing factory in Boulogne, we meet the central protagonist, Alice (Sandrine Kiberlain), as she is made redundant. Having left her boyfriend and moved back in with her parents, her excited anticipation of a different future is soon deflated by the harsh realities of a job interview in which she expresses her desire to be a singer. She has sex on the beach with the interviewer and he gives her money so that she can leave. On her arrival in Lyons Alice books into the Ideal Hotel and becomes part of its nomadic community, starting a tense relationship with Bruno (Giovaninetti). After a row, in which he rejects emotional commitment and she criticises his lack of agency, Alice finds work in a bar. As Bruno seeks her out, the final sequence posits a fragile new identity for them as a couple.

The film, released in the immediate context of the national demonstrations and strikes that dominated France in 1995, represents a clear engagement with a sense of social and personal alienation through its portrait of the frustrations of a generation confronting poverty and the consequent suppression of opportunity and self-expression that accompany economic deprivation. Reviews welcomed the film's 'inscription of a social reality, that of unemployment' (Vassé 1996: 21) imposed by its stark reminders of the personal alienation caused by reductive definitions of self through economic discourse. The vulnerable situation of the female working class dominates the first sequences of the film as a strong documentary style is established through a fixed camera which, sharing the point of view of an unseen male interviewer, documents the responses to questions of a series of women. For these scenes Masson used unemployed local women who improvised their responses to questions in mid-close-up, yet the interviewer remains unseen, allowing the consequently disembodied male voice to represent wider structures and hierarchies of the (gendered) economic frameworks of capitalism. The commodification of women as economic objects is articulated both through the ironic narrative framing of the interview process and through the inclusive visual framing of their coats hung on hooks behind them suggesting parallels of unstable interchangeability. The questions suggest the construction of a career path suited to a fixed model (marketable skills) and posit illusory choices ('why choose this company?') that remain laughably inappropriate to the desperate economic context. Spectatorial unease at the mismatch between such empty rhetoric and the women's personal situations is strengthened by a *mise en scène* which positions us alongside the interviewer. The challenge to discourse which claims paid work as the dominant vector of self-definition is voiced by the women themselves who admit that when working they 'think of nothing', refuse to identify personal qualities that commend them in this context and privilege escapism over ambition.

This opening sequence thus exemplifies what Beugnet describes as an illustration of Althusserian descriptions of power, a power imposed through a play of conventions and normalisation which denies the specific material contexts in favour of supposedly neutral discourses of career marketing and consumerism (Beugnet 2000: 201). The vulnerable interviewees are confronted with the grim choice of either betraying their humanity and self-expression by faking enthusiasm for a dead-end job or proving themselves somehow generically 'unsuitable' by the expression of 'inappropriate' desires and needs. This discursive scenario is followed by a stark representation of the kind of work available to them. The camera's slow tracking along the noisy production line of a fish-processing plant emphasises the dehumanising uniform of the workers and their largely undifferentiated status, in form and colour, from their factory environment. The cut to close-ups of piles of dead fish replicates the colours of pervading greyness and despondency and suggests a similar lack of control and identity amongst the (women) workers. The news of Alice's redundancy is presented in brief fragmented form and her emotional response is displaced to the later careers interview as, breaking down with frustration, she repeats her need for an outlet of self-expression.[5] This scenario does not, however, replicate the power-play of the interviews in the opening sequence of the film, as the discussion, filmed here in shot-counter-shot rather than with a static camera, reveals the interviewer to be equally disturbed by the encounter. His invitation to Alice to demonstrate her singing voice proves inadequate admission of the inhumanity of the situation and his later comments that she should leave while she is still young suggest wider empathy and resignation.

The film's title evokes directly Hawks's 1945 film noir classic *To Have and Have Not* and its first onscreen pairing of Bogart and Bacall, whilst its syntax also recalls Godard's *Sauve qui peut (la vie)* (1979). Beugnet's excellent detailed comparative study of the two films identifies the intertextual markers of Godardian style: captions, the syntax of the title, references to Bogart, use of slow motion and the freeze frame (Beugnet 2000: 194). The opening sequences discussed above also establish Godard and Masson's shared 'regard critique sur certaines des structures de pouvoir qui contrôlent et déterminent les relations entre individus dans notre société'[6] (Beugnet 2000: 198). The stylistic influences are clear and persist throughout Masson's oeuvre to date, yet there remain important differences also in the context and import of their use. Her captions do not feature abstractions or political maxims, as is common in Godard, but rather assert the recognisable geographical setting of the action and thus reinforce documentary aesthetics and the direct engagement of the narrative with the contemporary social and economic climate of mid-1990s France.

---

5 Alice's description of herself as 'an exhausted giraffe' highlights this sense of her unsuitability to the scale and landscape of banal routine.

6 'critical examination of some of the structures of power which control and determine the relationships between individuals in our society'.

Challenging exploitation

One of the major, and most problematic, themes of Godard's work of the late 1960s, the prostitution of humanity through capitalism as represented by analogies with female sexual prostitution, is markedly present here also as it features in the sequences which introduce us to the character of Bruno. A brief shot of him at work on a building site is followed by a longer sequence in which he passes a line of prostitutes who all make him different offers. The use of tracking shots (and their scarcity elsewhere in the film) creates a telling parallel between the prostitutes and the women workers on the factory production line. The construction of a response overwritten by economics is signalled further by the starkness of Bruno's first words of the film 'Combien?' (How much?) and echoes Alice's pragmatic response to her redundancy (Tarr with Rollet 2001: 66). The conventional fetish-istic framing of the prostitute's body as she and Bruno have sex reinforces the encounter as one of disengaged, alienated commerce, an episode which strengthens Bruno's personal isolation as he approaches women in the street to assuage his loneliness. Godard's recurrent adoption of (female) sexual prostitution as a metaphor for the wider prostitution of humanity endemic in capitalist economies results problematically in many of his central female protagonists being reduced to their sex. Although she foregrounds such parallel mechanisms of prostitution, Masson's film avoids this pitfall through an insistence upon the psychological and emotional consequences for *all* characters of the alienation caused by primary (self)identification as an economic object. Following the conspicuous consumption of champagne (alone, she could only afford coffee) Alice has sex with her interviewer, yet the clichéd models of exploitation are here mitigated by her assertion of control and agency. Her explicit statement 'C'est moi qui vous baise, d'accord?' (It's me who's screwing you, okay?) disrupts their pre-existing hierarchical relationship and although the visual markers of crashing waves and a mid-shot of a couple alone on a windswept beach project cinematic clichés of romance, this idiom is swiftly undercut by his ambiguous payment. The close-up of the banknotes in profile against the sky suggests not a sensationalist discomfort with the suggestion of sexual prostitution but rather a mutual recognition by both parties that capital has replaced romance in its substitution of illusory escapism with the provision of a pragmatic escape route.

The conventional filmic traits of romance narratives continue to be modified throughout by the construction of Alice as dominant desiring subject and, although the use of parallel editing to introduce the character of Bruno anticipates the conventional establishment of a romantic couple, it is the striking use of a zoom in a point of view shot centred on Alice that marks their first meeting.[7] In contrast to the mid-shots used in the sex scene between Bruno and the prostitute, the sexual consummation of Alice and Bruno's relationship is dominated by extreme low-lit close-ups of skin and limbs that are neither clearly gendered nor identified as belonging to Bruno or Alice. Beugnet identifies this sequence as representative of a 'cinema of sensation' in its foregrounding of a haptic visuality through the evocation of the texture of skin and suggests that as such it signals a temporary but positive liberation from socio-cultural representations of the (gendered) body (Beugnet 2007: 96). It can be argued further that this haptic mode may also signal a rejection of the economic structures that underlie such representations with their combination of illusory individualism and alienating objectification. Masson engages further with the conventions of the close-up in the early sequences of *En avoir (ou pas)* as Alice's face is often hidden from the camera and the dominant close-ups are those of her nape or of her hair falling across the side of her face. Such a motif can be seen to resist conventions of access and exposure, a strategy which Beugnet describes as the 'denial of disclosure (*stratégie du retrait*)' (Beugnet 2007: 100) in reference to the contrast between the use of the medium close-ups employed to reinforce the alienating experience of the interview and the paradoxical narrative denial of the subjectivity of the series of anonymous interviewees, and the lack of access to close-ups of the main protagonist (Beugnet 2007: 101). Yet there remains an ambiguity to such shots as, although they deny the conventional suggestion of access to a protagonist's thoughts and emotions, they also construct an equally powerful fetishism as that displayed through a full facial close-up. Indeed the repeated shots of Kiberlain's neck in the early sequences of the film, shots that can be read as conveying mystery and vulnerability, recall the obsessively recurrent close-ups of Binoche's nape in *Mauvais sang* (Carax, 1986) and its persistence as part of her early star image. Such contrasts are not maintained, however, as Alice's

7 Masson describes the zoom as marking a 'look of love' (Herpe and Kohn 1996: 22).

interview, although filmed in shot-counter-shot rather than through a fixed, disembodied point of view, employs conventional medium close-up to give us unrestricted visual access to her distressed self-expression. Indeed the contrast constructed here is between the interviewees' forced complicity in the charade of careers opportunity and Alice's refusal either to conceal her distress or to silence her desires.

Tension remains, however, between such a positive reading and the interpretation of romance narratives as signalling the dependence of women on men's economic and sexual agency. Romance provides the lure of (im)probable denouement in some films of this period and serves as a perennially effective shortcut to upbeat narrative closure. Its conventional status as a transcendental force that stands in opposition to the impact of social context on individual subjectivity can be seen as problematic in films now canonised as representative of this period, such as *Chacun cherche son chat* (Klapisch, 1996).[8] The final sequence of *En avoir (ou pas)* may seem to posit romance as a transcendent solution to the individual alienations experienced by both Alice and Bruno, yet they remain contained within the social. Holmes reminds us that romantic closure is often accompanied by physical displacement to

> a location more explicitly coded as fantasy: the couple find themselves alone in a luxurious house, or simply in a pastoral rather than urban space. Here, in a world clearly marked out as imaginary, the utopian pleasure of perfect complementarity, and of desire uncomplicated by social or practical constraints, can be fantasized. (Holmes 2006: 123)

In *En avoir (ou pas)* a sense of a distance from the real is suggested not through a fantasy setting (indeed the couple have left the utopian space of the Ideal Hotel) but through the striking use of soundtrack and the glorious slow-motion of Kiberlain's luminous backwards glance towards the camera. Indeed the use of slow motion in the final sequence and the accompaniment of an overwhelming final song (a device also found in Masson's later films) suggest the conventions of romantic closure (the creation of the uniquely suited couple, transcendence of practical problems) mitigated by the assertion, in both films, of a female subjectivity scored by a striking female vocal (compare the presence of Portishead's 'Glory Box' in the closing sequence of

8 The transcendence of social context via romance is more problematic here as it posits Chloe's exit from the city spaces so central to the narrative to a future non-urban domestic environment as more suited to female subjectivity.

Chacun cherche son chat to the emphatic use of P J Harvey's 'The Dancer' to close *En avoir (ou pas)*).

Is romantic closure thus restricted to a reading of recuperative transcendence that sweeps economic and social alienation before it, reliant on culturally pervasive tropes of myth and denial? In her recent definitive account, Diana Holmes argues for an ethical recuperation of the (literary) tropes of romance, describing it as 'a means of imagining the ideal relationship with the Other, and of exploring or rehearsing the conflicts between individual desire and all that contains and limits that desire, in particular the demands of society' (Holmes 2006: 7). Whilst other established feminist readings of romance may see its dominant modes as enacting reductive socio-cultural restrictions on the expression and representation of (female) agency and desire, Holmes argues for a recognition of the discourse's engagement with female subjectivity and with wider patterns of privileging non-consumerist constructions of identity: 'In more everyday terms, romance is a genre that aspires to the reconciliation of individual freedom with a capacity for emotional attention to the other person, and with commitment' (ibid.: 141). The consolidation of the romantic couple in *En avoir (ou pas)* is not signalled by the use of the establishment of sexual intimacy between them as narrative closure; it is rather the combination of this assertion of their subjective desires with their integration into the collectivity of the crowd (a combination prefigured by their first date at the football match)[9] that is emphasised in the closing shots of the film. It remains this clear situating of the romance narrative (as assertion of subjectivity) within the realm of the social that provides the final image of the film.

Masson's engagement with conventions of the close-up may suggest a film concerned primarily with individual subjectivity, yet *En avoir (ou pas)* provides striking representations of relationships that are defined neither by economic structures nor by the exclusivities of the couple and which play as large a role in Alice's subjective agency and well-being as the onset of the romance narrative. Unlike many films of this period, the central protagonist is seen to enjoy a close relationship with her immediate family. Her mother (played by Claire Denis) is presented as a generous and caring community

---

9 Masson describes the football match as the only place where you can find people expressing passion in public – in contrast to her experience of student demonstrations (Herpe and Kohn 1996: 28).

presence and supports Alice's negotiation of the complex relationship between economics, employment and self-esteem. The political engagement of her father (played by Daniel Kiberlain) and her parents' successful marriage are also represented as positive forces. The brief glimpse of Alice's familial background is, however, contained in the early sequences of the film, and the social context which fuels narrative development is that which Alice finds by chance when she arrives in Lyons. The tracking shots that accompany her arrival in Lyons represent the literal bright lights of the city as an exotic and uncanny fairground. The melancholy music and the close-up of the neon sign signalling the Ideal Hotel seem overdetermined and, whilst the spectator may anticipate this as a cruelly ironic destination, the closely framed spaces of the hotel, which contrast so markedly with the cold grey landscapes of Boulogne, constitute a tolerant social microcosm. This multi-ethnic, non-hierarchical community overseen by the guardian angel figure of Joseph (Roschdy Zem), in which the cleaner (Lise Lamétrie) distributes supportive advice to all and lends the manager money, is characterised by soft lighting and inclusive group framing and seems to be protected from the harsh socio-economic environment that prevails outside its walls. In marked contrast to other realist films of the same period which feature a central female protagonist (for example *Oublie-moi* (Lvovsky, 1994) and *Les Gens normaux n'ont rien d'exceptionnel* (Ferriera-Barbosa, 1995)), Alice's sense of alienation is not expressed through a sense of a physical crisis of the female subject in urban space, characterised by manic displacement and an inability to negotiate the physical environment. Indeed, scenes in which Alice is seen outside of the hotel are dominated by the mid-shot which emphasises the proximity of other people (rather than isolation) and scenes of physical movement (Alice's dance and the slow-motion football sequence) are associated with fluid and assertive self-expression rather than with flight or distress.

Masson's stated aim in making *En avoir (ou pas)* was to provide a portrait of her peers:

> A generation with no illusions, no points of reference, no political ideologies ... I didn't want to register the failure of a lost generation, but inspire a little hope, encourage young people to not just give in to things but to pay attention to their survival instincts and find the energy to act positively on their own destiny. Hope is other people. (Baudin 2000: 26)

Masson's explicit challenge to Sartre's infamous existentialist maxim, 'Hell is other people', confirms her manipulation of narrative tropes (romance narrative) and filmic conventions (the close-up) that suggest the glorious transcendence of the individual to insist both upon the inherent link between subjectivity and socio-economic structures and the importance of an intimate solidarity.

The second film in this apparent trilogy, *A vendre* (*For Sale*) was released in 1998 and achieved moderate box office success in France (488,000 admissions). The central protagonist, France Robert[10] (Sandrine Kiberlain again), fails to show up at her wedding, having left with the contents of the jilted groom's safe. The pragmatic Lindien (Jean-François Stévenin) asks his friend, the private detective Luigi (Sergio Castellito), to track her down. Luigi's quest starts with her childhood home and the episodic narrative structure is triggered as the stops on his search alternate with flashbacks to her experiences in those same locations. As Luigi's tour retraces her tracks through Champagne, Roissy, Paris, Marseilles and Grenoble, their trajectories gradually converge. France Robert's journey is accompanied by involvements with a series of men yet all of these provide experiments in the evolution of her imposition of economic representations on all relationships, including charging the men for sex (yet not working as a prostitute). Luigi's own state of mind becomes unstable as he is drawn to the Parisian scene of his failed marriage and ex-wife's new relationship and identifies increasingly with the object of his search. On finally tracking France down they have sex and he lets her escape by giving her enough money to leave for New York, where she reaches a dead end with neither work nor shelter. The last scene shows Luigi on the phone from Genoa,[11] having apparently abandoned his quest, offering to buy France a return ticket out of New York.

The narrative structure and main protagonists clearly reflect the influence of film noir on Masson's oeuvre.[12] *A vendre*, whilst not conforming to the conventional profiles of the main protagonists, exploits a classic narrative model of *film noir*; the private detective sent

---

10 Her name suggests parallels with the nation state and evokes the English near-homonym 'robber'.

11 It is notable that the central male characters in both *En avoir (ou pas)* and *A vendre* are Italian, yet this seems to be a trait that subverts caricatures of machismo masculinity to denote the vulnerable status of the outsider in France.

12 Indeed she describes the central couple of *En avoir (ou pas)* as detectives in search of their own identities (Herpe and Kohn 1996: 22).

to apprehend the *femme fatale* who has disappeared with her lover's money. Indeed, a brief sequence in the main protagonist's bedroom focuses on the rows of crime novels that fill her shelves, and Masson signals the importance of definitive noir themes as humiliation in *En avoir (ou pas)* and betrayal in *A vendre* (Audé and Garbanz 1998: 29). Although the punishment of the *femme fatale*'s sexual and economic agency is conventionally posited as normative closure, some iconic examples, such as *Out of the Past* (Tourneur, 1947), feature a detective who falls in love with the *femme fatale* and, like Luigi, fails to bring about the punitive ending. Stating her preference for 'genre films', Masson specifies that 'l'idée de l'enquête, de la quête, est pratiquement dans tous mes films ... Le film policier est une forme simple, un mode "mineur", qui me permet d'explorer des sujets majeurs'[13] (Masson 2008a). The adoption of the 'minor' mode of the detective film or the wider intertext of film noir (a category which is itself notoriously difficult to define) enables Masson to engage here with the 'major' subjects of the corruption of personal relationships by economic models of exchange and the hierarchies perpetuated by both the social construction of gender and the consequent economic status of women. Film noir predicates the foregrounding of dynamics of sexuality and power structures and, if, following Dyer, we see that 'sexuality, both as knowledge and solution, is also the means by which men and women are designated a place in society and are kept in their place' (Dyer 1986: 26), it is clear that Masson's film is able through this 'minor' generic mode to address the socio-cultural and economic status of women across a network of tropes of gendered discourses from consumerism to sexuality. As Luigi condenses France's two years of travelling into one month of his own, the film's episodic form provides parallels between differently gendered experiences of the same environments, constructing France as both the object of investigation and the subject of her own resistance to definition as (sexual) object. The noirish structure of the film, dominated by a long flashback in which Luigi's meetings with her acquaintances trigger further flashbacks, adds a tragic poignancy to France's quest as, for significant sections of film time, the audience knows the outcome of relationships before they are played out before us.

13 'the notion of the enquiry, the quest, is in almost all of my films ... The detective film is a simple form, a "minor" mode which enables me to address major subjects.'

The character of Luigi remains closer to the masochistic and abject masculinities of classic film noir (see Krutnik 1991) than to the 'sexualised fall guy' (Williams 2005: 106) of neo-noir thrillers of the 1980s and 1990s. In contrast to France's commodification of sex, he has been celibate since his wife left him two years ago and rejects sexual advances from a series of women whom he encounters in his search for France. Žižek reminds us that 'the very presence of the detective guarantees in advance the transformation of the lawless sequence into a lawful sequence: in other words the reestablishment of "normality"' (Žižek 1993: 58). Luigi's presence, however, problematises this function and does nothing to bring about narrative coherence and closure. The notion of lawfulness is further challenged as, although France's only criminal act is the theft of Lindien's cash, it is implied that her real lawlessness lies in the demystification of romance and associated social structures through her insistence on revealing the inherent links between socially sanctioned relationships and the economics of sexual prostitution. Luigi's summaries of his investigative progress, the delivery to dictaphone increasing the effect of a *voix-off* (Rouyer 1998: 25), posit a pseudo-scientific, objective structure ('question, answer, conclusion') in marked contrast to the subjective and misogynistic nature of his comment that focus is shifting 'd'une connasse à une autre' (from one stupid bitch to another) and the increasing dominance of abstract questions, such as 'A quoi ça sert d'aimer?' (what's the point of loving?) which serve to align his investigation with France's journey. Luigi is a private detective, a status often compared unfavourably with that of the official police[14] as having a more ambiguous relationship to the law and one in which he often tracks the clandestine sexual activity of others for financial reward. In a self-reflexive development of this motif Luigi uses his time in Paris tracking France to spy on his ex-wife, his position as voyeur of his own exclusion ironically emphasised by the screen-like expanses of the slick, glass home extension that he had paid for. Luigi moves from voyeur to intruder however as he enters his ex-home and imposes his uncomfortable presence on the new family unit in a desperately parodic simulation of sexual intimacy. His sense of ultimate impotency explodes however as he uses his symbolically overloaded gun to demand details of the sexual prowess of his replacement. This

14 Indeed Luigi's ex-wife, herself a lawyer, comments on the disreputable nature of his work.

episode, framed explicitly in the glass-walled space as a performative act, serves as a focal point for the crisis in Luigi's own identity: a crisis which accelerates his growing identification with France, a transfer exhibited through his attempts at occupying her physical space by renting the same rooms in which she stayed. However, whilst access to her physical movements may be easily acquired, access to her motivations remains elusive and Luigi's voiceover becomes an obsessive mantra as he repeats the rewardingly ambiguous phrase 'Je suis France Robert', which exploits the shared form of the verbs 'être' and 'suivre' to assert not only that he is following France Robert but also that he performs *being* France Robert.[15] Luigi's meeting with her, which would conventionally implicate the errant woman in a punitive closure and establish the detective's superior knowledge, has, on the contrary, a destabilising effect. Having played out his own complex set of sexual and economic substitutions (by replacing her client, having sex with her and paying), he takes her to the airport and allows her to escape. Thus the predictable climax of his quest and the long-anticipated meeting of their two narratives leads to the collapse of Luigi's 'regime' of serial refusals (his repression of sexual and other appetites) and the embrace of an excess which leads him to break his own monetary contract, betray his 'mission' and his friend, and pay so far above the 'asking price' for sex with France that she can fly to New York. This apparent crisis triggered by a return of the repressed culminates in his attack on his professional identity and illusory omniscience through the destruction of his office and his return to his native Italy (and to his mother).

Luigi's detective and narratorial skills, impaired by misogyny and alienated withdrawal from human relations, ensure that he is incapable of asserting self-knowledge. Lindien's cryptic statement that he was attracted to France because 'she knows' posits a transgressive knowledge that haunts Luigi's investigation and undermines any claim to omniscience. France's superior insight into the rampant hypocrisy of patriarchal constructions of sexual relationships, her ambiguous (generic) status and the absence of identificatory triggers for the spectator prevent both Luigi and the audience from knowing her. Luigi's initial projection of her motivations construct her as the classic *femme fatale*, mirroring accepted analyses of the figure of the

15 Such transferences between them are also signalled by France's adoption of
   Luigi's sunglasses.

femme fatale as representing the threat to man's sovereign subjectivity posed by the agency of female desire and thus 'not the subject of feminism but the symptom of male fears about feminism' (Doane 1991: 2). However, as the film progresses, France demonstrates few of the necessary traits of this identity such as: 'a lust for exciting sex, a desire for wealth and the power it brings, and a need to control everything and everyone around her' (Dickos 2002: 162). France can be aligned with the dangerous agency of the *femme fatale*, the supposedly seductive mystery in which she 'cannot be clearly located in the opposition between master and slave' (Žižek 1993: 65), yet here this signals not control but an ambiguous anxiety. Whilst the film's open ending does not clearly suggest that France has ultimately become 'the victim of her own game' (ibid.: 65), her assertion of control over the economic regulation of sexual activity is undermined increasingly by experiences of humiliation and the recurring contrast made between her selective attempts at empowerment and the lack of choices open to 'real' prostitutes. Masson thus exploits the conventions of film noir to create a demystification of the subordination of women across both the gendered cultural discourses of film noir and romance and the dominant economic structures of contemporary France.

In her discussion of the generic structures of romance, Holmes suggests an essential contrast between this mode and the detective narrative asserting that, in romance,

> unlike the heroes of popular male genres (for example the lone detective of *noir* fiction), the selfhood achieved by the heroine is very much defined by her relationship with another: it is by loving and being loved that she achieves a happy ending. (Holmes, 2006: 16)

A vendre builds connections and resonances between the two genres as both France and Luigi attempt to protect themselves from others, driven by an abject fear of rejection to reduce all behaviour to economic motivations. France, her heart already broken, defends herself from the discourses of romance by putting all sexual (and sentimental) activity on an economic footing.[16] This strategy preserves her role as both controlling subject (unlike most scenarios of prostitution she selects the client) and sexual object in a socio-economic climate in

---

16 In response to her parents' concerns about her debt to the family business, she reconfigures their relationship by calculating how much she has cost them and repaying in instalments.

which sex is easily detachable from its role in defining relationships to serve as a proto-consumer activity (Bauman 2003). Yet, whilst France's transactions are effective in their persistent demystification of the socio-economic structures of romance and marriage, they remain resolutely ambiguous in their failure to provide either economic wealth or personal freedom. The increasingly problematic nature of her 'freedoms' is articulated through the recurring alternation of sexual encounters with scenes of athletic training, suggesting at first that the latter offers truer self-expression.[17] Yet France's running becomes increasingly contained and regresses from a tracking shot of her running in open countryside to a long fixed shot of her pounding a deserted track and finally to a stubbornly static and bitterly ironic shot of her on a gym treadmill, dressed not in sports kit but in a dress chosen by Lindien and going nowhere fast.

France's demystification of the economics of romance begins as a refreshingly subversive strategy over which she seems to enjoy unquestionable control. As her journey progresses however such strategies of empowerment become increasingly illusory and alien-ating as, throughout the film, she occupies a markedly lower economic and professional status than the men she sleeps with. Abandoned in the Roissy Hilton by a businessman who applied the entrepreneurial diktats of 'establishing a project, fixing a goal' to her seduction, France finds work in a supermarket and starts a relationship with the local bank manager (Roschdy Zem). She responds to his declaration of love by quoting a price for a night with her and dismisses any moral or practical distinction between paying for dinner, flowers and paying her directly for sex and claims further that financial commit-ment indeed stands as the only credible guarantee of his desire. Sex between them is not shown, but a close-up of banknotes on the bedroom floor (recalling the beach scene in *En avoir (ou pas)*), estab-lishes the conflation of libidinal economies and financial transac-tion. Next seen in central Paris, France seems to have achieved social integration as a rare mid-shot emphasises her happy inclusion in a multi-ethnic market crowd, interacting as part of a community rather than party to an oppositional economic transaction. The chicken that she now keeps as a pet seems at first to provide a positive contrast to the shots of bare chicken carcasses and taxidermy that dominated

17 It is notable that the shock of her first romantic betrayal prevents her from competing in a race.

Luigi's visit to her moribund hometown. However, the sense of solidarity established in these brief sequences has little impact on the fixity of France's allotted position in dominant hierarchies and as soon as she re-enters work through her next job, as cleaner in a bourgeois household in which sexual infidelity appears the norm, she is defined emphatically as economic and sexual object. The move from accepting cash payment for her cleaning (tucking notes into her skirt in lap dancer fashion) to negotiation of sexual services to the husband (Pierrot) is swift, yet France fails ultimately to maintain either sexual or economic control. Cliché-ridden intimations of romance in the inclusive framing of shots of the couple sharing fruit in a luxurious bed are quickly dismissed as, ignoring France's protestations that she does not enjoy anal sex (he reserves the privilege of such choices for his wife), the husband insists that the paying client gets whatever he wants.[18] The following static close-up in which France is held face down on a highly mirrored table (a shot privileged by its selection for the film posters) foregrounds the ambiguity of her position as, even whilst she is forced to face her own image as passive object, it remains unclear whether her protest morphs to pleasure. Her position as commodified sexual object is reinforced by the doubling of her image in the mirrored surface and by the husband's accompanying descriptions of sex with other women. This sequence forms a stark contrast to France's conversation with a prostitute,[19] whose assertion of the economic motivation for her work was mitigated by her refusal of anal sex in comparison to France's situation in which her motivation and control are undermined. Coste's lucid analysis of the film's 'scenes of taming' reveals the men's strategies which rely on their allocating France a conventional position as wife or kept mistress (Coste 2005: 186) yet, even when subjugated, her presence remains disruptive. This affair ends when France's refusal of normalising romantic discourse becomes too disruptive for the seasoned seducer as she responds to his question 'why do you sell yourself?' with the more troubling retort 'why do you pay?' Further attacks on the husband's sexual and economic status (France suggests that his wife gets her extra-marital sex for free) trigger an immediate assertion

18 Such a combination recalls *Naked* (Leigh, 1993) in its focus on the gender inequalities and misogyny inherent in capitalist structures and in which the yuppie landlord insists on anal sex with his economically vulnerable tenant.
19 The only people with whom France establishes friendships are prostitutes.

of hierarchies as he calls to check on his wife before rejecting France. The conflation of serial hierarchies is further revealed as, disappointed that she is not upset ('tears are not included in the price'), the husband compensates by asserting economic power and firing her from her cleaning job.[20]

The impact of such episodes in which France moves from a selective, assertive negotiation of sexual agency to explicit humiliation is represented in a striking almost silent sequence of France in her chaotic room – her absolute freedom having led to absolute solitude. The long take in mid-shot of her dishevelled distress and slumped naked body constructs a frank and explicitly non-erotic representation made all the more striking by her steady return of the camera's gaze, a look that contains both tearful defiance of the objectifying gaze and a plea for acknowledgement of her existence through the presence of the other. France's failure to occupy the position of seller (highlighted by her thankless cold-selling job) leads her to attempt to be a client. She offers to pay for company (ironically, her male colleague is happy to sell sex but *not* affection) and buys time from the prostitute, Mireille (Chiara Mastrioanni), the same woman from whom Luigi buys not sex but information in the film's opening sequences. France's attempted identification with Mireille is short-lived however as France, dressed in the accessories of mass-produced erotica, masters selling technique[21] yet fails the interview as her motivation (the desire to reduce all relationships to economic transactions) is dismissed as rendering her unsuitable for such work.

The final episodes appear to serve as a mere coda to the climactic meeting of the two central protagonists, yet they provide France with defining experiences of absolute freedom, absolute exploitation and possible rehabilitation. More importantly, these sequences constitute a reflection on the position of the filmmaker (and spectator) in relation to constructions of voyeurism and empathy. France's utopian

20 The force of this 'buyer's market' is highlighted as, when Luigi visits the household, the first shot isolates another woman's torso and legs as she cleans; a nameless, fetishised replacement who is also made to request payment in the scene.

21 Evocations of conventional representations of desire persist in the film through nightclub scenes filmed with red filters and with pulsating dub soundtrack. The diegetic status of this scene is unclear and it serves as a marker of filmic conventions of the erotic.

destination, New York,[22] brings only increased alienation and the intervention of two figures, prostitute and artist, clarifies the exchange mechanisms in which she seems trapped. A male prostitute offers France help yet, indebted by his action, she accompanies him as (paid) voyeuristic accessory for his next job. Confronted with the brutality of the client's exploitation, and the trace of her own humiliation (the client pushes the male prostitute against a full-length mirror), the constructs of empowerment through which she viewed her own sexual transactions are revealed as illusory. In a final unravelling of her equations, the economic transaction fails to compensate as the client refuses to pay.

The brutal free market recuperation of France's initially empowering quest is countered, however, by France's successful negotiation of the non-commodification of her own subjectivity. A woman painter pays France to pose for her in a conventionally feminine dress, but, criticising the painter's lack of engagement with her sitters, France shames her into returning the portrait. The artwork thus becomes a gifted object[23] that transcends economic exchange values and, in its status as portrait, asserts the subjectivity of both artist and sitter. The suggested parallel between the position of the painter and that of both director and spectator as cultural mediators and bearers of a potentially objectifying gaze is clear. Masson asserts that:

> La peintre, c'est moi, c'est nous qui avons regardé cette fille en voyeur et qui l'utilisons comme elle a l'intention de le faire: elle la paie cinq cents francs pour la pose, comme nous, nous donnons à un sdf dans le métro.[24] (Audé and Garbanz 1998: 30)

France's defiance has evolved from the angry but mute return of the cinematic gaze to an articulation of her needs.

The generosity of the painter is echoed in Masson's resolutely ambiguous ending which offers France another chance at forming a relationship outside of the structures of consumer transactions. In striking similarity with the closing sequence of Lvovsky's *Oublie-moi*,

22 The use of reggae soundtrack and France's Rastafarian hat provide clumsy notation of her status as exoticised outsider.

23 Elsewhere in the film, gifts are contaminated by discourses of dependence, guilt and appropriation.

24 'The painter is me, it's all of us who have watched this girl as voyeurs and who use her as the painter intends to do: she pays her 500 francs for posing, just like us when we give money to a homeless person in the metro.'

the isolation of the central female is tempered only by a disembodied male voice whose identity is identified with romantic escapism and role play. There is some justification in reading Luigi's passive wait for France to return as a displacement of conventional gender roles (Coste 2005: 192), yet her mobility remains dependent on his payment of a ticket out of New York. Indeed, this final conversation premises the assertion of Luigi's financial control and his mirroring of Lindien's desire to bring her back, suggesting, in turn, the reinstatement of the overarching structure of male desire to stage 'little more than an elaborate love story, in which the heroine plumbs the depths to find a hero willing to accept her and love her for what she is' (Tarr with Rollet 2001: 239) and in which the rebellious self-selling nomadic heroine is economically and socially recuperated. Whilst other women-centred road movies, from the haunting solitudes of *Sans toit ni loi* (Varda, 1985) to the violent trajectories of *Baise-moi* (Despentes, 2000), disrupt the notion of linear progression, here it is Luigi's intervention that prevents France from ending up where we first see her, returned, as a misplaced commodity, to the jilted groom. France's previous lack of regard for romantic convention, combined with her newly acquired sense of a self which exceeds economic definition, may persuade the spectator of the illusory status of a normative happy ending. The film resists easy resolution; however, its central concerns, including the frank portrayal of the unambiguous and persistent feminisation of poverty, the pernicious layers of social exclusion and the continuation of gendered divisions of labour, foreground the inherent connections between economic structures and (gendered) subjective experience. France's response to her oppressed position in gendered economic hierarchies proves ultimately alienating yet provides temporary respite from the more conventional allocation of the role of victim in its presentation of the damage wrought by 'economic and sexual liberalism' (Coste 2005: 185). Discussing *Rosetta* (Dardennes, 1999), Osganian describes how the violence of the central female protagonist

> subvertit le cadre socialement acceptable de l'identification aux victimes et déplace la revendication sociale du statut ou d'identité, vers la demande politique d'une reconnaissance de l'individu comme sujet désirant.[25] (Osganian 2003: 52)

25 'subverts the socially acceptable framework of identification with the victims and shifts from the social demand for status or identity to the political request for recognition of the individual as desiring subject'.

The messy cultural violence of France's struggle to defend herself against such structures achieves a similar displacement. Masson indeed suggests that France

> ne se fait pas avoir, mais elle n'a plus rien elle-même. Elle finit par abandonner et s'abandonner à quelqu'un en prenant le risque d'être déçue et trahie, mais en même temps elle retrouve un rapport à l'autre.[26] (Masson 1998)

The ambiguity of the ending occludes the attribution of victim status to either protagonist and thus offers a space in which both France and Luigi might overcome their respective alienations to risk an openness to the other.

The romantic uncanny: *Love Me* (2000)

The necessarily dangerous acceptance of risk in embracing the other provides an ambiguous ending for *A vendre*, but it is the traumatic consequences of rejection that are central to Masson's next film, and final part of the Kiberlain trilogy, *Love Me* (2000), the English title of which alludes to the Presley song that recurs within it. The establishment of a 'family' of actors and collaborators is characteristic of the generation of filmmakers evoked in 'le jeune cinéma' and whilst the presence of Sandrine Kiberlain is the prime example in Masson's oeuvre, Stévenin and Clément reappear within the trilogy and beyond. Kiberlain's star identity remained closely connected to these three films, and descriptions of Kiberlain's star persona as a 'mélange de force têtue, d'ironie acide, de capacité à s'abstraire dans le rêve') (Audé 2002: 183) (a mixture of stubborn energy, of sharp irony, of the ability to leave herself behind and enter a dream) reflect closely the central characteristics of these protagonists. Masson's stated casting preferences also support such slippages between character and actor that are central to constructions of star identity: 'j'aime moins la capacité d'un acteur à devenir telle ou telle autre personne que sa capacité à n'être que lui-même'[27] (Douin 2001: 17). Yet, in Masson's work, 'being yourself' remains a complex and resolutely performative endeavour.

26 'escapes being had but no longer has anything herself. She eventually gives up and gives herself to someone, running the risk of disappointment and betrayal, but also rediscovering a relationship with the other.'
27 'I am less impressed by the ability of an actor to become this or that other person than their ability to just be themselves.'

A summary of *Love Me*'s narrative proves both extremely difficult and arguably counterproductive. The enigmatic central character, Gabrielle Rose (Kiberlain) seems to be two different women in two different times and places as the narrative switches between the attempts of a glamorous amnesiac to seduce the fading singer Lennox (Johnny Hallyday) in Memphis, and apparently the same woman's struggle to hold on to a job, friends and her own sanity in a dilapidated Le Havre. Gabrielle Rose, lost and alone in Memphis, is tracked by a sinister figure, Carbonne (Stévenin), who, as both detective and assassin, has also abducted a teenage girl, Mademoiselle Rose, from an orphanage. The latter could be Gabrielle Rose's daughter, her younger self or a fantasy double as the relationship between the characters and temporal and spatial transitions in the film remains unclear.[28] Gabrielle Rose continues her obsessive pursuit of Lennox but, after several tender yet inconclusive encounters, he rejects her and hands her over to Carbonne. The amnesiac's repeated blackouts act as transitions to another time and space in which the same woman works in a shabby 1950s Americana bar in Le Havre and lives in a caravan filled with posters of Lennox. We learn that this Gabrielle Rose never knew her father, lost her mother at a young age and was brought up in a state institution, yet now claims to be haunted by her mother and her younger self. Preparing for an audition as a singer, she plans to go to Memphis and visit Graceland. Stévenin appears in the last sequences of the Le Havre episodes as a psychoanalyst worried for Gabrielle Rose's health. Having met an enigmatic English sailor (Julian Sands) and, after a dramatic denouement in which mother and younger self vanish and the assassin/analyst kills her amnesiac double, she tracks the sailor down in Taipei.

The two modes of the film, associated with Memphis and Le Havre respectively, are initially distinct but become increasingly interwoven as the narrative progresses. The Memphis scenes are associated with the colour red and an oneiric film language of sweeping tracking shots, smooth camera movement, dramatic lighting and the reflexive foregrounding of *mise en scène*, whilst sequences in Le Havre are characterised by natural light, muted colours and a static camera. A visit to the 'club de solidarité' in Le Havre, which sets a more brutal realist mood with its use of non-professional actors, hand-held camera and

---

28 Indeed the film's credits refer to one role only – Kiberlain as 'la jeune femme'.

zoom on posters for the group 'SOS suicides', serves as an effective reminder of the very real problems of the local community, but this documenting of the human and social consequences of economic deprivation serves as a counter to Gabrielle Rose's escapism as she rejects their offer of 'human kindness' in favour of romance. Settings which appear to have solely realist motivations are drawn from the cinematic imaginary, and the run-down clubs, jetties and docks, whilst reflecting economic decline, remain timeless and generic in their accommodation of both realist and fantasy modes (Audé 2002: 183). The recurrent use of nostalgic 1950s Americana creates an eerie set of connections between the dingy (and uncannily misspelled) 'Solitair's bar' in Le Havre, Memphis and the crooner, Lennox. The undermining of the classical functions of setting is encapsulated in a shot in which Gabrielle Rose poses in front of Presley's birthplace, Graceland, only for it to be revealed as a flimsy backdrop. Indeed, the undermining of certainties of spatial and cultural references is extended to the making of the film as Masson asserts that the budget did not stretch to any shooting in the USA (Masson 2000).

The loss of reliable location for characterisation and narrative frameworks supports the explicitly performative nature of the identity of the central protagonist. This is established in the striking opening sequence as, in a lengthy long shot, Gabrielle Rose emerges from a caravan on a deserted beach and sashays towards the camera miming to 'Heartbreak Hotel'.[29] In a costume of pink 1950s nostalgia, she teases the camera in apparently playful performance, yet the humour of this quirky opening is soon undercut by her disturbingly over-literal interpretation of the lyrics as she mimes stabbing, shooting and cutting her own throat to the refrain 'I feel so lonely I could die'. The editing, which positions the sequence between a bleached-out image and a fade to black, further questions its status as real event or fantasy episode. Such episodes encourage a Butlerian reading of gendered identity as a socio-historical construct maintained in tropes of role, masquerade, imitation and performance. Butler argues that 'There is no gender identity behind the expressions of gender, ... identity is performatively constructed by the very "expressions" that are said to be its results' (Butler 1990: 25), revealing that there can be no performer

---

29 This performativity is reinforced by Gabrielle Rose's wish to be a singer, a desire which continues that of both Alice and France Robert in the preceding two films and provides an interesting parallel with Kiberlain's own recent singing career.

prior to the performance. Gabrielle Rose and her double repeatedly perform snatches of the same song, 'Love Me Tender', and this serves as the mantra of their desperate attempts to secure a projected and idealised (paternal) male subject of desire. The status of the projected double as bewildered amnesiac makes the lack of essential or stable (gender) identity all the more striking and highlights Masson's persistent critique of the pernicious artificiality of socio-cultural constructions of love through romance.

Father-substitute Lennox is the object of obsession for both the adolescent and adult Gabrielle Rose, [30] the latter attempting to form a love relationship with him within this highly stylised unconscious. His image dominates the film both through the frequency of close-ups (maintained in the huge posters that dominate Gabrielle Rose's caravan) and the impact of his steady return of the camera's gaze. He is associated with black and blue in sharp contrast to her eponymous pink, and with Presley's 'Love Me Tender', the lyrics of which are rendered sinister through repetition (John Cale's dissonant 'Heartbreak Hotel', heard before the final sequence, has a similar impact). When Lennox appears in the 'real' setting of Le Havre, and the two perform the film's only full rendition of 'Love Me Tender' as a duet, the establishment of an imagined or real relationship with the father figure brings no closure. Masson's casting of Johnny Hallyday in the role of Lennox constructs another referential layer as the film exploits his pre-existing status in the French cultural imaginary and his familiar star image. His status as the 'French Elvis Presley'[31] is exploited as, in addition to the construction of multi-layered connotations of Lennox/Hallyday's fading, eroticised glamour, his accented delivery of Presley classics in English creates an aural uncanny which complements the spatial and temporal defamiliarisations discussed above.[32] The uncanny permeates the narrative and *mise en scène* of the film through unstable and multiple identities, manipulation of proper names, repetition and apparent déjà vu and functions as 'a metaphor for a fundamentally unliveable modern condition' (Vidler 1992: x). More specific Freudian markers of the uncanny, notably the presence

30 In fact an offhand comment from Gabrielle Rose's 'mother' suggests that Lennox could be her father.

31 Indeed the film's title recalls Presley's film *Loving You* (Kanter, 1957).

32 This sense of an aural uncanny is established in early sequences which, set in Memphis, are delivered in unsubtitled English by a French cast.

of the double, are central to the film through the unresolved multiple identities of the main protagonist.[33] Cinema as a form has been linked to the construction of the uncanny owing to its inherent capacity to produce simultaneously an affective drive to identification and a distancing recognition of its own artifice. Thus the spectator, faced with enigmatic figures trapped within a seemingly unknowable narrative and prevented from identifying with central figures, may yet enjoy the imposed freedom of concentrating on the construction of *mise en scène* and performance. Such liberating constraints recall Lynchian strategies that are particularly prominent in *Lost Highway* (Lynch, 1997) and *Mulholland Drive* (Lynch, 2001), films that also feature the doubling of central female characters. The repeated representation of scenes of performance, audition and miming are often introduced by recurring fades to black that provide a rhythmic effect and alternative narrative support in the face of the denial of clear narrative progression. Lynch's *Wild at Heart* (1990) also features a central character, Sailor Ripley, an Elvis-obsessive whose performance of 'Love Me Tender' closes the film. Masson's film may, however, be seen as a riposte rather than a homage to this last film as, whilst they share hyperreal opening sequences and enigmatic central female characters, *Wild at Heart* remains problematically misogynistic in its representation and containment of female subjectivity within resolutely (violent) patriarchal structures of desire. Gabrielle Rose's double and *Love Me*'s other uncanny effects are not only catalysts for a reading of the film as revealing postmodern identities as plural and unfixed, but follow the strategies of Russian Formalism and Brechtian alienation effects (Royle 2003: xi) in employing the uncanny for political ends through the 'making strange' of discourses of romance and gendered desire in order to foster a complex spectatorial critique of both.

The performative episodes provide scenarios in which identity can be both suspended and multiple, yet they are countered by insistent demands for narrative and genre coherency. The character of Carbonne (Stévenin) occupies the dual roles of detective and therapist, roles which share the central strategy of asking others to construct their stories. His name, in its evocation of carbon paper, suggests doubling, transference and the establishment of documentary or archival traces,

---

33 Freud's discussion of the uncanny, one of his rare engagements with aesthetics, links the anxiety caused by the uncanny to the castration complex and fear of mortality.

whilst visual and narrative associations with iconographic elements of film noir (enigmatic solitude, guns, shiny black cars) posit him as the ultimate detective, facing the extreme challenge of reconstituting a case narrative from the fragmented memories of an obsessive amnesiac.[34] A clue as to the dual identity of analyst and detective is indicated playfully in the final sequences by the brandishing of a toy gun and, in measured defiance of Masson's explicit advice to 'follow the character, not the story. You are being taken inside the character's head' (Masson 2000), we can claim a reading of the film which posits Carbonne as an analyst who compels Gabrielle Rose to come to terms with abandonment by her father, consequent damaging obsession with him as idealised love-object and the death of her mother. This reading would suggest that the failed audition for work as a singer[35] triggers a breakdown in which Gabrielle Rose retreats into fantasy projections of her identity alongside that of the lost father and mother. Such a reading is supported by the prominence given to two sequences that provide a *mise en abyme* of the film's main concerns. Gabrielle Rose, surrounded by huge posters of Lennox, is transfixed by a television interview in which a psychologist explains the function of love, likening it to a madness in which the love object becomes the ideal being who corresponds to what we lack. Further fragments provide explicit commentary of her position which describes those suffering (parental) abandonment as 'des victimes de blessures profondes et irréparables qui peuvent cicatriser avec notre aide – mais qui sont en souffrance pendant toute leur vie'.[36]

The film's denouement, however, is not that of an explicitly therapeutic or discursive cure; rather the noir elements resurface to enable a dramatic representation of the aims of analysis. Carbonne arrives with the amnesiac double, her 'mother' and 15–year-old self to find Gabrielle Rose standing at the end of a jetty (a location glimpsed at the start of the film in clear reference to Marker's seminal deconstruction of memory). Gabrielle Rose is saved as Mademoiselle Rose snatches

---

34 Other noir references include the character Terry Lennox in Chandler's *The Long Goodbye*, a man with multiple identities who, accused of both murder and suicide, turns out not to be dead (Masson, 2000). Lennox's room is also the 'Robert Mitchum Suite'.

35 Note that in *En avoir (ou pas)* Alice sang in English and that France Robert wanted to be a singer.

36 'victims of deep and irreparable hurt whose scars can heal with our help, but who will suffer throughout their whole lives'.

the sailor's address (signifying a future love) from the amnesiac and brings it to her. Having aligned herself exactly with the profile of her older self, the teenager then slips into the water, disappearing at the same moment that Carbonne shoots the amnesiac at point-blank range. The consequences of such radical interventions in the unconscious are witnessed in the realist setting of Le Havre as Gabrielle Rose regains consciousness on the analyst's couch and requests the sailor's address before leaving. Thus we might construe that the whole film is the (retro) projected psychodrama of her analysis and that the romantic narrative closure signals the successful treatment of her inability to negotiate the consequences of paternal abandonment. Yet, as throughout Masson's oeuvre, closure remains illusory and the film's final sequence echoes the ending of *En avoir (ou pas)* in its assertion of female subjectivity through point of view, combined with a gloriously problematic romantic mood. This ambiguity is heightened further in *Love Me* by the spectator's enduring doubt over the nature of the final sequence. Gabrielle Rose's journey to Taipei (to trace the enigmatic sailor (Sands) encountered in Le Havre) would seem to present a perfect example of the fantastical displacement that allows romantic closure to function, yet fantasy remains relative here as Taipei may represent a paradoxical engagement with the real after the troubling spatio-temporal interpenetrations of a banal Le Havre and an other-worldly Memphis. The impact of this final sequence owes much to its accompaniment by the intervention of Presley's inimitable voice (a voice whose marked absence has haunted the film) singing 'I Can't Help Falling in Love with You'. This could remain simply a clumsy signal that this new love, in contrast to earlier cover versions, is indeed 'the real thing', but Presley's voice, through its global recognition and clear association with the industrialised production of popular culture, remains troubling in its simultaneous signification of both (relative) authenticity and (nostalgic) fantasy. Even as a swooning slow-motion sequence shows the new couple gazing wordlessly into each other's eyes, the apparent romantic closure of Gabrielle Rose's paradoxical engagement with the real is further tempered by our knowledge that she believed her father was a sailor and that the trip to Taipei, whether real or imagined, may constitute a further episode of dysfunctional obsession. The function of romance in *Love Me* remains thus tantalisingly suspended between realism and fantasy as the conventional narrative and cinematic boundaries separating the two have been dismantled. The primal romance between daughter and (lost) father provides a model of the 'grand amour' which may signal an obliteration of the self and estrangement from socio-economic reality, yet it remains unclear whether the detective work of the film noir analysis has 'normalised' Gabrielle Rose's desire. The central protagonist's double identity presents a singular quest for the investigator or spectator and could be construed as positing conventional notions of female identity as enigma, yet, whilst her name evokes the infamous mystery of *Citizen Kane*'s Rosebud, she remains subject of (and subject to) her own desires, rather than the mute object of those of others.

Masson's trilogy, although not devised as such from the outset, reveals a consistency of themes and strong sense of development. The striking central female protagonists of all three films embark upon journeys of escape, evading overdetermining origins to search for a sense of self. The journeys become more complex in form, from Alice's linear spatial trajectory to France Robert's more extensive itinerary (rendered circular by the overarching structure of the flashback), to Gabrielle Rose's obsessive distortions of time and space. As these physical displacements become more fragmented and non-linear, so the concomitant quests for identity become more ambiguous and open-ended. Whilst Alice continues to assert personal agency in the face of socio-economic determinism, France Robert's attempts to bracket out the personal lead to the painful realisation that she cannot occupy the sole position of either economic subject or object without losing her humanity. Gabrielle Rose loses sight of even the most basic markers of identity in her quest through the mythical landscapes of the unconscious before reaching a far-flung (and far-fetched) destination that may be simply a new stage-set for the same cyclical narrative. These quests share the common goal of establishing a functional, female desiring subject, a position which is negotiated through the use of slow motion, zoom and the freeze frame, elements which assert the place of the subjective and encapsulate the insistence on the simultaneous existence of the real and the fantasy in Masson's films. The trilogy is notable also for its juxtaposition of frank depictions of socio-economic hardship (from the canning factories of Boulogne sur mer in *En avoir (ou pas)* to the compared alienation of prostitutes and cleaners in *A vendre* and the harmful impact of unemployment in *Love Me*) alongside the self-reflexive use of the generic conventions and iconography of both film noir and romance.

The juxtaposition of such seemingly opposed modes and the consequent rejection of a wholly naturalist vision are central to Masson's consideration of the role of (filmic) representation and its relationship to the political. Dismissing naturalist attempts to represent unemployment ('Il n'y a pas le chômage, mais comment les gens vivent le chômage' (Rouyer and Vassé 2000: 24) ('Unemployment' as such does not exist – but personal experiences of unemployment do), she asserts the importance of maintaining a personal, subjective focalisation. A belief that the political is personal thus remains at the contestatory heart of Masson's filmmaking, through a style that supports the representational hybridity of subjective experience rather than the framing of political discourse within solely realist conventions. The central role of love in the trilogy is also presented within this framework as central both to socio-economic survival and to the emotional imaginary. Whilst it remains clear that the couples' attempts to consolidate sexual identities may 'account for their positive "romantic" endings' (Coste 2005: 187), it can also be asserted that the role of romance in this trilogy functions in a wider context. Diana Holmes advocates a rehabilitation of the central tropes of the romance narrative as politically and personally advantageous, asserting that it

> deals with serious ethical questions: how to reconcile the fierce egoism of sexual and emotional drives with social responsibility, how to negotiate the boundaries between self and other, between loving desire and possessive control, between fascination with and fear of difference. (Holmes 2006: 19)

Such combative negotiations are central to the three films of this trilogy, yet the scene of romance is clearly portrayed not as a transcendent solution to such struggles but as the main arena in which it takes place. The swooning ambiguity of the endings of all three of these films, which suggest at once the liberating assertion of (female) desire and the accompanying dangers of both escapism and appropriation, posits the powerful strategy of risking the self as an opening, rather than a closure, of their respective narratives.

Memory and identity: *Je suis venue te dire* (1996)

Between the filmings of *En avoir (ou pas)* and *A vendre*, Masson made a short film which serves as a parallel and more personal exploration of the ambiguities of desire and risk. The film also stars Kiberlain and constitutes an intimate account, filmed on video, of the narrator's shifting sexual identity and sense of dislocation from the outside world.[37] Masson describes the film as providing the outlook of 'quelqu'un enfermé en soi-même et chez soi, qui voit la vie dehors sans réussir à y participer'[38] (Audé 2002: 182). The narrator writes to another woman, who may have been her lover, and recounts the story of a break-up in ten letters,[39] an account which combines intensely poetic memory with the writer's everyday present, evoked mainly through sound and music. Masson describes the film as seeking the very definition of love, through the questions: 'Quelle est la différence entre l'amitié et l'amour, est-ce que l'amour est le désir, peut-il y avoir de l'amour sans désir?'[40] (Audé and Garbanz 1998: 28). A dislocated interplay between sound and image presents desire as simultaneously constructed and sensually immediate: for example, whilst the voiceover analyses the narrator's previous sexual preference for men as a consequence of social inhibition, the image reveals a slow-motion sequence of two women kissing. The narrator's reference is to Calaferte's notorious novel *La Mécanique des femmes* (1995), a work interesting here not only for the suggested counterpoint of its reductive investigation of female sexual desires but also, more importantly, for its fragmented diary structure, which is echoed in this film.

The film, whilst intimate in tone, is also a formal exercise in the representation of memory and (cinematic) point of view. The film's search for a means of representing memory is made explicit through the serial framing via the round portholes out to sea. The circular form serves as a *mise en abyme* of the camera lens as the narrator, wondering how to capture the ocean, raises the parallel question of how to film the shifting tides of emotion and subjective time. The ocean itself, filmed without the conventional, relativising marker of the horizon, evokes the impossibility of capturing the intangible and,

37 The narrator's apparent isolation from the outside world represented through the shots from her apartment window recall Cabrera's alienated night watch in *Demain et encore demain* (see Chapter 1).

38 'someone who is closed off within themselves and within their home, who can see life outside but doesn't manage to take part in it'.

39 This structure evokes a series written by the poet Marina Tsvetaeva in 1922; *Neuf lettres avec une dixième retenue et une onzième reçue.*

40 'What is the difference between friendship and love? Is love desire? Can there be love without desire?'

whilst the languid voiceover suggests that revisiting the past remains an ill-fated enterprise, the film persists in interrogating the inscription of memory in the present. The alternation of shots between a remembered holiday and the narrator's Parisian apartment soon gives way to the dominant use of lap dissolve through which layers of image are built up to form an interpenetrating strata of memories. This recurrent use of the lap dissolve, which also superimposes video footage of the sea over (unexplained) stills, engages with the suggested limits of the cinematic, adopting an exploration of the ontology of the moving image not through its haunting absence (as in *La Jetée* (Marker, 1962)) but through the combination of the still and the moving image to suggest that the structures of memory incorporate both snapshot and narrative. The role of the image is further challenged as the narrative critique of retrospective distortion is matched by recurring zooms into extreme close-up which undermine pictorial and narrative coherence. Further attempts at evoking the processes of subjective memory are present in the use of sepia filters to preserve a nostalgic Venice and red filters to evoke the perceptual distortion wrought by the emotional saturation of an image.

The film presents as an intimate diary form yet the letters, even those unsent, retain an explicit addressee. The initial privileging of the act of writing (bold red captions announce each letter accompanied by the graphic presence of the titles and the sounds of writing) is gradually supplanted by creativity of filming as a more public therapeutic act.[41] The culturally constructed nature of these letters is evident in the citing of cultural intertexts as the narrator charts the failure of the relationship to emulate such icons of romantic adventure as Paul and Jane Bowles in Morocco and Bogart in Algeria. In continuation of the central role of music in Masson's work, the title constructs a clear reference to one of Gainsbourg's best-known songs 'Je suis venu te dire que je m'en vais' yet the curtailment of the title and the visible change in gender of the narrative voice retain the song's dramatic melancholy whilst leaving the film haunted by an unrepresented rupture. The shortening of the title, and the resultant tension between present proximity and future absence, reinforces the film's representation of the non-linear relationship between narrative and memory. The use of Bogart's iconic signature phrase 'You

41 This can be compared with the therapeutic act of filming the writing self in Cabrera's *Demain et encore demain* (1997) – see Chapter 1.

must remember this...' (heard in English) serves as further evidence of Masson's passion for film noir, yet also encapsulates the central concerns of *Je suis venue te dire* as the narrator is compelled to narration yet incapable of representing a coherent account of this memory.

Je suis venue te dire offers an autofictional twist as a close-up of Kiberlain reading is accompanied by the voiceover recounting the couple's shared dream of finding someone who could incarnate the characters of their stories and mentions 'the giraffe', an image that Alice uses to describe herself in *En avoir (ou pas)*. This tentative construction of links between interdiegetic and extra-textual identities is pursued in Masson's next film through its extended engagement with star identity as a mode that entails the blurring of such categories.

Layering identities: *La Repentie* (2002)

Masson was approached by producers looking for a film to mark Isabelle Adjani's return to the big screen as, despite her status as one of the dominant female stars of 1980s French cinema, she had not made a feature film since starring in *Diabolique* (Chechik, 1996), a differently diabolical remake of Clouzot's *Les Diaboliques*. *La Repentie* is based loosely on a novella of the same name by Didier Daeninckx which features a female protagonist trying to escape her criminal past and which can be seen as indicative of a more general return to history via the use of the detective narrative in contemporary French literature (Forsdick 2001: 336). *La Repentie* maintains Masson's interest in combining the narrative trajectories of film noir[42] and romance. The film, far simpler in narrative structure than its predecessors, begins with two men in prison discussing revenge on a woman who betrayed them both, before cutting to the mysterious Charlotte (Adjani), who arrives at a station and changes her disguise before catching the next train to Nice. Once in Nice, unable to find work in luxury boutiques, she shelters at the epitome of luxury, the Hotel Negresco. A wealthy, enigmatic lawyer with a troubled past of his own, Paul Viard (Sami Frey), offers her work as his companion and despite their mutual self-hatred, entrenched defence mechanisms and the deathly surroundings of wealthy Nice, they fall in love. When Charlotte's past catches up with her in the shape of the vengeful Karim (Samy Naceri),

42 Generic projections are present in the casting as Adjani and Frey starred together in the neo-noir *Mortelle randonnée* (Miller, 1983).

she returns to Paris, where both Karim and Paul track her down and Paul inadvertently kills Karim. In a seeming return to her maternal roots, Paul and Charlotte leave for Morocco, where her despair at rejection by her mother is countered by Paul's expression of love and the reinstatement of her real name, Leila. They share a night of intimacy in Casablanca, before the police find them and Leila sacrifices herself by confessing to Karim's murder, leaving Paul to wait for her return.

In an interview included in the DVD release, Masson describes *La Repentie* as an 'unidentified cinematic object' that received a markedly negative reception from critics who, frustrated at not finding an easy generic label for the film, reduced it to the self-indulgent obsession of a director with her star and luxury locations (Guilloux 2002: 44). The film's main location of the wealthiest parts of Nice does indeed run counter to the dominant use of more depressed economic sites by filmmakers of this generation, areas that indeed also dominate Masson's earlier work. In response to criticism that the film is in thrall to luxury, Masson claimed the importance of representing all realities (Masson 2003) and points out that the characters' search for happiness in the materialism of 'la belle vie' are revealed to be deluded. Criticism of the film extended to suggestions that Masson sought reflected glory via Adjani yet, whilst the film is uneven in both tone and pace, it can be read as an articulation of wider anxieties around the disruption of Adjani's star image (Higgins 2008: 3). *La Repentie* is indeed dominated by the presence and image of Adjani, yet the film involves a more knowing engagement with her star identity than that acknowledged by its critics. Adjani's star persona remains one of the most complex in contemporary French cinema, and one that engages questions of racial identity rather than the reduction of the female star to issues of sexuality. Starting from Dyer's analysis of the role of whiteness in the construction of stardom, Austin provides a lucid examination of the development of Adjani's star image from one associated with whiteness, luminosity (and associated traits of purity and innocence) to the 'hysteria surrounding her ethnicity' (Austin 2006: 133) that followed the revelation of her Algerian descent. Austin's conclusion that Adjani's star identity is successful in its accommodation of both whiteness and 'the foreign body' (ibid.: 33), is countered by Higgins's suggestion that, rather than representing a reassuring resolution of oppositions, the interaction between Adjani's role and star identity in *La Repentie* encapsulates the anxiety-inducing ambiguity of a character who remains both 'never more exotic than in France and never more French than in Morocco' (Higgins 2008: 9). Both analyses remain valuable here as a context to what must be seen as the film's explicit *mise en abyme* of the construction of star identity that succeeds in implicating the spectator as voyeur through a series of performances in which the camera foregrounds the objectifying look of others. Such a move recalls the function of the opening sequence of Godard's *Le Mépris* in which Bardot performs a reflexive commentary on the camera's fetishisation of the (female) star body and, whilst such explicit verbal commentary is not present here, Masson's framing of Adjani as performer fulfils a similar purpose.

The changes made to the central figure of Daeninckx's novella (mixed heritage, the return to North Africa) can be seen to reference Adjani's life (Higgins 2008; 3) yet important differences remain as Masson's heroine returns to Morocco (rather than the more politically sensitive site of Algeria) and seeks maternal rather than paternal recognition. The film should be read as an engagement with constructed star identity rather than with biographical fact, and this element builds upon the exploration of discourses of identity formation present throughout Masson's oeuvre. Questions of identity and representation dominate as the film is punctuated with visual portraits of women, ranging from the huge canvas in the hotel lobby of a woman reduced to the voluptuous folds of her red dress that signify wealth as well as objectification, to the ghostly, pale triptych of Paul's dead wife that dominates his deserted villa. The film stills on Karim's wall enjoy multiple significations that evoke simultaneously his obsession with Charlotte, an acknowledgement of Adjani's star identity and its exploitation in the artifice of the film that we are watching (the stills are deleted scenes). In a move that acknowledges the conflation of the audience's desire to see the mysterious, intradiegetic stranger with their desire to see Adjani on screen, a full facial close-up is delayed. Her face, hidden by hat and sunglasses, remains unseen as she changes her clothes in the station toilets, her star identity deferred through a knowing series of fetishising close-ups of her breasts, eyes and lips which, because of the necessary lack of onscreen observers, establishes our spectatorial voyeurism.[43] These partial glimpses are

43 Adjani's Yves Saint Laurent wardrobe, in its overdetermined evocation of both her past (and future) heritage roles and the iconography of the classic *femme fatale*, suggests a character not wholly anchored in realist narrative.

undercut as the close-up, when it comes, is not a conventional celebratory star shot but one of Charlotte/Adjani in profile, looking away from the camera, as she rejects the attention of a persistent fellow traveller and, by implication, challenges the spectatorial gaze. On her arrival in Nice, the multiple mirrors in the luxury boutiques highlight the underlying spectatorial irony roused not by Charlotte's failure to find work but by the fact that Adjani, central to many Vuitton advertising campaigns, should pass unrecognised.

The importance of the look as bearer of meaning is central to Masson's continued exploration of the tension between the liberating construction of identity through reinvention and the invasive role of others as its reductive arbiters. Charlotte repeatedly rebuffs those who claim to recognise her and, in verbal parallels to the fetishistic shots discussed earlier, reduce her to the sexualised markers of both character and star.[44] Before their first public appearance together Charlotte rehearses her chosen persona and her 'spectacular' dress is matched by the use of slow-motion to film her entrance. Charlotte/Adjani thus remains the acknowledged dominant visual focus throughout the film yet, in a move central to Masson's engagement with discourses of identity, is also situated as the bearer of the (erotic) gaze, able to function as both object of desire and desiring subject. Indeed her assertive occupation of both positions is enforced when she shocks the admiring hotel manager by asking if he can deduce by looking at her how long it is since she had sex, thus challenging his reduction of her to fetishised object by implicating her own desire. The freedom afforded by a musical halt in narrative flow and an escape from the morbidly imperial interiors of the Hotel Negresco[45] to a Moroccan wedding party further foregrounds Charlotte's agency. Her encounter with the 'bel étranger' (Ari Päffgen) and their silent mutual fascination is founded not on a reductive recognition of shared ethnic origins but on a correspondence between the status of an iconically charged Päffgen (the son of the stars Nico and Alain Delon) and Adjani. The communication of desire between Charlotte and Paul is conveyed by the mapping of looks in which the camera position is aligned with Charlotte as he, in beautifully composed close-up, provides a silent tender return of both her gaze and that of the camera.

44 This is to be contrasted with her own family who pretend not to recognise her.
45 The filmic representation of Nice as a site of dehumanising wealth, beginning with *A propos de Nice* (Vigo, 1930), is well-established.

The lengthy static sequences of the film in which identity is assessed and fixed are countered through the representation of movement in dance. Dance remains a significant feature in all of Masson's film, signalling in *En avoir (ou pas)* and *A vendre* a fleeting liberation from the constrictions of definition as socio-economic objects and, in the opening sequence of *Love Me*, the suspension of reality, which establishes the film's complex layering of identities and narratives. Dance in *La Repentie* remains a site of tension between a seemingly authentic self-expression and a knowingly performative construction of identity. The mixing of film noir and romance, and the inclusion of musical interludes that suspend narrative flow through the foregrounding of their own artifice, continue to evoke a Godardian self-reflexive hybridity. Such intertextual touchstones are rendered more specific through the visual referencing of Anna Karina (Charlotte's sunglasses and hairband) and *Pierrot le fou* (the blue beauty mask), which anticipate a doomed *amour fou*.[46] The frequently heavy-handed interpretative use of music in the film is also underwritten by reference to its selection and function as, daunted by the sinister Hitchcockian atmosphere of Paul's modernist villa, Charlotte chooses a light-weight Gene Pitney track to break the mood and then a Joe Cocker love song to tempt Paul to dance with her. The lengthy sequence in which Charlotte reacts to her failure to find a job by kicking off her shoes and dancing on Nice's famous Promenade des Anglais is a self-reflexive performance which suggests the ambiguous coexistence of self–expression and liberation through (improvised) movement and the objectification of the same by the crowd of onlookers, a public clearly bemused by this spectacle.[47] The foregrounding of the public gaze provides a further example of the *mise en abyme* of the spectatorial position and reinforces a discomfort triggered both by the length of the sequence and the apparent suspension of fictional narrative development. The series of dance sequences which punctuate the film map the development of Charlotte's relationship with others as she progresses from dancing alone for a crowd, losing herself within a crowd (at the wedding), a failed attempt to engage Paul in dance and the final sequence in which the anticipated romantic resolution is

46 Frey of course starred alongside Karina in *Bande à part* (Godard, 1964).
47 Masson filmed without extras wherever possible and this scene, as well as others in supermarkets, beaches, railway stations and cafés, was filmed amongst the general public.

represented through a series of lap dissolves of them dancing together in the Casablanca hotel room.

In common with Masson's other heroines, Charlotte is engaged on a quest for self-determination, an attempt to evade existing and reductive constructions of identity.[48] However, the achievement of mobility and self-invention comes at great cost, as the protagonists' alienation and solitude are resolved only through a risky engagement with the (romantic) other. Charlotte, defined by the desiring gaze of others and hiding her own origins as second-generation Maghrebi immigrant, adds another interpretative layer to the quest in *La Repentie* through the evocation of Adjani's star identity. Yet, as is the case for Masson's preceding heroines, neither salvation nor redemption is to be found in adopting an identity defined by others. Adjani's whiteness is indeed highlighted in the film through the contrast with her all-black attire, yet this contributes mainly to the vampish and vampiric look shared by Charlotte and Paul as they remain comically pale and fully clothed on the beach, languish in the mausoleum-like spaces of the hotel and mix with the living dead at the suffocating gatherings of Nice's wealthy elite. Higgins rightly reads *La Repentie* as providing 'a progressive dismantling of Adjani's French identity' (Higgins 2008: 13), yet, whilst Charlotte becomes increasingly associated with Morocco in the film, this alternative site provides neither sanctuary nor stability of identity. Morocco haunts Charlotte, represented both through her pursuer, Karim, and through its illusory promise of authentic identity. Masson's heroines are all drawn to the sea as a marker of potential limitless displacement, yet the presence of the Mediterranean in *La Repentie* has further specific connotations as it permits the visualisation of the metaphorical return to origins evoked by the French homonyms of the mother and the sea (*mère/mer*). The importance of this potential return is prefigured in a sequence in which Charlotte strolls on the beach at dusk framed, not within the realist movement of the hand-held camera, nor the contextualising motivation of the mid-shot, but through a sweeping use of steadicam which permeates the scene with a sense of euphoria, reinforced by the use of Souad Massi's 'Raouï'. The sequence of the Moroccan wedding serves less as an anticipation of a return to her origins than as an ironic sensual counterpoint; Morocco itself proves

48 Indeed the choice of aliases in the surnames of 'Delarue' (literally 'of the street') and 'Duchemin' ('of the road') signifies her nomadic identity.

to be neither picturesque nor hospitable. A seemingly trivial sequence in which Paul imposes an uncomfortable lunch with his parents is intriguing for the 'confession' that Charlotte delivers in which she admits that she is not from Paris but from Créteil (an area with a large migrant population of North African origin), and that she has been in prison for theft. She refers explicitly to racist prejudices against 'arabes' but, in a combination of denial and provocation, ambiguously confesses that she too is intolerant. This revelation of origins, which evokes reaction to Adjani's own paternal lineage as discussed earlier, is undercut immediately in a visit to a North African market which, whilst aligning the couple's status as outsiders with that of the migrant population and prefiguring their flight to Morocco, does not suggest integration. Paul's error in his romanticised reading of Charlotte's identity is clear as he returns to search for her there only to receive her call from an anonymous hotel in the Parisian *banlieue*.

The most explicit engagement with Charlotte's Maghrebi lineage is presented in a troubling sequence in which, alone and distressed, her raincoat disguise contrasting sharply with the traditional henna motifs covering her face and hands, she slumps in a hotel bathroom The visual mixing of the iconographies of French film noir and North Africa is accompanied by the aural hybridity of Natacha Atlas's cover of Brel's 'Ne me quitte pas'. The scene's abstraction and isolation from the largely chronological narrative suggest a projected fantasy function that foreshadows her final unsuccessful return to Morocco.[49] This uncanny undermining of her quest is strengthened as Charlotte's visits to her father in Créteil and to her mother in Morocco are marked by the appearance of doubles who suggest representations of her younger self but, rather than nostalgic comfort or narcissistic validation, provide only hostile observation. Charlotte's physical features have served as indelible reminders of her identity, yet her family pretend not to recognise her and the absurd role play, in which she masquerades as a go-between, is answered by the open hostility of her sister (Maria Schneider) and the melancholy muteness of her father (José Giovaninetti).[50] The long journey to her mother's

---

49 In the DVD commentary Masson explains that the idea for this scene came from Adjani.
50 José Giovanninetti's cameo appearance provides another enigmatic star presence evoking his Resistance role, criminal past and association with male stars of classic French cinema.

door also proves futile. The mother (Farida Amrouche) speaks only Arabic yet her daughter's translation of the ambiguous yet devastating response that she has 'come to the wrong place' fails to disguise primal rejection as a banal error of address. Charlotte's rejection by the mother(land) is visualised as the Beckettian spectacle of her struggling across wasteland in her ubiquitous black lace dress and heels, dragging her identity in a cumbersome wheeled suitcase behind her. The incompatibility of the sand and her black attire and the heightened sound ensure that she remains no less alien to Morocco than to the luxury spaces of Nice. The brutal failure of a quest for identity in the reclaiming of ethnic, familial or spatial origins leaves Charlotte and Paul mutually dependent upon the construction of their identity as a couple. Having seemingly resolved this, however, their literal and metaphorical new dawn is thwarted by the return of the film's thriller element as Charlotte is arrested. Her wearing of a bright blue djellabah and the police's use of her real name, Leila Imbert, suggests yet another attempt to fix identity (here also evoking reductive discourses of ethnicity and criminality) yet her sacrifice of freedom for Paul suggests her final status as the penitent of the film's title.

La Repentie's luxurious settings, older central characters and slower pace creates a very different mood to that of Masson's earlier films, yet the central concerns remain consistent. Charlotte's quest for identity encounters the suffocating alienation of materialist constructions of desire and the illusory sanctuary of familial and cultural origins. The film's closure, in line with that of her earlier works, suggests that the agency and subjectivity are constructed through an openness and engagement with the (romantic) other. The ambiguity of the ending, suggesting a heady mixture of punishment, dependence and redemption, again allows room for spectatorial doubt. The French verb 'repentir', which in common usage signifies 'to repent', also translates the art term 'repentimento' – the revealing of a painting that has been covered over by a later work, a term which provides a fruitful metaphor for the film's treatment of identity. *La Repentie* thus points not towards the uncovering of an essential identity but to the revelation of the multilayered nature of such representations (of the female subject, of the female star) over which protagonist, star, director and spectator exert an ambiguous and partial control.

Creative identity and the negative in parenthesis: *Pourquoi (pas) le Brésil* (2004)

Despite the box office appeal of its central star, *La Repentie* was a commercial failure and its negative critical reception caused problems of both funding and morale for the director. In an increasingly reflexive turn, the ensuing challenges become the subject of Masson's following film which shifts engagement with constructions of identity on to a higher level of self-referentiality in its questioning of the relationship between creative representation and lived experience. *Pourquoi (pas) le Brésil* (2004) addresses a director's response to the challenges of funding and filming an adaptation of Christine Angot's novel *Pourquoi le Brésil?* A personal friend of Masson,[51] Angot remains a literary and media phenomenon whose work is emblematic of the contemporary cultural turn towards 'radically self-revelatory cultural production by women, which reconfigures the public/private divide' (Jordan 2007: 201). The creative and explicit employment of elements from the author's life (including graphic narrative detail and the use of real names) has been attacked as sensationalist, unethical and even open to legal action under French privacy laws, yet it remains both provocative and empowering in its assertion of self-expression and its challenging of dominant representations of interactions between the individual subject and others.[52] Angot's oeuvre, which addresses her own experience of incest abuse by her father and her conse-quent radical refusal of all structures of secrecy, can be seen to serve testimonial and therapeutic purposes that transcend the reductively solipsistic to address universal taboos and silences.[53] Masson's film does engage with the thematic concerns of Angot's text but, rather than performing a straightforward adaptation as transposition (a move rejected as producing a mere 'illustration du texte') the central conflict of the film's narrative resides in the tension between Masson's attempts to adapt the book (seen as betrayal) and the book's power to

51 Masson's husband is Angot's editor and, in a further self-referential twist, Masson is mentioned in Angot's novel *Pourquoi le Brésil?* in reference to an earlier collaborative project.
52 Holmes cites *Vendredi soir* (Bernheim, 1998) (made into a film by Claire Denis) and *Pourquoi le Brésil?* (Angot 2002) as examples of postmodern texts 'struc-tured by the romance script' (Holmes 2006: 116).
53 Jordan argues that Angot's work also, problematically, privileges tropes of vulnerability and shame (Jordan 2007: 203).

adapt her life. A director faced with mounting debts receives a call from a famous producer proposing a film adaptation of Angot's novel *Pourquoi le Brésil?* The autofictional novel interweaves an account of a tempestuous relationship between Angot and Pierre-Louis Rozynes[54] with explorations of the difficulty of writing and being a writer in contemporary France. After first refusing this 'impossible' task, 'Masson' decides to proceed, but produces a script that uses the suggested adaptation as a catalyst for reflection on the relation-ship between lived experience and artistic creation, between funded commission and creative liberty. The script is roundly criticised by producers and actors alike, the casting proves problematic and as the film goes ahead this attempted adaptation causes the director to question the nature of her creative agency. Such insecurities trigger an erotic fascination with her children's Jewish doctor, and her home-life deteriorates as she struggles to make a film. Money runs out and she disappears, re-emerging in the final sequence having reassessed the connections between her work and her life.

The negative in parenthesis of Masson's title, *Pourquoi (pas) le Brésil*, thus signals an acknowledgement of the commissioned adap-tation contained within her ultimate achievement in producing the negation of such a project, the *not* making or anti-adaptation of Angot's text. Masson's reaction to the proposal describes the book as 'inadaptable' and this becomes a fruitful term for approaching the film in its close link to the French adjectival form '*inadapté*', which also signifies maladjusted, unsuitable or inappropriate, and is a term with which Masson confronts her own approach to filmmaking and indeed her wider identity.[55] The film's narrative complexities and recurrent *mises en abyme* of the processes of its own making are sufficient to ensure spectatorial *distanciation* (and frustration), yet questions of identification and coherence are further complicated by the film's casting. Sequences filmed on video show Masson, deliberating over the filmmaking process, yet many of these sequences are 'adapted' and then filmed starring Elsa Zylberstein and Marc Barbé as her and her husband (I shall refer to the character as 'Masson' in these sequences). Furthermore, in sequences of the Angot adaptation that 'Masson' makes, the same two actors also play Angot and her lover.

54 Rozynes is ex-editor of *Livres hebdo*, cultural commentator and publisher.
55 It is also an adjective used by Angot to describe her lover in the novel (Angot 2002: 116).

In addition to reflexive meditations on the dynamics of influence between life and art, the film also presents a frank picture of the conflict between filmmaking as artistic practice and commercial investment. In the film, the producer Maurice Rey (his name an amalgam of those of Masson's own producers) exudes authority but becomes anxious over the film's poor fit with the programming priorities of television channels and consequent unprofitability. In unscripted additions to the sequences with a fictional producer, Masson includes video footage in which she asks the producer Alain Sarde and actors Francis Huster and Daniel Auteuil for their reactions to her script. Whilst Sarde is coldly dismissive, Huster angrily attacks script (and novel) for their lack of engagement with contemporary reality, a criticism which recurs elsewhere in the visual juxtaposition of 'Masson''s anxiety over her work with war reportage. In addition to the reductive nature of commercial models, the director must negotiate the disproportionate impact of star actors to the commercial success of a project. 'Masson' reels off an absurd wish-list of French stars and the impact of their inevitable serial rejections is represented in a shot of a white room filled with huge close-ups, evoking their overwhelming status as magnets for cultural consumption.[56] The elusive presence of stars is taken further in a rare moment of playfulness in the film in which Masson films a meeting with an ill-at-ease Daniel Auteuil in which they discuss her script. Despite his rejection of the project and the clear mismatch between his status and her budget, she thus manages to 'cast' him (as himself). His disquiet over whether their meeting constitutes a 'scene' and the redundancy of any move to remake the sequence with someone else playing Auteuil reveals the central concern of the adaptive processes between reality and art.

The film's economic constraints (it was shot in only five weeks for a budget of €1 million (Audé et al. 2004: 16)) meant that it eschewed the exotic locations featured in the novel (even substituting the Parisian Gare Austerlitz for Nancy station). The limited budget is central to the film's aesthetic as it provides the spectator with a much-needed navigational aid as the sequences in which Masson herself struggles to (not) make the adaptation were filmed later on video and so remain clearly visually delineated from the other sequences in which Zylberstein plays 'Masson' and which retain high lighting, spacious

---

56 She later reveals that she could persuade no female stars to take a role explicitly identified as that of a 'grandmother'.

white interiors and a more abstract mood. Masson challenges the associations between reality, experience and realism by imbuing the sequences adapted from Angot's autofictional text with a spare, white minimalist look, apparently inspired by an exhibition of hyper-realist painting and the desire to 'sublimate the object shown' (ibid.: 18), resulting in a Godardian stylisation of the real (Tobin 2004: 14). The contrast between the cool, white spaces of the love story and the domestic clutter of Masson's home in which she struggles to find space to work provide spatial underpinning to her avowed lack of emotional identification with the text. This block triggers a deliberate manipulation of her own reality in an ultimately deluded quest for 'emotional truth' through a search for new experiences including speed-dating, an erotic fantasy involving her children's doctor and even a 'site visit' to the apartment in which the relationship took place, yet in which no tangible traces of it remain.

The unsuccessful adaptation of Angot's story is gradually displaced by a different investigation of identity that emerges from Masson's recurring fascination with the dynamics of origins, fate and intervention. Whilst Angot's title might suggest the random choice of love object, it is taken from a letter from her abusive father (also called Pierre) and suggests other motivations linked to familial origins and Jewish identity (both Angot's mother and Rozynes are Jewish). Masson's parallel question 'Pourquoi le pédiatre?' (why the paediatrician?) encourages her to switch tracks away from construed romantic obsession to more 'meaningful encounters' with her grandmother and with the real paediatrician, Haïm Cohen (played in the sequences with 'Masson' by Pierre Arditi). These meetings converge around the common thread of Jewish identity and its role in (over)determining perceptions of the self. Yet, emerging questions, such as the problematic eroticisation of 'Jewishness', are left largely unexplored and Masson, unable to complete her film and faced with the growing exasperation of producer and husband, disappears. This crisis of creative agency compels her to dismiss the autofictional mode as both unsuited to her creative practice and damaging to her life: 'Ce livre me renvoie sans cesse à moi, et moi ce n'est pas le sujet d'un film' (this book keeps bringing me back to myself, and I am not the subject of a film). Her final statement, made from a station platform and which signifies imminent return not departure, could not be more explicit in its rejection: 'Je n'adapte pas, je ne m'adapte pas' (I don't adapt, I don't adapt myself). The film ends thus with a telling assertion of both the director's resistance to imposed projects and the film industry's multiple resistances to creative freedom. The film contains beautiful fragments, which are indeed adapted from Angot's text, yet their status as autofictional or even filmic narrative is overshadowed by the more engaging video footage of Masson's challenge to her own creative identity. The sequences in which she films herself in a mirror provide striking echoes of similar scenes in Cabrera's *Demain et encore demain*, however, whilst Cabrera's self-portraits assert her dual position as the legitimate object of the film's study *and* the creative subject of its making, Masson's shots, with their jerky, hesitant zoom, articulate a deeper ambivalence about the relationship between lived experience and creative agency.

Masson has continued to engage with the autofictional aspects of her work in her contribution to the collection 'X-femmes', a series of nine short films commissioned by the site SecondSexe.com and supported and shown by Canal +.[57] The series aimed to create alternative representations of sexual desire by and for women, yet Masson's film *Enculées* (2008) challenges representations of both narrative and erotic pleasure to focus on dominant discourses of sexuality. The newly redundant Claire (Hélène Fillières) seeks work as an escort girl and is thus forced to confront her attitude towards anal sex. Documentary-style sequences show her seeking advice from professionals before a prolonged alternative and solitary staging of desire on a deserted dance floor signals a more familiar Masson aesthetic. The film then cuts to Masson's statement that she could not shoot the sex sequences within her own narrative but preferred to film porn actors whom she then interviews about their experiences of anal sex and the erotic. The film's interweaving of the fictional and the real and its stubborn reflexivity constructs parallel anxieties around the dominant representation of sex as a 'mécanique du corps' (bodily mechanics) and the submissive role of the director in accepting any commission. It remains difficult to envisage the commercial or personal sustainability of such self-reflexive narratives, and Masson's tense and complex mode of filmmaking in *La Repentie, Pourquoi (pas)* and *Enculées* constituted an increasing inaccessibility. This ceased with the release of *Coupable*

57 The series includes films by actors (Mélanie Laurent, Arielle Dombasle), singers (Héléna Noguerra and Caroline Loeb) and directors (Lola Doillon, Tonie Marshall).

(2008), which marks the director's return to earlier generic interven-tion and to critical acclaim (including selection for the 2008 Berlin Festival).

Guilty pleasures

Coupable signals a renewed engagement with the interaction between the quest narratives of detective and romance genres that dominated the Kiberlain trilogy; the interweaving of trajectories of knowledge and desire are announced by the no-nonsense tagline from Kierke-gaard: 'sans le péché point de sexualité et sans sexualité point d'histoire'(without sin there is no sexuality and without sexuality there is no story). An introductory voiceover, denouncing the damage done by Western civilisation's investment in the myth of the *âme-soeur* or soulmate and its subsequent role in the socio-economic institution-alisation of love, provides a further explicit framing device. The plot continues Masson's exploration of the socio-cultural constructions of romance, imbuing an ostensibly realist narrative with elements of the uncanny to reveal 'à quel point le rapport amoureux est un théâtre ancré dans l'intime et dans le social' (Masson 2008a) (to what extent love relationships are scenes which are founded both in the intimate and in the social). The lead is played by Hélène Fillières (sister of the director Sophie Fillières) who starred in Masson's *Nulle part* (1993) which is also included on *Coupable*'s DVD release. In interview Masson stated that the central character can be seen as an older version of the figure in *Nulle part* who, 15 years later, remains 'aussi extrême, toujours inadaptée, toujours en quête d'idéal' (Masson 2008b) (just as extreme, still ill-adapted, still in search of an ideal'). Marguerite Marquet (Fillières) works as a cook for a troubled bourgeois couple, the Kaplans. She strikes a dissonant, almost mythical figure as she traverses the gloomy autumn landscape on her moped in a long embroidered gown, accompanied by her book and her case of chef's knives. When Paul Kaplan (Barbé) is found dead with a kitchen knife in his back she becomes the main suspect and is accused by the sinister Blanche Kaplan (Anne Cosigny). Thirty-four-year old Marguerite lives with her marriage-fixated parents and, disappointed at the loss of her lover and promise of escape, she becomes desperate to find someone. In a bid to mitigate his wife's financial aspirations, the divorce lawyer

Lucien (Jérémie Renier)[58] takes on the wife's defence but becomes fascinated with Marguerite, an obsession shared by the local detective, Berger (Denis Podalydès). The film explores the dogmas of romance and coupledom by juxtaposing different pairings of these characters and revealing Marguerite's disturbing impact on them all. Lucien, believing Marguerite to be guilty, and desperate to match her apparently radical stance, kills his wife and presents himself to Marguerite as newly *libre*. The inspector, having arrested Paul Kaplan's real killer, allows this emerging couple to escape before declaring his own love for Marguerite to camera. Despite her downtrodden background, Marguerite provides sharp, deadpan deconstructions of the conventions of coupledom – from her scathing critique of their displaced emotional investment in food and interior design ('mais comment meubler l'ennui?' (but how do you furnish boredom?)) to her frank reappraisal of Paul Kaplan's romantic 'offer' ('toujours lui derrière, toujours habillé, toujours un quart d'heure maximum' (always him behind, always fully dressed, always fifteen minutes maximum)). Her subsequent searches for a husband are both pragmatic and comic and find a counterpoint in the constructed nature of contemporary articulations of romance and of sensuality as explored via the figure of Lucien's wife, Dolores (Amira Casar) who, characterised by a performative and stylised sensuality, undertakes increasingly bizarre attempts to create the 'essence of love' in a perfume.

Masson claims that: 'L'enquête, ce n'est jamais le coeur d'un film, c'est son genre' (Masson 2008b) (The investigation is not the heart of the film, it is its genre), yet it is the nature of the investigation which shifts rather than its centrality, as the two central male characters, Lucien and Inspector Berger, increasingly conflate the identification of the killer with that of a potential soul mate. In classical film noir the central function of the detective in his labelling of the woman as object of his inquiry, rather than subject of her own narrative, remains emblematic of the overarching structure of patriarchal tropes of narrative to identify, commodify and contain her, yet neither of these detective figures achieves any kind of knowledge of Marguerite. Lucien's description of Marguerite as 'bizarre, radicale, idéaliste' recalls the radical transgressive trajectory of the *femme fatale* in which, as Žižek points out, she 'cannot be clearly located in the opposition between

---

58 Renier is best known for his work with the Dardennes – with lead roles in
   L'Enfant (2005) and *La Promesse* (1996).

master and slave' (Žižek 1993: 65) and thus triggers a crisis of knowl-edge for the detective. Lucien, seduced by what he wants to believe was murderous revenge for Kaplan's debased romantic intentions, kills his wife and declares himself Marguerite's liberated equal and soul mate. The narrative is punctuated with intimations of Inspector Berger's omniscience, yet the final sequence reveals that he is claiming not an instinctive identification of the murderer but a recog-nition of Marguerite as the love of his life – the displacement of the quest culminating thus in a displacement of identification. *Coupable* has no retrospective detective–narrator to provide omniscient reassur-ance for the spectator, indeed the narratorial 'voice of God' in the film is constituted by Michel Onfray's[59] *voix-off* as he describes the psycho-logical damage done by Western culture's dependence on the platonic concept of the soul mate. The detectives are not party to this knowl-edge but indeed remain the ultimate victims of its power.

Masson's films include striking use of music – often not simply to support a mood but to introduce haunting ambiguity and the sensuality of the voice that contests the dominance of the final image and of the visual or visible.[60] The final sequence continues Masson's penchant for swooning musical closure, yet, in contrast to the hybrid generic closures of many of her films, the final ambiguity is not centred on the fate of the female protagonist. Marguerite, innocent of Kaplan's murder (but perhaps guilty of indirect encouragement of Lucien's crime) has been allowed to escape all punishment and it is Inspector Berger who remains haunted by the romantic quest. Accompanied by mournfully romantic music (sung by the composer Jean-Louis Murat), in a melancholic double of the exhilarating, final dance sequence of *Beau travail* (Denis, 1999), Berger dances alone, free but lost in the incongruous cheap disco setting. As the credits begin he is partnered, in turn, by Masson and other cast members and the artistic construc-tion of the film bleeds once again into the fictional narrative.[61]

59 Onfray, also seen on television in *Love Me* expounding a treatise on the impact of parental abandonment, is best known for his *Traité d'athéologie* (2005) and the founding of the Université populaire which champions alternative approaches to philosophy.

60 There is not space in this chapter to discuss Masson's documentary on Jean-Louis Murat nor her recent '*portrait/fiction*' on the singer Benjamin Biolay, *Dans ta bouche* (2010).

61 Masson has since made a film for television (*Petite Fille*, 2009) starring Fillières as a 35-year-old shepherdess rejecting pragmatic alliances in the search for her one true love.

Masson's oeuvre provides an original and unsettling exploration of the social and filmic codes of socio-cultural constructions of gender and romance. These explorations are presented as quest narratives in which the female subject seeks to escape normative socio-economic definitions of identity, yet remains alienated by the void that this reveals. The ambiguous function of the conventions of romance in these films is both to reveal the reductive gendered constructions of identity and to suggest a way forward that involves risking the self in an openness to love and the other, suggesting that such closures posit not glorious isolation from the world, but a wider acceptance of the centrality of personal and social relationships. Masson's insistence upon the non-oppositional relationship between realism and the fantastic or the imaginary is of marked contrast to many prominent directors of this period and the perceived domination of the 'return to the real' in post-1990s French cinema,[62] asserting the importance of filming the 'côté théâtral de la réalité' (Masson 2008a) (the theatrical aspect of reality). The recurrent use of Godardian strategies, such as the juxtaposition of dissonant narrative moods and genres, the defamiliarisation of realist conventions of the use of music and *mise en scène* and the construction of an active spectator, ensures that her work remains both politically engaged and sensually engaging. The assertion of the inherent links between the political and the personal, between the economic and the subjective, is clearly common to the four directors discussed in this book and central to Masson's oeuvre, yet her insistence upon the imaginative and creative solutions to social exclusion take this further. As she explains:

> L'être humain est un tout, et je constate qu'en politique on isole l'individu selon le contexte – son travail, son intimité – comme je trouve qu'au cinéma, les films qui parlent de sentiments ont très souvent pour cadre la bourgeoisie. Tout ça mene à trop de simplifications, or ce qui m'intéresse, c'est justement la complexité.[63] (Masson 2008)

62 In contemporary, national contexts, Jacques Audiard maintains a similar engagement with the role of the imaginary in representing the 'real' of subjective experience.

63 'A human being is a whole entity, and I've noticed that in politics the individual is isolated according to a set of contexts – their work, personal life – just as I've noticed that in cinema, the films that deal with emotions are often set in the middle classes. This leads to too much simplification, whereas what interests me is complexity.'

Masson's challenge to the determination of identity by social origins is clear in her assertion that she despises the desire to 's'accrocher à un héritage' (Audé et al 2004: 18) (cling on to a heritage) and sees her work as countering that of dominant media which 'confortent les gens dans ce qu'ils sont ... les engluent dans leur identité. On doit renouer avec l'apprentissage d'un ailleurs' (ibid.: 18).[64] The drives of her central protagonists are encapsulated in Masson's description of actor Hélène Fillières (star of *Coupable* and *Nulle part*), each character presenting a 'personnage rebelle, prête à tout pour ne pas vivre une vie banale, soumise' (Masson 2008a) (rebellious character, prepared to do anything to avoid living a banal submissive life) and seeking fictional, even fantastical, responses to the hardships of contemporary social and economic exclusions. Whilst such responses remain unsettling and ambiguous in their embrace of both creative imaginary agency and conventional modes of (romantic) escapism, their insistence on challenging the dominant political and aesthetic discourses of contemporary narratives of social exclusion and alienation do offer narrative non-closures which enable the central female protagonists to escape the status of eternal victims. In a discussion of the most critically acclaimed and influential films of post-1990 Francophone cinema, that of the Dardennes brothers, Osganian outlines a particular trajectory in which this

> dénonciation de l'horreur de la condition sociale ... enregistrerait alors un glissement d'une vision en termes de rapports de classe vers une anthropologie négative reposant sur une vision irréductiblement pessimiste de l'homme scellée par un relatif fatalisme.[65] (Osganian 2003: 53)

Aligning herself more closely with the aesthetics of installation or conceptual art than the literary skills of the writer (Masson 2008b), Masson acknowledges the impact of dominant socio-economic contexts both on her protagonists and on her own creative practice. Yet her response to the inherent fatalism that might ensue in the face of the monolithic discourses of identity and genre is to contest dominant definitions of identity through a dual affirmation of the representation

64 'comforts people in what they are ... mires them down in their identities. We must rediscover how to learn about other possibilities.'
65 'denunciation of the horror of the social condition, ... would mark a shift from a vision defined by class relations towards a negative anthropology founded on a relentlessly pessimistic vision of mankind sealed by a relative fatalism'.

of an avowedly constructed real and the empowering creative forces of the imaginary.

References

Angot, Christine (2002), *Pourquoi le Brésil*, Paris, Stock.

Audé, Françoise (2002), *Cinéma d'elles 1981–2001*, Lausanne, L'Age d'homme.

Audé Françoise and Garbanz, F. (1998), 'Interview avec Laetitia Masson: on n'est pas neuf devant l'amour', *positif*, 451, 27–32.

Audé, Françoise, Eisenreich, P., Martinez, D. (2004), 'Entretien, Laetitia Masson. J'ai un côté rock'n'roll', *positif*, 523, 15–18.

Austin, Guy (2006), '"Telling the truth can be a dangerous business": Stardom, Race and Isabelle Adjani', in Stephanie Dennison and Lim S. Hwee (eds), *Remapping World Cinema, Identity, Culture and Politics in Film*, London and New York, Wallflower Press, 129–34.

Baudin, Brigitte (2000), 'Laetitia Masson; portrait d'une génération', *Le Figaro* (28 December), 26.

Bauman, Zygmunt (2003), *Liquid Love: On the Frailty of Human Bonds*, New York, Polity Press.

Bernheim, Emanuèle (1999), *Vendredi soir*, Paris, Folio.

Beugnet, Martine (2000), *Marginalité, sexualité, contrôle dans le cinéma français contemporain*, Paris, L'Harmattan.

Beugnet, Martine (2007), *Cinema and Sensation: French Film and the Art of Transgression*, Edinburgh, Edinburgh University Press.

Butler, Judith (1990), *Gender Trouble*, London and New York, Routledge.

Calaferte, Louis (1992), *La Mécanique des femmes*, Paris, Gallimard.

Coste, Béatrice (2005), 'The Soul of Woman Under Liberalism: Laetitia Masson's "A vendre"', *Studies in French Cinema*, 5 (3), 185–94.

Daeninckx, Didier (1999), *La Repentie*, Paris, Verdier.

De Bruyn, Olivier (2000), '"Love Me": Les fantômes de la liberté', *positif*, 469, 21–2.

Dickos, Andrew (2002), *Street With No Name: A History of Classic American Film Noir*, Lexington, University of Kentucky Press.

Doane, Mary Ann (1991), *Femme Fatales: Feminism, Film Studies and Psychoanalysis*, London and New York, Routledge.

Douin, Jean-Luc (2001), 'Angot / Masson, drôles de dames', *Le Monde* (13 April), 17.

Douin, Jean-Luc (2008), 'Réflexion sur les désirs inconscients des êtres', *Le Monde* (27 February), 19.

Dyer, Richard (1986), *Heavenly Bodies: Film Stars and Society*, London, BFI.

Forsdick, Charles (2001), '"Direction les oubliettes de l'histoire": Witnessing the Past in the Contemporary French Polar', *French Cultural Studies*, 12, 333–50.

Gaertner, Julien (2006), 'L'Azur à l'ecran. Un Arret sur images', www.cg06.fr/culture/pdf/rr178–lazur.pdf (accessed 10 December 2006).

Guilloux, Michel (2002), 'La Repentie', *L'Humanité* (17 April), 23.

Herpe, N. and Kohn, O. (1996), 'Entretien avec Laetitia Masson', *positif*, 419, 24–8.

Higgins, Lynn (2008), 'Rien à déclarer: Isabelle Adjani in Laetitia Masson's "La Repentie"', paper given at 'International Colloquium for Twentieth and Twenty First Century French and Francophone Studies', Washington DC.

Hirsch, Foster (1981), *Dark Side of the Screen: Film Noir*, Portland, Oak Tree Publications.

Holmes, Diana (2006), *Romance and Readership in Twentieth Century France*, Oxford, Oxford University Press.

Jordan, Shirley (2007),'Reconfiguring the Public and the Private. Intimacy, Exposure and vulnerability in Christine Angot's "Rendez-vous"', *French Cultural Studies*, 18, 201–18.

Krahenbuhl, Véronique (1998), 'Laetitia Masson: à bras-le-corps', *Femmes et Société*, 34, 10–14.

Krutnik, Frank (1991), *In a Lonely Street: Film Noir, Genre, Masculinity*, London and New York, Routledge.

Lardoux, Xavier (2002), 'La Repentie', *Etudes*, 396, 825.

Masson, Laetitia (1998), Interview at Cannes, www.cannes-fest.com/1998/ avendre2.htm (accessed 2 October 2005).

Masson, Laetitia (2000), Programme notes to the Berlin festival quoted on http: //geraldpeary.com/festivals/berlin_feb_2000.html.

Masson, Laetitia (2003), *La Repentie*, DVD commentary.

Masson, Laetitia (2007), 'La libre interview', http://letelelibre.fr/index.php/ 2007/12/la-libre-interview-de-laetitia-masson/.

Masson, Laetitia (2008a), 'La vérité ou presque', http://allocine.fr/film/ anecdote_gen_cfilm=121630.html (accessed 7 March 2008).

Masson, Laetitia (2008b), 'Coupable en liberté', www.evene.fr/cinema/ actualite/interview-laetitia-masson-coupable-a-vendre-.

O'Neill, Eithne (2002), 'La Repentie. Femme à l'ombrelle', *positif*, 495, 74–5.

Osganian, Patricia (2003), 'D' "Amerika rapports de classe" à "Rosetta". Sortie du naturalisme et subjectivation du réel', *Mouvements*, 27/28, 51–7.

Romney, Jonathan (2008), 'French Exceptions', *Sight and Sound*, 18 (5), 42–4.

Rouyer, Pierre (1998), 'A vendre. La gazelle et le détective', *positif*, 451, 25–6.

Rouyer, Pierre and Vassé, Claire (2000), 'Fantasmer Memphis au Havre', *positif*, 469, 23–7.

Royle, Nicholas (2003), *The Uncanny*, Manchester, Manchester University Press.

Tarr, Carrie with Rollet, Brigitte (2001), *Cinema and the Second Sex*, London, Continuum.

Tobin, Yann (2004), 'Pourquoi (pas) le Brésil. Faire un film (ou pas)', *positif*, 523, 13–14.

Vassé, Claire (1996), 'En avoir (ou pas). La girafe et son prince' *positif*, 419, 20–3.

Vidler, Anthony (1992), *The Architectural Uncanny: Essays in the Modern Unhomely*, Cambridge, MA, MIT Press.

Williams, Linda Ruth (2005), *The Erotic Thriller in Contemporary Cinema*, Edinburgh, Edinburgh University Press.

Žižek, Slavoj (1993), *Looking Awry: An Introduction to Lacan through popular Culture*, Cambridge, MA, MIT Press.

4

Marion Vernoux:
encountering difference

Marion Vernoux's family background (her mother's career in casting and her father's in theatre set design) triggered a fascination with performance and *mise en scène* that was not dependent initially on the medium of film. She did, however, leave school to pursue a career in cinema and found work as a production assistant in the mid-1980s. Following notable and diverse commercial successes as a writer, with productions that include the lyrics for the pop hit 'N'importe quoi' (Pagny, 1988) and the script for *Pacific Palisades* (Schmitt, 1990), Vernoux was encouraged to direct one of her own scripts and made her first short film for television in 1991. Her scriptwriting success has continued to develop alongside her directorial career and includes the script for the major critical and box office hit *Vénus beauté* (Marshall, 1999), co-written with her partner, the director Jacques Audiard. Reportedly frustrated by a comment from her teenage heartthrob Jacques Dutronc, in which he claimed that it is impossible for women to be both funny and sexy (Vernoux 2004), Vernoux has created, through her work across scriptwriting and directing, a series of formidable, largely comic roles for strong, female protagonists who challenge social and generic conventions in their search for self-expression. The role of humour and satire is central to challenges to the dominant social and filmic representation of women, as it holds the potential to defamiliarise and reveal the absurdities of social and gendered discourses, whilst maintaining a narrative and structural context that remains non-didactic and ultimately reassuring for a wide range of spectatorial expectations. Despite the Anglophone, distribution-led perceptions of French cinema as constituting predominantly 'art-house', and indeed auteurist, productions, comedy maintains its status as the most popular genre at the French box office. The highly evident, formulaic features of comedy are critically perceived as incompatible with auteurism's privileging of directorial creativity and thus occupy a lowly position in wider hierarchies of genre.

Vernoux's oeuvre maintains a coherent focus on the modes of transgression (potential and realised) present within the generic conventions of comedy and romance in films which exploit the common narrative device of the encounter to propel narratives and characters across social boundaries within a dominant generic focus on romantic comedy. The encounter is central to the generic conventions of both comedy and romance. In the former the accidental encounter provokes the comedic staples of mistaken identity, the plot structures of farce, odd couples, incongruity and slapstick, whilst the conventions of romance privilege the encounter, not as a catalytic accident but as central narrative evidence of the conjoined destinies of the romantic couple.

In a wider discussion of the generic affiliations of romantic comedy, Krutnik claims that whilst conceptualisations of romantic love can reflect socio-historical change in their articulations of wider shifts in socio-cultural constructions of gender, sexuality, identity and marriage, the romantic comedy continues to celebrate love as an 'immutable almost mystic force that guides two individuals who were "made for each other" into each other's arms' (Krutnik 2002: 138). Such a distinction demonstrates that romantic comedy, because of its predominantly conservative and normative approach to such issues, can thus provide a powerful popular and populist site in which to articulate and explore the changing social and sexual roles of men and women.[1] In this context, Vernoux's films reflect the advent of 'confluent love' (Giddens 1992: 24) in which the quest for romantic love aims to secure a relationship rather than a specific individual and is concerned with identifying the feasibility of 'for now' rather than the projection of 'forever'. Whilst Vernoux's narratives foreground repeated assertions of the dramatic potentiality of the unexpected (romantic) encounter, they also feature persistent rebuttals of 'le couple en tant que concept, comme le refuge principal' (Chauville 1998: 210) (the 'couple', in terms of a concept, as main refuge) and perform serial deconstructions of the romantic couple through a

---

1 Other contemporary examples include *Gazon maudit* (*French twist*) (Balasko, 1995) and *Pas très catholique* (Marshall, 1994).

dismissal of the classical tropes of romantic predestination and an accompanying insistence on the haphazard nature of human encounters. These films foreground the role of wider social groupings and identities which both permeate and puncture romantic discourse as more accurate and potentially more positive modes of constructing identity.

Vernoux's first film provides ample early evidence of such concerns. The playfully titled *Pierre qui roule* (1991) was produced for television by Arte and focuses on a young widow, Marie (Marianne Denicourt), who, after a year in isolated mourning, decides to throw herself at the first man she meets, the unsuspecting, unassuming and woefully unprepared Pierre (Benoît Regent). The plot device of Marie's self-imposed solitude permits Vernoux to construct the first of her many self-confessed *emmerdeuses* (troublemakers), whose disregard for all social convention, and for the wishes of others, creates chaos around her. This film marks the first appearance of what becomes a consistently transgressive presence in Vernoux's work, that of a figure whom Rowe describes as the 'unruly woman' and who remains

> willing to offend and be offensive ... her sexuality is neither evil and uncontrollable nor sanctified and denied ... The unruly woman often enjoys a reprieve from fates that often seem inevitable to women under patriarchy, because her home is comedy and the carnivalesque, the realm of fantasy and inversion, where, for a time at least, the ordinary world can be stood on its head. (Rowe 1995a: 10–11)

The unruly woman is thus an important device in an oeuvre which uses the generic accessibility of the (romantic) comedy to address and challenge social convention, yet seeks to avoid the conventional denouements and reductive representations of gendered identity inherent to these generic frameworks.

Desperately seeking solidarity: five women and a camper van

The focus of Vernoux's first feature film continues to explore the struggle of an 'unruly woman' to assert her transgressive agency whilst also achieving some form of social reintegration, here through a reassertion of sisterly solidarity and the mother–daughter relationship. *Personne ne m'aime* (1994) was nominated for a César for best first film and this refreshing play on the road movie largely permits the displacement of explorations of female identity from domestic space. It also can be differentiated from the recurring form of the '*film d'errance*' (nomadic film), which provides a central characteristic of post-1990s French cinema through the often circular wanderings of lone, alienated individuals (as exemplified in Masson's oeuvre – see Chapter 3), through its representation of a collective journey that recruits and bonds female characters as it progresses to stage 'un véritable microcosme féminin' (Gillan 1996: 263) (a real feminine microcosm) on the move. The central female characters, from a range of different class and cultural backgrounds, overcome initial differences that provide the staples of comic tension, to share experiences and create a cross-generational, cross-class solidarity that challenges patriarchal structures of authority. In accordance with the conventional central device of the road movie, two sisters set out on a geographical and narrative quest to catch a cheating husband, yet, as they pick up other female characters their quest becomes a multiple and often chaotic search. Whilst some claims for the film's impact, which suggest an alignment with the Blier grotesque (De Bruyn 1994: 50) seem misplaced given the problematically reductive gender stereotypes that dominate Blier's work, the film does succeed in removing its female characters from domestic and familial structures and asserting their identities as sexual and social agents whose transient and pragmatic desires emerge unfettered by romantic or social convention.

Annie (Bernadette Lafont) is thrown out of her lover's apartment and criticised by her ex-partner Lucien (Jean-Pierre Léaud) for her continuing estrangement from her daughter, Marie (Lio). In further scenarios informed by the rupture of traditional family structures, Marie prepares her daughter for her father's remarriage and Annie persuades her prim sister Françoise (Bulle Ogier) to join her in a trip to the Normandy coast to check whether the latter's husband is with his mistress. After an overnight stop in which Annie drinks herself unconscious and Françoise sleeps with a salesman who provides her with tranquillisers, they are joined on their trip by the hotel manager, Cricri (Michèle Laroque), who abandons both her business and her ineffectual husband. She is joined by the hotel worker Dizou (Maaike Jansen) who, unlike the others, seeks not rupture but a mythical meeting in her first glimpse of the sea. Their chaotic brief stop in a faded resort sees Françoise acquiring a gun, Annie having sex with a local man who passes out and is abandoned on a bench, CriCri dictating the terms of a relationship that will provide her with a child and Dizou reaching the sea. Some narrative coherence and the original motivation for the trip re-emerges when, brought together by a lost girl who turns out to be Annie's granddaughter, they discover that Françoise's husband, Paul, is having an affair with his niece, Annie's daughter, Marie. Mother, daughter and granddaughter are happily reunited and Françoise uses the van, the symbol of the women's independent mobility and solidarity, to knock down her husband.

This low-budget film, filmed in Super 16, constructs multiple references to the style and icons of the Nouvelle Vague with the casting of Léaud and Lafont, recalling the central couple of *La Maman et la putain* (Eustache, 1972). Clear engagements with more specific intertexts are difficult to trace however as the film does not attempt the lucid integration of interpersonal relationships and socio-political contexts so central to Eustache's film and suggestions of the film as staging a projection of the status of his protagonists into middle age would seem ill-founded. The film is dedicated to 'Catherine et Jeanne' and, whilst it would be reductive to view the central characters as older versions of the Nouvelle Vague icons Deneuve and Moreau, Lio's gamine look and the tracking shots that accompany her running across a railway bridge and through urban space provide explicit echoes of *Jules et Jim* (Truffaut, 1962) and Dizou's desire to see the sea for the first time clearly evokes *Les quatre cents coups* (Truffaut, 1959). These specific intertextual references are complemented by Vernoux's wider use of techniques associated with key films of the Nouvelle Vague such as 'use of a lightweight handheld camera, location shooting, and the occasional direct address to camera' (Tarr with Rollet 2001: 243). The film differs greatly from the dominant resistance of the Nouvelle Vague (with the important exception of Varda) to any sustained reworking of gender roles and its central characters defy the assertion of a generational conflict. The women in *Personne ne m'aime* are presented as sexual subjects and, whilst the road trip is triggered by the desire to find and confront an absent man, the female characters remain, ultimately, defined by shifting relationships with one another. Whilst the locations of conference hotels and a deserted seaside resort may appear to conform to the gritty northern settings of the 'new new wave', Vernoux's stylised, Godardian use of primary colours accentuates the carnivalesque energy and adventure of the central group rather than asserting any convincing contextualisation of their behaviour in an environment of socio-economic decline.

The film begins with a series of parallel and flashback sequences which foreground the breakdown of the mother–daughter relationship over the serial failures of romantic partnerships. The parallel editing suggests not only clear similarities between the apparent failures of relationships between the sexes across generations but also a pattern in which the female characters internalise social judgements that blame romantic rupture on the reluctance of the female partner to subscribe to dominant models of femininity. Early sequences catalogue the characters' disillusion in the face of romantic discourse as Annie's bruises mark her failed relationship, Lucien regrets the ravages of time on the couple and Marie recounts a clichéd *coup de foudre* involving the (lost) love of her life. This initial temporal fragmentation and sombre mood of the narrative is countered by the emergence of the classical comic duo, the central 'odd couple' of Annie and Françoise who, although genetic sisters, seem to share no sisterly feelings nor indeed any common values or traits. Françoise is sketched rapidly as an uptight bourgeois hypochondriac, reliant on high-maintenance beauty regimes and tranquillisers to get her through the day and wedded to the (overstated) pinkness of a highly stylised domestic femininity. She is appalled at her sister's 'loutish' behaviour as Annie smells, swears, spits and reveals equal reliance upon alcohol as her sedative of choice. Whilst providing a series of effective 'odd couple' gags (which include Annie trying to set her prudish sister up with a younger man only to discover that she has made her own arrangements) this binary fades as the sisters' oppositional identities become diluted by the presence of other women.

Whilst conventions of the road movie dictate a liberation from past selves through the access to expansive landscapes, central sequences of *Personne ne m'aime* take place within the camper van as a supportive, privileged space in which differences can be dismantled and relationships reformulated, often simply in accordance with the seating arrangements of each stage of the journey. The social reconfigurations offered by this space and represented in the close framing of characters and lack of shot-counter-shot can thus be aligned with the use of the van in *Nadia et les hippopotames* (Cabrera, 1999), and with the failure of the car space to provide a socially unmarked shelter for the ambiguous couple dynamic in Vernoux's *Rien à faire* (discussed later in this chapter). This construction of shared space is complemented by the use of intradiegetic music as the women achieve wider harmony through their collective singing of ballads that articulate the frustrations of socially sanctioned gender roles.[2] The conflictual stereotypes of the early sequences gradually break down as the women find pleasure in solidarity and such shifts are not only reflected in the increasingly non-confrontational dialogue but rendered visible through the sharing of clothes and the consequent realignment of their appearances. Whilst Annie begins as an *emmerdeuse extraordinaire* (a real troublemaker), acting as carnivalesque clown through assertions of the 'unfeminine' bodily symptoms of her binge drinking, she becomes increasingly supportive to others and confronts her desires rather than hiding behind the temporary oblivions provided by alcohol. She ultimately acts as a restraining influence on Françoise as the latter mutates from uptight pill-popping bourgeoise into gun-toting avenger. Similarly Cricri's admission that she wants to have children leads her to dictate terms to a mystery man over the phone rather than to regret her abandoned husband. Dizou, however, remains a disappointingly reductive character as the happily married, working-class mother of eleven, who is overcome by the beauty of the sea, struggles with technology and maintains a nurturing and unconflicted role in relation to all. If her inclusion were intended as a counterpoint for the more assertively independent characters it remains largely unconvincing.

The dominant focus on the evolving identities of an all-female group is supported by a reversal of conventions of (narrative) agency as the male characters and male bodies of the film are associated with stasis and extreme inertness. This trope culminates in the final sequences of the film as Paul is left helpless on the ground having been hit by the van and the unconscious body of Annie's local lover is left propped on a bench. The film language of both sequences asserts the women's agency as a low-angle point of view replicates Paul's bewildered gaze as he surveys the group of women standing over him

2 Notably here Ferrat's 'On ne voit pas le temps passer' with its regret for a life remembered primarily through gendered domestic work. 'Entre les courses et la vaisselle, Entre ménage et déjeuner, Le monde peut battre de l'aile, On n'a pas le temps d'y penser' (Between the shopping and the washing up, between housework and cooking, the world may fall away, there's no time to think of that).

and the predicament of Annie's erstwhile lover forms a final, comic contrast to the movement and colour of the women's van as it speeds blithely past him. The fates of the husband and lover who have been rendered immobile (indeed unconscious) by their encounters with the women remain secondary to the film's privileging of the two concurrent solidarities asserted in the family reunion of three generations of women and the women's group identity which dominates the closing sequences.[3] Unlike the problematically temporary parameters of subversion often prescribed by comic narrative structures and by the Bakhtinian carnivalesque, there is no indication in the film's denouement that the women, having satisfied their desire for adventure, are bound to return to the 'normalities' of their respective domestic settings. The film's often nostalgic aesthetic is not accompanied by the ultimate return of conventions of gendered identity and sexual difference that characterise the narrative closures of many Nouvelle Vague films and, whilst Vernoux's central protagonists and their associated star identities may recall images of their younger selves, they serve to challenge the cinematic invisibility of older women, by insisting upon a reinstatement of their independence, mobility and narrative agency.

Bizarre love triangle: *Love etc* (1996)

Vernoux's stylistic preoccupation with the Nouvelle Vague and continuing engagement with the conventions of the romance narrative dominate her next feature film, yet the solidarities of transgression described above remain hauntingly absent here. *Love etc* (1996) is adapted from the Julian Barnes novel *Talking it Over*,[4] and tracks the episodic development of a triangular romance in which two close, male friends fall in love with the same woman, forming an explicit parallel with the central plotline of *Jules et Jim* (Truffaut, 1962) and the more contemporary *Comment je me suis disputé ... (ma vie sexuelle)* (Desplechin, 1996). Pierre (Charles Berling) castigates his friend Benoît (Yvan Attal) for his timidity and lack of success with women. Benoît begins a relationship with Marie (Charlotte Gains-

---

3 This solidarity is reinforced by the women's recurrent and explicit articulation of themselves as a group – 'We stay as a group, agreed?' 'Let's regroup.'

4 Confusingly, Barnes's sequel to *Talking it Over* is titled *Love etc* yet this remains the title of the translation of the first novel into French.

bourg) through personal ads and, following introductions and the important revelation that Benoît used Pierre's photograph in his ads, the trio spend holidays together. On the couple's wedding day, Pierre realises that he too is in love with Marie and pursues her, even taking a hotel room opposite the couple's apartment in order to spy on them. Marie rejects Pierre's declarations yet, having allowed him to watch her work in her studio, she attempts to seduce him. A confrontation soon ensues in which Benoît reveals that he has known about their 'relationship' for some time and accuses them both of deception and betrayal. A coda sequence sees the three protagonists, their relationships reconfigured, return to their seaside haunts to see in the new millennium together.

The isolated world of the triangular relationship, evoked by tight framing and lack of long shots, and into which superficial secondary characters intervene only briefly, provides little acknowledgement of socio-economic context or geographical location. Boulogne sur mer, whose bleak post-industrial landscapes recur in many of the films discussed in this volume, is reduced to a nostalgia-tinged backdrop for nods to the Nouvelle Vague. Vernoux attributes her motivations in making the film to an explicitly nostalgic desire to 'raconter une histoire d'amour avec de grands sentiments romantiques, comme celles que je regardais au cinéma du dimanche soir à la télé: les Sautet, les Lelouch, les Truffaut' (Pliskin 1996: 23),[5] yet the film hesitates awkwardly between the often irritating predictability of the roles cast by the clichéd triangular relationship and more ambiguous elements which signal the undermining of such romantic discourse. Marie and Benoît's relationship is characterised from the outset by compromise and the comically unromantic. Marie's depressing remark on her first date with Benoît on the importance of 'recognising your limits' is supported by her pragmatic habit of sleeping with her married neighbour. The symptoms of the central couple's burgeoning love, signs that would conventionally permit them to transcend the everyday and invest greater meaning in a conjoined existence, are reduced to domestic banalities (Marie's resolute cleaning) and the grotesque (Benoît absentmindedly eating cat food). The couple are linked not by the conventional, anticipatory device of parallel montage, but rather by repeated tracking shots and camera movement from right

5 'to tell a love story with grand romantic emotions, like those I used to watch on Sunday evening television: films by Sautet, Lelouch, Truffaut'.

to left, a motif normally associated with a lack of narrative progress. These elements undermine the notions of absolute compatibility, predestination and all-conquering love associated with the romance script and work in tandem with a central recurrent theme within the film – that of the difference between appearances and reality – the former aligned here with deceptive photographic images. The couple's meeting is triggered by Benoît's personal ad, yet the catalyst turns out to have been Benoît's use of a photograph of Pierre. The posed wedding photograph reveals uncomfortable truths through its snapshot of both the body language of the three characters and the voiceover which articulates their thoughts as Marie praises Benoît's dependability, Benoît is astonished at having attracted Marie and Pierre realises his true feelings for the bride.

Much of the impact of Barnes's novel comes from the use of three first-person narrators, and the insight provided by this device into their contrasting subjective interpretations of the same events. The coexistence of the three narrative voices is partially maintained in the film's sporadic use of different voiceovers, yet better reflected in the striking use of point of view shots at moments of romantic and dramatic tension and the recurrent motif of the power of the subjective gazes of all three characters and the lines of desire and betrayal that these construct. Pierre's confident mode of casual flirtation is demolished by his discomfort under the scrutiny of Marie's gaze as she takes his photograph, and he wreaks revenge for this when, having picked the honeymoon couple up from the airport, he reasserts his presence through the oppressive watching of Marie through the rear view mirror – a surveillance which obliges her to seek refuge in feigned sleep. As Pierre is linked with the photograph and the confident desire expressed through the close-up, Marie is associated with mid-shot composition and painting. The sequences that take place in Marie's studio contain little dialogue and are dominated by careful composition and the interplay of desiring gazes. Having imposed distance and passivity on Pierre, Marie is free to watch as he sleeps, his gaze in turn constructs a striking composition of his very own 'adoration', in which Marie's face is framed alongside the portrait of a saint. The negotiation of mutual desire articulated in this network of gazes forms a striking contrast with the predominantly manipulative and divisive function of the gaze in the rest of the film. This reaches an almost comic apogee in the voyeuristic strategy adopted, first by Pierre and then by both men as they both rent rooms in the same hotel from which they can spy on the other couple. Such spatial constructions, which engage with the incongruities between proximity and knowledge and foreground the framing of both men at their identically shuttered windows, retain clear elements of classical farce. Yet this surveillance does not ultimately focus on competing couples but culminates in a sequence in which both men simultaneously watch Marie, joining forces against an isolated object of desire. The sequence remains sinister and oppressive in tone as Marie is identified as a marker of their desire and, consequently, as the conventionally gendered, fetishised locus of betrayal.[6] Vernoux exaggerates the romantic cliché of the tensions between the triangular romance and the resolution via establishment of the couple, revealing their mutual dependence on the objectification of the woman in order for the male protagonists to remain agents of their own desire.

The film's references to Nouvelle Vague tropes evokes *A bout de souffle* (Godard, 1960) as the opening sequence sees Pierre and Benoît framed together, filmed from the back seat as they drive through Paris, and Pierre's surreal address of apparent strangers recalls the confident, self-ironising quality of Belmondo's early star identity. The tracking shots that accompany the initially playful trio recall *Jules et Jim* (Truffaut, 1962)[7] and *Love etc* can be read as an updating of this narrative in a frame that questions the conventions of romance and a reading of the 'etc' of the title as a dismissive and irreverent response. Yet, despite this subversive potential, the film struggles to avoid the clichéd narrative consequences of the conventional triangular romance in which, despite the superficial unconventionality of the relationships, the woman remains fixed in a position as the object of (shared even universalised) desire and mediator of an unacknowledged desire between the two men.[8] Vernoux stated that her principal focus was the vulnerability of the male characters and that she felt least affinity with the character of Marie (Vernoux 1998: 23), indeed the opening scene described above establishes the two

6 An earlier episode in which Marie, desperate to conceal the traces of Pierre's excessive bouquet (and associated declaration of love), eats the remaining petals could also be anticipated as farce but remains sinister.

7 Indeed in Barnes's novel 'Pierre' jokes that their situation mirrors that of Truffaut's film.

8 Vernoux insisted on the importance of Pierre's appeal to both sexes as 'séducteur universel' (Pliskin 1996: 23).

men as the primary couple, framed together in the intimacy of the car interior. Vernoux's Marie is not the assertive creative artist of Barnes's novel and, although Gainsbourg's feisty performance and considerable screen presence dominate the early sequences of the film, the character of Marie becomes increasingly objectified and silent. Both male protagonists insist on her function as sexual object; Pierre rejects her sexual agency as an inappropriate response to *his* great passion for her and Benoît punishes her (imagined) sexual infidelity through the imposition of a submissive role in hostile sex. During the final confrontation Marie is confined to the background of the frame as observer and trophy and Vernoux's intervention in the novel's ending, which introduces a sentimental closure in which the trio reunite to see in the millennium together, suggests an eerie harmony founded on Marie's continuing elision by a conversation that posits future paternity as a competitive male discourse.

Chauville's criticism of Vernoux's 'parti pris d'évacuer tout discours social' (Chauville 1998: 210) (tendency to evacuate all social discourse) represents a limited response to the two films discussed thus far as it posits a narrow notion of social discourse. *Personne ne m'aime* addresses questions of ageing and cross-generational and inter-class solidarity alongside a *mise en abyme* of the social conventions of gendered identity. *Love, etc,* whilst it struggles to liberate the central female character from the role of sexual object, succeeds in undermining conventionally farcical elements of the *liaison à trois* to construct a more sinister mood that reveals the oppressive response to the threat posed by such a relationship to patriarchal constructions of masculinity and romantic exclusivity. The tone of the final sequence remains unassured, and divergent readings of the ending – as the celebration of friendship beyond romantic rivalry, or the assertion of the two rival male subjects through their combined objectification of Marie – remain plausible. Thus, the narrative's ambiguous closure suggests that, on the very eve of a new millennium, the central female character remains trapped in dominant and reductive socio-cultural constructions of gendered identity.

A more assertive and lucid engagement with the marriage of social cinema to the main drives of popular romantic comedy is central to Vernoux's next release, *Rien à faire* (1999). Its central themes – an acute attention to the registers of different discourses, the different functions of domestic space and the tension between the empowering potential of reimagining the self and the difficulty of negotiating the clichés of the popular imagination – are evident in Vernoux's short film *Dedans* (1996). Scripted by Stéphane Galas and one of ten competitive entries selected by Arte on the theme of love 'in the time of AIDS',[9] the film centres on a young, HIV-positive man (Eric Caravaca) who imagines what his life might have been like without his illness, and constitutes an extraordinarily moving and understated piece whose tone and aesthetic differ radically from the dominant modes of Vernoux's feature films. Vernoux describes how, on approaching the project, she was reminded of the importance of bearing witness to the lives of ordinary people facing extraordinary situations. Galas's stated intention was to reject the clichés of melodrama and excess that accompanied the media representation of HIV-positive people, to show a man who, alone in his room, plays out his desires to camera, fully aware of the painful differences between the joyful hypotheses of his performance and the present realities of his life.

> J'ai décidé d'écrire un personnage qui ne serait ni dans la détresse, ni dans la folie, ni dans l'excès, un mec qui, simplement, au lieu de rêver sa vie, d'une manière passive, la jouerait, tout en restant conscient qu'il ne fait que l'interpréter, tout en mesurant combien ça lui pèse que ce ne soit pas vrai.[10] (Galas 1996)

The film thus counters a homogenised notion of victimhood in which the individual subjectivity of the sufferer is erased, to represent someone who remains 'the same good colleague, the same close friend, the same bastard, the same party animal' (Galas 1996). The dominant narrative mode of the film is quickly established as a man facing a static camera enumerates a list of simple desires in which the repeated poignancy of the use of the conditional perfect tense, 'J'aurais aimé ... (I would have liked to ...)' foregrounds both the assertion of his desires and the haunting acceptance of their increasingly hypothetical nature. The conditionality of his speech is both supported and underscored by his physical actions as he comically simulates a nightclub scene by dancing, flashing a torch and addressing imaginary

---

9 *Dedans* was included in the series 'L'Amour est à réinventer' and first shown on television in December 1996.

10 'I decided to create a character who would be neither distressed, nor mad, nor excessive, a bloke who, instead of passively dreaming about his life, would act it out, remaining aware throughout that he is only acting the part, remaining aware throughout of how painfully he realises that none of this is true.'

friends. His apparent isolation from a world he now describes as 'impossible' is confirmed by the serial framing of a shot from his window of children playing and the emotional impact of his simple desires escalates to the shatteringly succinct statement 'J'aurais aimé vieillir' (I would have liked to grow old). The delivery of these simple sentences to camera in close-up remains extraordinarily moving, yet Vernoux mitigates the potential for constructions of victimhood by creating the alternation of different modes of delivery in which filmed sequences are shown on his television screen.[11] This device, along with the inclusion of the camera set up in some shots, asserts his creative agency and control, whilst also marking out the poignancy of the finished product of the film, projecting us as future spectators who can but bear witness to the projected desires upon which he can perhaps no longer act.

Rien à faire: (all) consuming romance

The performative nature of identity and desire and a decisively pernicious mismatch between fantasy and reality are expanded in Vernoux's next film which provides a re-examination of a classic trope of romantic discourse, that of the couple who overcome socio-cultural barriers or taboos to be together. *Rien à faire* centres on a couple from different socio-economic backgrounds who meet and embark on an affair as an indirect consequence of their shared joblessness. The couple, Marie-Do (Valeria Bruni Tedeschi) and Pierre (Patrick Dell'Isola), meet with increasing frequency until, after Pierre undergoes a humiliating job interview, their friendship becomes a sexual relationship. This is maintained in episodic fashion until Pierre's news of his new employment shatters Marie-Do's illusions of the nature of their liaison and she flees from their first weekend away to return home. The film maintains an intimate tone and could be read as a rather whimsical portrait of the apparently liberating effect of unemployment on a couple who, following the narrative trope of victory over social, racial or economic obstacles to achieve their establishment as primary, exclusive relational unit, find love (or at least mutual attraction) despite their different class backgrounds and

11 See also Cabrera's assertion of different filmings and filmers as discussed in Chapter 1.

economic circumstances. The central romantic event of the fated meeting is also present through the uncanny reprises of Christophe's 'Les Mots bleus'. However such a reading overlooks the film's incisive critique of the reduction of individuals to their socio-economic status through the suggested parallels between discourses of consumer targeting, product branding and advertising and the trajectories of the romance narrative within the film. The tension between two such readings of the film is encapsulated in the title as 'rien à faire' may indicate that it is only their jobless situation of having 'nothing to do' that provokes the chance conditions for an affair, or rather that 'rien à faire' denotes that 'nothing can be done' and thus that resistance is futile in the face of a romantic destiny that transcends circumstance.

Vernoux's parents were militant communists who, having lived in the working-class suburb of Garges-lès-Gonesse (Sarcelles), moved into the bourgeois milieu of central Paris when she was a teenager. Vernoux recalls that the shock of this change in her personal socio-economic environment served as a catalyst for both her political beliefs and the idea for this film. She recounts: 'Deleuze disait "Etre de gauche, c'est regarder un peu plus loin que chez soi" – cette histoire pourrait se passer à Garges. Sept kilomètres de Paris, ce n'est rien en apparence, en fait c'est énorme'[12] (Melinard 1999). Representations of jobless characters are numerous in iconic films of 1990s French cinema and are usually situated within discourses of severe economic and social precarity (*La Vie rêvée des anges* (Zonca, 1998)) and violent exclusions (*La Vie de Jésus* (Dumont, 1997)). Whilst sharing the seemingly obligatory setting of northern France with these films,[13] *Rien à faire* adopts neither Zonca's captivating combination of naturalistic spontaneity and narrative suspense nor Dumont's stark naturalist mode. Indeed, in contrast to many films of the period which introduce unemployment as one facet of a more generalised alienation further framed within a rites-of-passage narrative centred on young protagonists (see Masson, Chapter 3), Vernoux's study of the impact of unemployment features two middle-aged central

12 'Deleuze said "Being on the Left means looking beyond your own neighbour-hood" – this story could take place in Garges. Seven kilometres from Paris seems like no distance at all, but in fact it's immense.'

13 The film is set in Boulogne sur mer whose canneries, bleak landscapes and mournful skies (also prevalent in Masson's oeuvre) stand as shorthand for economic deprivation and decline.

characters with normal levels of social integration who both occupy parental roles within conventional family units. Vernoux's explicit intention was to address the limited cinematic representations of the unemployed, as she explains: 'Les chômeurs restent un tabou en France. Tu peux parler des marginaux... Mais on ne peut pas traiter des chômeurs ordinaires, pas révoltés, qui subissent leur sort dans un coin' (Melinard 1999).[14] Indeed, unemployment is a decisive factor in the identity and narrative of the central protagonists, providing both the catalyst for their meeting and a framework for the shifting structures of dependence that evolve between them.

The intersections between romance, economics and subjectivity are multiple in the film. It is clear from the beginning, indeed from the pre-credit sequence, that the discourses of romance are ever-present in Marie-Do's life and in everyday cultural consumption. Indeed there are several suggestions that romance is an ambiguous and artificial cultural mode that has infected Marie-Do's now expansive free time at home, creating an Emma Bovary figure (Mérigeau 2000) who has lost touch with harsher realities.[15] The clear romantic discourse of the television show that distracts Marie-Do's daughter from her schoolwork, and is dismissed as 'ces conneries' (this bullshit) by her husband, invades the home and underwrites the television and radio programming which provides Marie-Do's domestic company. Even at the job centre, Marie-Do and her long-term adviser discuss personal relationships rather than (illusory) employment opportunities.

The most striking signal of the pernicious and joyless nature of an alienating investment in romantic discourse is witnessed in the film's remarkable pre-credit sequence, which remains both privileged by its very removal from the main narrative and disturbingly opaque in tone. This sequence shows Marie-Do in the bathroom, singing a romantic ballad, 'Les Mots bleus' (Christophe, 1974), into her telephone, a sound eerily echoed via the transmission of her live performance on the radio. Meaning is deferred as we discover only later in the film that Marie-Do enters radio phone-in competitions

---

14 'the unemployed remain a taboo in France. You can talk about marginalised characters ... But you can't discuss the ordinary jobless who don't rebel and who suffer their fate quietly, out of sight.'

15 It is notable that Emma Bovary's avid material consumption and attempts to emulate an idealised 'lifestyle' are markedly different from those of the economic constraints of Marie-Do's situation.

in which prizes are awarded to those who can most accurately reproduce song lyrics on air. The song itself, a pop hit reinterpreted by many performers, describes an unrequited and unarticulated love, which seems both resident in a potential future and lost in nostalgic fantasy. Yet it is the striking delivery of the song and the impact of film language in the sequence, rather than the lyrical content, which arrests spectatorial attention. Marie-Do's performance remains both hesitant and deliberate, both touching and ridiculous as, encouraged by the disembodied voice of the male presenter, she sings in her cramped bathroom for an unseen and unseeing audience. A mobile camera tracks into the bathroom mid-song, and reinforces our initial voyeuristic position through Dominique Colin's startling use of scope close-ups of her nervously clenched hands and hesitant smile. Whilst the lyrical and filmic framing of the song implies performative structures of identity, there is little conventional sense of performance owing to the lack of physical movement and her emphatic turn away from the mirror. In parallel to the intradiegetic audience who have no visual access to her performance, the cinematic spectator is also denied the conventional codes of performance of the female body that would include tropes of physical display and fetishistic camerawork. The distinctive sound, due to both the poor acoustics of the room and the relaying of her voice, emphasises the use of direct sound to suggest authenticity, yet the resultant eerie echo of her words constructs a sense of alienated rupture between speaking subject, body and text. In work on the intimate and the use of *chanson* in film, Massera points to the combination of nostalgia and projected desire in which 'La production culturelle se substitue aux présences et aux expériences de l'être ensemble' (Massera 2004: 134), engineering 'une absence du sentiment de soi au présent'[16] (ibid.: 133). The sequence thus affirms the cultural resonance of the impossible romantic encounter (the song's refrain of '*une rencontre*') yet undercuts its projections of desire by the alienation communicated through the film language. Such examples serve as both a marker of the impact of such cultural discourses whilst also enacting a more mischievous *mise en abyme* of Vernoux's own generic fidelities, pointing out the constructed nature of romance and disrupting spectatorial identification. The reprises of commercial recordings of the song later in the film are used as ironic

16 'Cultural production is substituted for presence and the experience of togetherness' ... engineering 'a lack of a sense of self in the here and now'.

counterpoints to accompanying sequences set in the supermarket where Pierre explains the use of such music to slow the brain and thus facilitate the possibility of further consumer seduction.

The (pre)occupation of Marie-Do's free time by romantic narrative, and the apparent lack of fulfilment in her marriage, thus construct a vulnerable predisposition to the discovery of romance as one offer amongst many found in the supermarket aisles. Pierre's status as branding executive and his ironic patient explanations of the tricks of product placement in large retail environments underlines this conflation of discourses. The post-Fordist shift in human relationships, what Bauman refers to as the 'radical overhaul of kinship structures' (Bauman 2003: 51), attests to the weaker material and social imperative to link sex and falling in love to lifelong union. Such a move arguably increases individual sexual freedoms, but at the cost of presenting relationships as consumer activities: 'only sustained until a better product appears, satisfying the confident, active, curious aspect of the self, but also producing anxiety and fear' (ibid.: 51). In this film the generic conventions of romance act as devices which reveal the interconnectedness of the personal and the economic through the revelation of the pernicious spread of consumer and market dynamics to the realm of personal (here sexual) relationships. Vernoux's central protagonist learns the harsh lesson that cross-class romance cannot withstand the more powerful economic narratives carried within the consumerist discourse that identifies and fixes her as economy brand. The ideal worker projected by post-Fordist economics must embrace the achievement of ultimate individual flexibility (of contractual conditions, hours and location), and collective institutions (such as trade unions) are disempowered by the economics of deregulation and market forces (Bauman 2007: 14). Romance is arguably particularly suited to such explorations as its generic conventions foreground the individual above all group identities as the couple are deemed to possess unique and exclusive compatibilities which ultimately transcend wider (collective) differences. Indeed Marie Do's infidelity is linked to disillusion with her husband's union activism (a focus on the group rather than her as individual) and the obvious disappearance of the solidarities of the Fordist enterprise in which, through collective protection and stable (albeit hierarchical) environments, 'solidarity made some kind of capital out of labour' (Bauman 2007: 60).

Conventions of the romance dictate that the couple will eventually overcome externally imposed barriers (here, those of class) to construct their own exclusive environment that transcends public constructions of time and space. Marie-Do and Pierre remain (in his motivational jargon) '*hors poste*' (in between jobs), and lack of work creates a sense of the suspension of conventional parameters of routine time and space, a move aggravated by Pierre's loss of role as sole financial support for the family and his apparent concomitant loss of sexual function at home. Bonnet admires the lovers' construction of a new space: 'la membrane protectrice créée par leur union qui parvient à les arracher du réel' (Bonnet 1999: 36) (the protective membrane created by their union which succeeds in taking them away from the real) yet, whilst the nature of their extra-marital affair necessitates the improvised use of public spaces, the temporary spaces that they attempt to construct fail to protect them from the (economic) real. Many of the spaces portrayed, particularly the recurring supermarket, would seem to fit the ethnologist Marc Augé's influential identification of the 'non-places' that dominate late capitalist topographies (see Augé 1992). These places are characterised by transience, consumption of material goods and lack of social function, and therefore, Augé argues, present human individuals as homogenised consumers, passengers or visitors. However, despite the surface credentials of spaces associated with the couple in *Rien à faire*, a series of of ugly mass-produced environments juxtaposed neatly with their hesitant intimacy as Augéan *non-lieux*, the couple do not function within them as undifferentiated, homogenised consumers, but are persistently reminded of their different economic capacities and class origins.[17] Vernoux thus foregrounds the failure of romantic discourse to transcend class and economic identities through the representation of their struggle to find time, space or discourse that could accommodate them both without hierarchy.

The use of the car as narrative site recalls a close intertext to *Rien à faire* in *L'Emploi du temps* (Cantet, 2001), in which a redundant middle-class *cadre* lies to his family about a new job and travels the country, living in his car.[18] His car thus becomes a last indicator of

---

17 Indeed Augé's construction of the *non-lieu* remains problematic in its lack of consideration of differences of class, race and gender on the relationship between an individual and the constructions of both space and place.

18 The film does not adopt the tragic ending of the true story on which it is based in which the man's fear of being found out was so great that he killed his family.

his own threatened and conflicted masculinity and a 'uterine space' in which he is protected from socio-economic realities (Archer 2008: 144). Pierre's car lacks this defensive function yet the recurrent use of shots that foreground the car interior, rather than point of view shots out through the windscreen, construct an intimate space that supports his invitations to Marie-Do and provides the setting for their first kiss. The car interior has been prevalent in recent film (from Denis's *Vendredi soir* (Denis, 2002) to *10* (Kiarostami, 2002) as a site of renewed intimacy, a space of potential proximity with the other. Indeed it can be seen to have undertaken a paradoxical displacement of the road or external landscape as a coded space in which journeys of identity and self-expression take place. The multilayered significance of Pierre's car is thus implicated as new-found intimacies remain inseparable from power relationships in a space that remains associated with his role as driver, head of the family and high-waged commuter. The filming of their meetings in the car achieves an ambiguously inclusive framing that suggests simultaneously intimate proximity and contrasting juxtaposition. The rejection of conventional shot-counter-shot used in filming these conversations permits the visual reinforcement of the gap revealed between their respective life experiences, personal discourses and economic status. Marie-Do accompanies Pierre to interviews, yet the in-car, performative role play used to prepare him for interview is disrupted by the economic real (the revelation of his salary) and class alignments (his unwelcome jokes at the expense of a manual workforce). The failure of the car to function as romantic bubble is identified in narrative terms as well as through cinematographic means. Marie-Do accesses free driving lessons for the unemployed, yet her early attempts to drive Pierre's car lead to near-collision and the awkward unravelling of the couple's romantic exclusivity. In a later episode her comically dysfunctional driving on a country lane provides ironic commentary on the clichéd romantic setting of the rural sunset. The final breakdown of the car as privileged site of their relationship is triggered by Pierre's (deferred) news that he has found a job, and the consequent abrupt transformation of their first weekend away together into their last. The rupture is enacted by the newly qualified Marie-Do who appropriates his car and, distraught but safe, drives home alone.

As the couple struggle to find private space that is not saturated by the social and economic discourses that separate them, so they also fail to assert themselves as special individuals in the face of wider externally defined, group identities. In the supermarket, Pierre disrupts conversation to deliver mini-lectures on the science of product placement and consumer psychology integral to his training as brand manager, underlining a reduction of the individual to groups defined by malleable patterns of economic behaviour. The 'space of choice' as he ironically labels the supermarket, further foregrounds the socio-economic definition of the two central protagonists through their choice of products. Indeed the mix-up of bags that follows their first meeting results in their bewildered respective families considering their lack of consumer familiarity with fine wine or with the substandard nutritional fare of economy pâté, and meetings in the supermarket café reveal Pierre's often callous touristic gaze. As the relationship becomes sexual, the pair meet at a house where Marie-Do works as a cleaner. Whilst this location has all the appearances of private, domestic space it is not their space and contains the threat that Marie-Do, unskilled, uncontracted worker, would lose her job if they were discovered. Pierre's observation of her working (as ambiguous sexual display) can be read as an enactment of conventional fantasies (and histories) that conflate paid female domestic labour and sexual availability (fantasies which are enacted in Masson's *A vendre* (see Chapter 3).

Vernoux's casting is brave as Bruni Tedeschi's star identity and past roles encourage an audience to anticipate dramatic, physical confrontation and the explicit externalisation of emotional crises. Here she is cast effectively against type as Marie-Do remains reflective and passive for most of the film, her troubles mainly contained, her alienation surfacing not in violent contestation but in her ready belief of the romance script and a consciousness of the concomitant objectification of the (female) body through her sporadic preoccupation with diet and exercise. On New Year's Eve, the camera initially frames Marie-Do's drunken dancing as temporary liberation, yet the insistent cutting of this with point of view shots and her rebuke to her husband for never looking at her invoke more complex structures of observation and alienation in which her agency is undermined. Marie-Do's gradual realisation of her own inescapable function – commodified as economy brand to get Pierre through his identity crisis until his economic profile is reinstated (tellingly through a job as *luxury* brand manager) – precedes their final rupture. Marie-Do's unequal investment and status in the relationship is represented by her unreciprocated Christmas gift for Pierre. The cigarette lighter is recognised as a familiar object in the discourses of modern adulterous romance (triggering suspicion or confession), as an ironic reference to the figure of the *femme fatale* and as a clichéd metaphor for the ignition of desire. This lighter's spluttering malfunction undercuts all of the above and highlights rather the unsuitability of its budget branding, marked by its disposability and brevity of use in parallel with Pierre's relationship with Marie-Do herself.

The film does not suggest that Marie-Do is alone in being defined by her socio-economic status above all else, but does suggest that she is more limited in her choices and that such constraints leave her more vulnerable to escapist cultural discourses. Some sympathy is elicited for Pierre as *cadre* (executive) without a purpose, indeed his need to perform as 'unique offer' and display his 'selling points' to potential employers and successive self-reinventions in the face of impassive superiors and critical peers suggests a loss of humanity. Pierre's over-identification with work and his proud self-branding as *suractif* contrast sharply with Marie-Do's acceptance of a welcome break from unrewarding work. However, whilst Pierre is presented as the victim of managerial jargon (a (female) interviewer makes him identify his weaknesses only to assert them mockingly as his strengths), the motivational slogans of his job-seeking group remain uncomfortably close to those of the romance script ('Il faut savoir séduire. You have to know how to seduce').

The most famous cinematic representation of a (very British) cross-class illicit affair remains *Brief Encounter* (Lean, 1945).[19] Yet as Lean uses the railway station as public space in which the couple attempt to construct private time and a metaphor that provides ironic projection of the journeys they will never make together, *Rien à faire* employs the supermarket as the site par excellence of product choice, consumer leisure and the pervasive presence of economic branding. Following the supermarket logic, Vernoux succinctly confirms that 'Marie-Do et Pierre ne sont pas dans le même rayonnage' (Mérigeau 2000) (Marie-Do and Pierre are not on the same shelf). An optimistic reading of the film might highlight the 'possibility of shared, human resistance to the alienation it (unemployment) provokes' (Tarr with

19 The trope of the encounter is also supported in the different reprises of the ballad 'Les Mots bleus' whose chorus repeats the words 'une rencontre'.

Rollet 2001: 138), yet the film exceeds this to reveal the pernicious impact of socio-economic disparity on all aspects of experience and the creeping consumerism which infects personal relationships and supports the further reification of such brandings. The suggestion that love provides a 'palliative answer to the blessing/curse of human individuality' (Bauman 2003: 17) is rejected here as constructions of individuality are revealed as flimsy and temporary in the face of economic constraints and social structures. The pessimistic interpretation in which Marie-Do becomes a victim of the dual discourses of romance and consumerism can, however, be tempered by the suggestion of change that is carried in the final sequence. Marie-Do's brutal realisation of the unshakeable inequalities and short sell-by date of the relationship triggers an assertion of agency, independent mobility and an embrace of the future represented in her new skill by driving home alone. Pierre follows, but failing to locate Marie-Do and excluded by the homogenous façades of the tower blocks in which she lives, he is removed from the frame. Marie-Do is rarely framed with friends in the film yet, as she responds to the neighbour who has taken her in, a new sense of intimacy is constructed, one which may promise a more enduring solidarity and community than that of either the romance of consumerism or the consumerism of romance.

Reines d'un jour: multiple encounters

Securing funding for Vernoux's next production was much less difficult – yet this was, tellingly, a consequence not of the relative box office success of *Rien à faire* but rather of the more apparently straightforward generic categorisation of *Reines d'un jour*. Vernoux is not widely denoted as an *auteur* yet this film serves as a prime example of definitions of an intermediate category of 'comédies d'auteur' (Moine 2005: 228) in its upholding of the traits of a national heritage of comedy originating in the *boulevard* tradition as opposed to the *comédie d'action* seen as Hollywood model (ibid.: 224). The film is an assured and at times dazzling ensemble comedy, which provides a surprising juxtaposition of slick entertainment and emotional depth. The plot's episodic linking of interrelated characters takes place over 24 hours in Paris and, whilst Sellier identifies narrative polyphony as characteristic of French women making films in the 1990s which put 'the subjectivity of the 'auteure' on the backburner in deference to an empathy for the characters' (Sellier 2003: 220), such structures were also enjoying critical success in film more widely (for example *Short Cuts* (Altman, 1993) and *Magnolia* (Anderson, 1999)). The polyphonic structure has an impact on romance elements of the plot as spectatorial anticipation of the emergence of the couple is frustrated by the potential for multiple pairings and encounters.

Following a customer complaint about ruined wedding pictures, Marie (Hélène Fillières) is sacked from her job in a photo shop only to find out that she is pregnant as a result of a drunken sexual encounter with the groom, Pierre (Jonathan Zaccai), at that same wedding. Meanwhile the groom's sister, the speech therapist Hortense (Karin Viard), is trying desperately to arrange a night with one of two lovers, Ben (Melvil Poupaud) or Shermann (Gilbert Melki), while her husband Antoine (Philippe Harel) is away. The bus driver Luis (Sergi Lopez) learns that his wife is leaving him and takes off across Paris with bus and passengers. Maurice (Victor Lanoux), a faded celebrity television chef who has turned to drink, waits all day for a meeting with a lover he has not seen for 25 years (Jane Birkin) but then does not answer the door to her. Hortense, humiliated by an unromantic meeting with both lovers, drug-fuelled escapism and rejection by Luis, creeps home exhausted and disillusioned only to discover that her husband has returned early but, asleep beside the babysitter, has not even noticed her absence.

Announced clearly by the lyrics of Brassens's 'Le Vent', which accompany both opening and closing credits, the film reveals a continuation of Vernoux's fascination with chance and the unforeseen consequences of accidental meetings. These 'rencontres' (encounters) persist as challenges to the construction of fated (romantic) destinies as the characters' often physical collisions engender mistakes, misdemeanours and misunderstandings rather than any coherent negotiation of identity. The characters fall victim to a series of accidents and coincidences, yet when asserting their right to very different choices (the future of a pregnancy, choice between lovers, response to separation) they share no more than a common vulnerability to 'option paralysis', this inability to make decisions suggesting a delimiting deferral of all assertions of agency and identity. Vernoux's approach to the 'chassé-croisé' (toing and froing) structure thus has a different trajectory from the suggestion of the 'six degrees of separation' that connect individuals across a city, as the film foregrounds rather their lack of communication and integration into wider social networks. The tension between the isolated needs of the individual and the ceaseless movement of the city is articulated through recurrent shots in which the central characters remain frozen against a background of moving traffic or crowds. The multiple locations and storylines of the film serve as ironic counterpoints to foreground the lack of time or place in contemporary society for meaningful communication – a lack so marked that Luis's wife takes advantage of having accidentally boarded his bus to inform him that she is leaving him. Hortense's job as speech therapist provides ironic comment on the inability of all central characters to articulate their own desires or to listen to others. Her increasingly hysterical use of the mobile phone serves no narrative purpose as her embarrassed lover deletes her repeated messages whilst seated at the same table with her and his wife. The conventionally farcical device of the phone with multiple lines enables Hortense to switch between conversations with two lovers, yet, rather than suggesting a ludic control of her situation, it results in panic and disappointment.

The film returns to the dynamic mood of *Personne ne m'aime*. The casting of Karin Viard, as outspoken and unconventional 30-something Hortense, is central to the comedic premises of the film as it follows Viard's breakthrough role in *La Nouvelle Eve* (Corsini, 1999), described as the 'most commercially successful woman's film to address the question of romance through a modern screwball comedy' (Tarr with Rollet 2001: 177). Yet, unlike the figure of the unruly woman described earlier in this chapter, Hortense is neither 'unfeminine' nor grotesque but rather an apparently successful, well-groomed bourgeois professional. Indeed, the unravelling of this identity through the comic interventions and complex storyline displaces the focus from her transgression of social 'norms' and assertion of sexual agency to reveal an anxious and performative interiorisation of her own desirability to others. The film foregrounds a pragmatic attitude to the social and romantic conventions of marriage, from the grotesque collapse of the wedding cake to the groom's marking of his 'special day' by sexual infidelity, but no successful alternatives are suggested. Whilst it remains striking that, in contrast to *Personne ne m'aime*, the film features little female solidarity (Marie and Hortense both confide frankly in male colleagues), Hortense and Marie dominate the narrative and the male characters are largely passive, inarticulate, ineffectual or even risible. The two central female characters provide contrasting responses to the role of chance in their lives. Hortense's assertion of her right to sexual freedom is hampered by the hysterical consequences of her debilitating inability to make choices between lovers. Marie's more reflective mode combines a triumphant dismissal of romantic convention with a central engagement with unplanned trajectories.

Vernoux's definition of comedic writing as 'C'est balancer un chat du 7ème étage et voir le nombre de tours qu'il va faire sur lui-même avant de tomber sur ses pattes'[20] (Vernoux 2004) is evident in the converging strands of the narrative which gradually draws the characters together, ending with a series of meetings in the same building. The film employs the escalating rhythms and pace of farce to include the key elements of husband, lover, mistress, confidant and the slamming of doors (Vernoux 2001). Yet, whilst the classical farcical situations of misrecognition, coincidence and duplicity provide many comic moments, the tone of the film is increasingly melancholic, as Hortense remains paralysed, rather than liberated, by illusionary choices. Classic comic devices and the unlikely contrivances of the plot are supported by serial non-realist interludes. Indeed, Vernoux's description of the film as a 'fantaisie autorisée' (Vernoux 2001) is echoed in the characters' investment in imaginary scenarios rather than any meaningful engagement in the complex detail of their lives. Several encounters feature markedly non-realist dialogue as, in the wake of her car crash, Marie reproaches the woman who has hit her for her good looks, tasteful clothes, luxury car and happy family life. More disconcertingly still, the woman responds with a frank evaluation of the impact of these attributes on her relationships with others which is more reminiscent of the politicised reflexivity of early Godard than contemporary comedy. Access to Hortense's inner monologue provides a conventional comic insight to the gap between private thoughts and socially permissible utterances, but also foregrounds the role of fantasy in her obsessive planning of alternative romantic encounters. Maurice's serial fantasies provide gloriously comic cameos for Jane Birkin, yet their noisy and colourful humour is undercut by Maurice's melancholy but vengeful silence when, faced with her real

20 'throwing a cat out of a seventh floor window and seeing how many somersaults it can do before landing on its feet'.

arrival, he refuses to answer his door. Hortense's drug-fuelled vision of rowing a boat under moonlight (suggesting agency, fluidity and romance) ends in chaos and embarrassment. Slow motion is also used to comic effect to highlight the gap between the character's imaginary sense of control over the world (for example, Hortense's beatific glide through the waiting room after having arranged a date with her lover) and the fragile subjectivity revealed in such spatial and temporal disconnection.

The film thus presents a group of touching anti-heroes who retain their humanity despite the increasingly burlesque situations that they face. The final sequences' tight, assertive framing of characters together in shared domestic space, repeats the suggested positive trajectory of the narrative closure of *Rien à faire* as the hectic chase around the city ends not with a series of romantic couplings but with the assertion of communication and tolerance between neighbours. Such a trajectory reflects the suspension of conflict and construction of community that Rowe defines as essential to all comedy in its important 'impulse towards renewal and social transformation' (Rowe 1995b: 44).

Isolated incidents: *A boire*

Vernoux's following comedy turns away from such multi-protagonist adventures to focus upon three misfits whose forced and predominantly drunken stay in a ski resort turns apparent social incompatibility to an ambiguous mutual dependency. With its star leads (Emmanuelle Béart, Edouard Baer and Atmen Kélif), increased budget (€4.4 million) and accessible comedic plot, the film was expected to capitalise on Vernoux's rising mainstream profile following the popular success and considerable critical appreciation of *Reines d'un jour*. Yet *A boire* (2004) was largely unsuccessful at both box office and in review. The film is set on Christmas Eve in a ski resort (filmed in off-season Val d'Isère) where the central encounter is that of three central characters who collide on the slopes. Inès (Béart) is unaware that her rich boyfriend has had an accident and believes he has gone home, leaving her with a huge hotel bill. The alcoholic doctor, Pierre-Marie (Baer), has fled his failed marriage to work at the resort and, bored and frustrated after having broken his arm on his first day skiing, Seb (Kélif) is learning

German in preparation for his forthcoming marriage to his Stuttgart-based Algerian fiancée. Vernoux's original intention of writing a comic buddy movie specifically for two of France's most popular contemporary comedians, Baer and Kélif (Widemann 2004), was driven by the plot device of the narrative potential of alcohol as a liberator of self-expression and behaviour,[21] yet these elements were modified as her interest turned to the loneliness for which this drinking compensates. Béart's role was originally written for Viard.

The opening sequences of the film construct a documentary mood as the muted dialogue and hand-held camera which accompany Pierre's inappropriate drunken demeanour at a children's party that triggers his expulsion from the family bear witness to the damage caused by alcohol addiction. The ingenious credits sequence in which Pierre wanders up and down a moving escalator provides a striking metaphor for the loss of control and paradoxically euphoric transport provoked by his alcoholism. The film soon, however, adopts a different generic register as the recognisable comic character archetypes of 'la blonde, du bougon et du naif (Vernoux 2004) (the blonde, the grouch and the innocent) emerge within an episodic structure of farcical set pieces presented in a delimited physical and social environment. Describing ski resorts as 'aussi artificielles que les villes dans les Westerns hollywoodiens' (Vernoux 2004) (just as artificial as the towns in Hollywood westerns), Vernoux suggests a location in which non-realist developments of plot and character can be accommodated, yet, whilst the loss of further temporal and spatial precision conveys the alcohol-induced disorientation of the central characters, this also prevents coherent development and constructs a sense of a lack of convincing transgression.

Vernoux's claim that her work pushed her characters 'vers la gêne, le ridicule, la faible estime de soi – parce qu'ensuite on peut les réparer' (Vernoux 2004) (towards unease, ridicule, low self-esteem – because then they can be mended) is most evident in this film. The characters in *A boire* have reached rock bottom but their continuing lack of communication renders them one-dimensional as differences of gender, class and ethnic background become superficial markers, seemingly evacuated by their drunkenness. The characters adopt predictable roles. Béart is largely convincing in this comic role, yet

21 A device she admired in Cassavetes's provocative *Husbands* (1970) (Widemann 2004).

Inès's response to her dilemma, as she attempts to pay the hotel bill through explicit prostitution with the hotel manager and implicit sexual promises to acquaintances, compares unfavourably with the ingenuity of classic screwball heroines. Pierre's melancholy in the face of family breakdown and career suicide induces passivity and inarticulacy, whilst Seb's Muslim identity apparently evaporates in favour of a deferred drunken adolescence as his ethnic difference is reduced to a comic toast to a relative who he loudly proclaims was the first Algerian to walk on the moon. This undermining of difference creates not radical new connections but a concomitant loss of any potential for transgression. Vernoux countered criticism of the film's portrayal of alcohol consumption by offering a wider view on her moral stance in filmmaking that she describes as asserting 'un point de vue politique qui parle de transgression' (Vernoux 2004) (a political point of view that articulates transgression). However, the suggestion that the characters' persistent inebriation might lead to a liberation of identity and transcendence of difference, thus facilitating the encounter with the other which remains central to Vernoux's work, is hampered by the lack of character development and the consequent lack of credibility of their emerging relationships. Seb's naivety in believing that fellow drinkers remain best friends when sober is perhaps not shared by the audience who find it difficult to invest in the development of any of these relationships.

The lengthy final sequence, in which the three characters are framed together on the back seat of a bus leaving the resort, hovers ambiguously between melancholy and redemptive ending and merits further attention. There is little narrative closure as Pierre has neither job nor home, Inès leaves before her boyfriend's absence is explained and Seb remains lost. There is no dialogue, but a silent exchange of glances which suggests a future romantic relationship between Pierre and Inès whilst positioning a sleepy Seb, who has been problematically infantilised throughout the film, as child in a dysfunctional new family unit. The unlikely trio are obliged to flee with no trajectories other than the initially random and increasingly desperate choice of each other, reinforced by the close framing of the final sequence to exclude all contexts. Vernoux's model of the transgressive encounter is here stripped to its basic elements of physical proximity, from the ski-run collision, through off-piste drunkenness to the shared bus seat of the ending. Outside the artificial setting of the resort, the suggested narrative projections of the buddy movie or the romantic comedy come adrift, and the subsequent implication, that the relationships of this triangular version of the 'odd couple', frozen here in the final shot, are possible only in a closed and inebriated environment, lends a chilling ending to this uneven comedy.

The force of nostalgia: *Rien dans les poches*

Vernoux's most recent project to date is a two-part series made for television[22] which combines a historical chronicle that compares the lives of two women (the mother born in 1962, the daughter in 1985) with key melodramatic elements (family secrets, betrayal and revenge). Two years in the writing, the films' attention to period detail is reinforced by the intercutting of archive footage of historical events and the filming of other sequences in Super 16 and with a Bolex camera. The multi-protagonist scope of *Reines d'un jour* is combined with a core of female characters and a central protagonist and *emmerdeuse* Marie (Emma de Caunes), described by Vernoux as 'allergique à toute tentative de normalisation' (Vernoux 2008) (allergic to all attempts at normalisation).

The narrative tracks the life of the central character Marie from 1979 to 2007 as she leaves her mother and the suburbs for central Paris, founds a successful pop band (Les Poux) and falls in love, first with Maurizio who has fled Italy because of his political affiliations and then with the HIV-positive director Etienne who dies before the birth of their daughter, Esther. Marie becomes a television presenter and runs her own business, a concept boutique, with her new partner Marcel in a Parisian 'bobo' (bourgeois bohemian) paradise. She leaves her job, the relationship fails and, now with a new lover, she becomes increasingly estranged from her daughter as she embarks upon a comeback. A serious car accident sees her renounce this and achieve a final reconciliation with daughter and ex-partners alike.

Filmic nostalgia is evident throughout Vernoux's early work through the strong intertextual and visual references to the Nouvelle Vague, but here it is focused on more recent history and collective memories of the last forty years. The film's persistent appeal to a collective memory of the 1980s is supported not only by the frequent

22 It was also Alain Chabat's first production for television.

use of pop songs from the time but also by references to the arrival of iconic objects such as the microwave oven, Rubik's cube and the instamatic camera. Whilst several of the characters clearly reference well-known figures from the popular culture of 1980s France (Les Poux recall Rita Mitsouko, Etienne Faber can be read as Cyril Collard and Rita as Jenny Bel'Air), the casting also includes stars of that pop scene as Nicolas Bogue plays Lolo, Caroline Loeb has a cameo as the tour manager and, in a neat generational shift, Lio plays Marie's mother, rather than the rebellious daughter of a defiantly Nouvelle Vague mother in *Personne ne m'aime*.

The common perception of nostalgia as a negative, conservative discursive and aesthetic mode can be extended through postmodernist views of nostalgia as constructing 'history without guilt' (Kammen 1991: 688). Yet this mode can be seen as a response to the contemporary fragmentation of communities as it suggests 'an affective yearning for a community with a collective memory, a longing for community in a fragmented world' (Boym 2001: xvi). Vernoux asserts that her main aim in this project was to 'raconter l'intime (moi, moi et moi) ET rendre compte du monde autour (nous, nous ET nous)'[23] (Vernoux 2008) and thus rejoin the personal and political, suggesting the recognised function of nostalgia as an important intermediary discourse that can connect personal and collective memory (Boym 2001: 54).[24] The rhythmic intercutting of archive footage which includes national references to the building of Les Halles, the arrest of Klaus Barbie and the elections of Mitterrand and of Chirac, and to global events such as the rise of Solidarity in Poland, the fall of the Berlin wall and the events of 9/11, succeeds in establishing historical setting and temporal linearity. These montages are rapidly cut however and, with the great exception of the arrival of HIV and AIDS and the development of an aggressive and self-serving celebrity culture, the events shown have no impact on the storyline, creating little sense of a tangible connection between the experiences of the main protagonists and the changing socio-economic environment.

23 'to recount the intimate (me, me and me) AND to take account of the world around us (us, us AND us)'.

24 The wording of Vernoux's statement does, however, recall the character Nader's theory of 'and … and …' an insistence on the possibility of 'having it all' – of being a good mother and a party animal, a has-been and a 'will-be'. This is a goal that Marie rejects.

In her extraordinary work on nostalgia and collective memory, Boym posits two kinds of nostalgia: a restorative mode, which desires the reconstruction of an original in an attempt to conquer time, and a reflective mode that provides a meditation on the passage of time and which embraces fragmented memory (Boym 2001). The rapid cutting between sequences of archive footage in *Rien dans les poches* suggests an affiliation with the restorative mode that provides a series of unproblematised, iconic snapshots, yet the creation of a nostalgic aesthetic in other sequences of the film which suggest partial access to Marie's memories through the use of Super 16 and the hand-turned Bolex camera constructs a more complex texture of sensual access to memory and suggests the reflective mode. Whilst the presence of such sequences that recall early home movies of the late 1970s and early 1980s fits well with the first half of the film, the continued presence of such techniques becomes puzzling and disruptive when employed to represent events that took place after 1992. This visual insistence on the nostalgic perception of current events thus comes to signify the central character's inability to move on from her own ambivalent attitude towards her early celebrity and self-designation as precocious has-been. It is suggested that the consequences of her early fame prevent her from growing up, thus presenting 'a sentiment of loss ... but also a romance with one's own fantasy' (Boym 2001: xiii).

The second part of the film builds a more consistent spectatorial identification with Marie and, after an eventful 25 years (in which she remains seemingly unmarked by time), the final sequence presents a harmonious pastoral scene of a bohemian group of self-proclaimed outsiders. The closure resists cosy triumphalism, however, as the characters remain bound rather too tightly by a sense of nostalgia for their past and a concomitant lack of security about their future. The narrative is thus underwritten by a strong sense of melancholy as, despite her established role as perpetual feisty survivor, Marie's direct rejection of the promise of 'having it all' seems also to rule out the progression of her life outside of this group identity. Vernoux's avowedly indulgent and entertaining nostalgia is seen therefore to articulate a more serious issue as Marie's decision to cancel her own comeback has, paradoxically, led to a stagnation of identity. The group surrounding her is widely representative of alternative energies of the post-68 generations yet has found little outlet for its desires other than the sanctioned commodification of the past, the reification of nostalgia and a chosen investment in a shared lifestyle rather than wider social and political engagement. Marie's personal intransigence is echoed in the film's sometimes clumsy but sincere portrayal of

> ... la mélancolie d'une génération coincée entre le dégoût d'une France giscardienne à l'agonie et la tutelle envahissante des héritiers de 68, sans que l'ombre d'un avenir radieux ne pointe jamais son nez à l'horizon.[25] (Icher 2008)

Thus the film reveals the therapeutic function of nostalgia as a response to the perceived impossibility of future utopian projections. The personal energy of the *emmerdeuse* or unruly woman and the potentiality of the transgressive encounter are thus contained and subsumed within an absence of discourses and structures of wider social and political engagements.

The close encounters that drive the narratives of Vernoux's oeuvre do not always prove to be of a transgressive kind. The early assertions of the accidental over the predestined and the insistence on the role of chance in the creation of new relationships reflect an engagement with the potential of the individual human agent to escape socio-economic definition, gender stereotypes and the discourses of romance. Such engagements are seen as involving delusion and failure and articulate the pitfalls of asserting an individual reconstruction of self over disappearing collective identities and struggles. The closing shots of each of Vernoux's films foreground such tensions between the individual and the group and, through close framing and the pre-credit cueing of emotive music, foreground the importance of relationships (and narratives) other than the romantic and the familial in the construction of identity. From the emphatic sisterhood of the end of *Personne ne m'aime* to the hesitant neighbourliness and class solidarity of the closing scene of *Rien à faire*, from the problematically interdependent trios of *Love etc* and *A boire* to the comforting community of friends in *Rien dans les poches*, these films use popular genre to explore the precariousness of relationships between the individual and the collective, between self and other. They do so, not through the tropes of violent confrontation and exclusion that dominate the filmic production of many of Vernoux's contemporaries but through

25 'the melancholy of a generation caught between disgust at the death throes of Giscard's France and the overpowering domination of the heirs of '68, with not the slightest glimmer of any brighter future on the horizon'.

an exploitation of the established generic codes of romance, played across familiar and increasingly entwined discourses of class identity and nostalgia.

References

Archer, Neil (2008), 'The road as the (non) place of masculinity: "L'Emploi du temps"', *Studies in French Cinema*, 8 (2), 137–48.

Augé, Marc (1992), *Non-lieux. Introduction à une anthropologie de la surmodernité*, Paris, Seuil.

Augé, Marc (1992), *Non-places. Introduction to an Anthropology of Supermodernity*, London, Verso.

Bauman, Zygmunt (2003), *Liquid Love: On the Frailty of Human Bonds*, London, Polity.

Bauman, Zygmunt (2007), *Liquid Times: Living in an Age of Uncertainty*, New York, Polity.

Bonnet, Sandrine (1999), 'Rien à faire', *Les Inrockuptibles*, 245 (15 December), 36.

Boym, Svetalana (2001), *The Future of Nostalgia*, New York, Basic Books.

Chauville, Christophe (1998), *Dictionnaire du jeune cinéma français*, Paris, Scope.

De Bruyn, Olivier (1994), 'Une certaine tendance du jeune cinéma français', *positif*, 399 (May), 48–50.

Galas, Stéphane (1996), 'Dedans: l'amour est à réinventer', www.archives.artetv.com/thema/19961202/ftext/dedans.html (accessed July 2006).

Giddens, A. (1992), *The Transformation of Intimacy: Sexuality, Love and Eroticism in Modern Societies*, Cambridge, Polity Press.

Gillan A. (1996), 'L'Imaginaire féminin au cinéma', *The French Review*, 70 (2), 259–70.

Icher, B. (2008), 'Ticket chic et choc', www.ecrans.fr/Ticket-chic-et-choc,5944.html.

Kammen, Michael (1991), *Mystic Chords of Memory*, New York, Vintage.

Krutnik, Frank (2002), 'Conforming Passions? Contemporary Romantic Comedy', in Steve Neale (ed.), *Genre and Contemporary Hollywood*, London: BFI, 130–47.

Massera, Jean-Charles (2004), 'Régression mon amour', in E. Lebovic (ed.), *L'Intime*, Paris: Ecole nationale supérieure des beaux Arts), 123–41.

Melinard, Michael (1999,) 'Avec Marion Vernoux, les chômeurs passent à la caisse', www.humanite.presse.fr/journal/1999–12–02–300482 (accessed 1 June 2007).

Mérigeau, Pascal (2000), 'L'Amour au supermarché', *Le nouvel observateur* (30 November), 158.

Moine, Raphaelle, 'Reconfigurations génériques de la comédie dans le cinéma français contemporain: l'émergence des "comédies d'auteur"', in Raphaelle Moine, (ed.), *Le Cinéma français face aux genres*, Paris, Association

Française de Recherches sur l'Histoire du Cinéma, 223–32.

Ostria, Vincent (2001), 'Reines d'un jour', *Les Inrockuptibles*, 432, 42.

Pliskin, Fabrice (1996), 'Nous trois', *Le nouvel observateur*, 1672 (May), 23.

Rouyer, Pierre and Vassé, Claire (2003), 'VBT: la foi et la richesse', *positif*, 507, 28–32.

Rowe, Kathleen (1995a), *The Unruly Woman: Gender and the Genres of Laughter*, Austin, University of Texas Press.

Rowe, Kathleen (1995b), 'Comedy, Melodrama and Gender: Theorizing the Genres of Laughter' in K. Karnick and H. Jenkins (eds), *Classical Hollywood Comedy*, London and New York, Routledge, 39–59.

Sellier, Geneviève (2003), 'French women making films in the 1990s', in R. Célestin, E. Dalmolin and I. de Courtivron (eds), *Beyond French Feminisms: Debates on Women, Politics and Culture in France*, Basingstoke, Palgrave Macmillan.

Tarr, Carrie with Rollet, Brigitte (2001), *Cinema and the Second Sex: Women's Filmmaking in France in the 1980s and 1990s*, London, Continuum.

Vassé, Claire (1996), 'Love, etc. Charlotte et ses Jules', *positif*, 430, 40–1.

Vernoux, Marion (1996), 'Dedans: l'amour est à réinventer', www.archives. artetv.com/thema/19961202/ftext/dedans.html (accessed July 2006).

Vernoux, Marion (1998), 'The Weakness that Squared off a Love Triangle', *The Independent* (20 March), 23.

Vernoux, Marion (2001), 'Entretien: "Reines d'un jour"'. http://cinema. alicadsl.fr/article/default.aspx?articleid=AR013753.

Vernoux, Marion (2004), 'Entretien: "A boire"', www.cinemotions.com/ modules/interviews/interview/1436 (accessed July 2007).

Vernoux, Marion (2008), 'Entretien: "Rien dans les poches"', www.commeau-cinema.com/notes-de-production/rien-dans-les-poches.

Widemann, Dominique (2004), 'C'est le film qu'il nous faut', *L'Humanité* (29 December), www.humanité.fr/html?id_article=453810.

Filmographies

Dominique Cabrera

L'Air d'aimer (**An Air of Love**) (1985) (13 min., col.)

Production company: L'Envol Productions
Script: Dominique Cabrera
Cinematography: Roger Millie
Sound: André Rigaut, Xavier Griette
Editing: Jean-Bernard Bonis
Music: Alain Jomy
Cast: Michael Lonsdale (Raymond), Frédéric Leidgens (Frédéric), Christine Sirtaine, Véronique Alain

La Politique du pire (***Worst Case Scenario***) (1987) (19 min., col.)

Production: L'Ergonaute
Script: Dominique Cabrera and Ariel Sctrick
Cinematography: Robert Millie
Sound: André Rigaut, Xavier Griette
Cast: Myriam Courchelle, Claire Fayolle, René Garallon, Frédéric Leidgens

Ici là-bas (**Here Over There**) (1987) (13 min., col.)

Production: L'Ergonaute
Script: Dominique Cabrera
Cinematography: Robert Millie
Sound: Edmée Doroszlai
Editing: Jean-Bernard Bonis

Un Balcon au Val Fourré (***A Balcony in Val Fourré***) (1990) (44 min., col.)

Production: INA, ISKRA Productions
Script: adapted from Ahmed Madani, 'La Tour spectacle'
Cinematography: Philippe Lubliner
Sound: Pierre Camus
Editing: Anne Richet

Rester là-bas (***Staying Over There***) (1992) (47 min., col.)

Production: La Sept, INA, Méli-Mélo Productions
Script: Dominique Cabrera
Cinematography: Jacques Bouquin
Sound: Franck Mercier
Editing: Dominique Greussay, Estelle Altman

Chronique d'une banlieue ordinaire (***Tale of an Ordinary Inner City***) (1992) (57 min., col.)

Production: INA, ISKRA Productions, Canal +
Cinematography: Jacques Pamart
Sound: Xavier Griette, Raoul Fruhauf
Music: Jean-Jacques Birgé
Editing: Estelle Altman, Dominique Greussay

Rêves de ville (***City Dreams***) (1993) (26 min., col.)

Production: INA, ISKRA Productions, Canal +
Cinematography: Jacques Pamart, Isabelle Razavet
Sound: Pierre Camus, Raoul Fruhauf, Xavier Griette
Editing: Cathy Chamorey

Réjane dans la tour (***Réjane in the Tower***) (1993) (15 min., video, col.)

Production: ISKRA Productions, INA
Cinematography: Jacques Pamart
Sound: Xavier Griette
Editing: Cathy Chamorey

Traverser le jardin (***Crossing the Garden***) (1993) (19 min., col.)

Production: Bloody Mary Productions
Script: Dominique Cabrera, Manuela Fresil

Cinematography: Hélène Louvart
Editing: Dominique Greussay
Music: Jean-Jacques Birge
Cast: Nelly Bourgeaud, Clovis Comillac

Une poste à la Courneuve (*A Post Office in Courneuve*) (1994) (54 min., col.)

Production: ISKRA Productions, Périphérie
Script: Dominique Cabrera, Suzanne Rosenberg
Cinematography: Hélène Louvart
Editing: Christiane Lack
Sound: Xavier Griette

L'Autre côté de la mer (*The Other Shore*) (1997) (92 min., col.)

Production: Didier Haudepin, Bloody Mary Productions, France 2
Script: Dominique Cabrera, Louis Mathieu de Vienne, Nidam Abdi
Cinematography: Hélène Louvart
Sound: Xavier Griette
Music: Béatrice Thiriet
Editing: Sophie Brunet
Cast: Claude Brasseur (Georges Montero), Roschdy Zem (Tarek Timzert), Marthe Villalonga (Marinette), Slimane Benaïssa (Boualem), Ariane Ascaride (Lulu), Marilyne Canto (Lisa)

Demain et encore demain (journal 1995) (*Tomorrow and Tomorrow*) (1997) (79 min., col.)

Production: INA
Cinematography: Dominique Cabrera
Sound: Dominique Cabrera
Editing: Réjane Fourcade

Retiens la nuit (*Hold Back the Night*) (1998) (67 min., col.)

Production: Agat films et cie, La Sept-Arte
Script: Dominique Cabrera, Philippe Corcuff
Sound: Gérard Lamps
Music: Béatrice Thiriet
Editing: Sophie Brunet
Cast: Ariane Ascaride (Nadia), Marilyne Canto (Claire), Thierry Frémont (Serge), Philippe Fretun (Jean-Paul)

Nadia et les hippopotames (Nadia and the Hippopotamuses)
(1999) (102 min., col.)

Production: Agat Films et Cie, La Sept-Arte
Script: Dominique Cabrera, Philippe Corcuff
Cinematography: Hélène Louvart
Sound: Xavier Griette, Philippe Fabri
Music: Béatrice Thiriet
Editing: Sophie Brunet
Cast: Ariane Ascaride (Nadia), Marilyne Canto (Claire), Thierry Frémont (Serge), Philippe Fretun (Jean-Paul)

Le Lait de la tendresse humaine (The Milk of Human Kindness)
(2001) (95 min., col.)

Production: Films Pelléas, Luc et Jean-Pierre Dardenne, Les Films du fleuve
Script: Dominique Cabrera, Cécile Vargaftig
Cinematography: Hélène Louvart
Sound: Xavier Griette
Music: Béatrice Thiriet
Editing: Francine Sandberg
Cast: Marilyne Canto (Christelle), Patrick Bruel (Laurent), Dominique Blanc (Claire), Valeria Bruni Tedeschi (Josiane), Sergi Lopez (Serge)

Folle embellie (Wonderful Spell) (2004) (100 min., col.)

Production: Les Films de la croisade
Script: Dominique Cabrera, Antoine Montperrin
Cinematography: Hélène Louvart
Sound: Olivier Calvert
Music: Milan Kymlicka
Editing: Sophie Brunet
Costumes: Nathalie Raoul
Cast: Jean-Pierre Léaud (Fernand), Miou-Miou (Alida), Morgan Marinne (son), Marilyne Canto (Colette), Julie-Marie Parmentier (Lucie), Yolande Moreau (Hélène)

Quand la ville mord (When the City Bites) (2009) (60 min., col.)

Production: Agora film, France 2, Arte France
Script: Dominique Cabrera, from the novel by Marc Villard
Cinematography: Hélène Louvart

Sound: Xavier Griette
Music: Béatrice Thiriet
Editing: Sophie Brunet
Cast: Aïssa Maïga (Sara), Samir Guesmi, Laurentine Milebo, Alain Dzukam-Simo, Assane Seck, Djeneba Kone, Gérald Papasian, Kadi Diarra

Ranger les photos (**_Sorting Out Photographs_**) (2009) (14 min., col.)

Production: Miniane
Directors: Dominique Cabrera and Laurent Roth

Noémie Lvovsky

Dis-moi oui, dis-moi non (**_Say yes, say no_**) (1989) (18 min., col.)

Production: FEMIS
Script: Noémie Lvovsky, Denyse Rodriguez-Tomé
Cinematography: Jean-Marc Fabre
Sound: Ludovic Herrault, Denis Maignan
Editing: Emmanuel Salinger

Embrasse-moi (**_Kiss Me_**) (1990) (11 min., col.)

Production: IMA Productions
Script: Noémie Lvovsky
Cinematography: Jean-Marc Fabre
Editing: François Gédigier
Cast: Emmanuelle Devos, Camille Japy

Oublie-moi (**_Forget Me_**) (1994) (93 min., col.)

Production: Les films Alain Sarde
Script: Marc Cholodenko, Sophie Fillières, Noémie Lvovsky
Cinematography: Jean-Marc Fabre
Editing: Jennifer Augé
Sound: Ludovic Herrault
Original music: Andrew Dickson
Cast: Valeria Bruni Tedeschi (Nathalie), Emmanuelle Devos (Christelle), Emmanuel Salinger (Antoine), Philippe Torreton (Fabrice), Laurent Grévill (Eric)

Petites (***Little Girls***) (1998) (90 min., col.)

Production: Arena films, La Sept-Arte
Script: Noémie Lvovsky, Florence Seyvos
Cinematography: Agnès Godard
Editing: Michel Klochendler
Sound: Marie Guesnier, Frédéric Ullmann
Cast: Ingrid Molinier (Inès), Julie-Marie Parmentier (Stella), Camille Rousselet (Marion), Magali Woch (Emilie), Jean-Luc Bideau (Emilie's father), Valeria Bruni Tedeschi (Emilie's mother), Marie-Armelle Deguy (Marion's mother), Christine Fersen (Stella's mother), Luis Rego (Stella's father), Marina Tomé (Inès' mother)

La Vie ne me fait pas peur (***Life Doesn't Scare Me***) (1999) (105 min., col.)

Production: Arena Films, Canal +, La Sept-Arte, Vega Films, TSI
Script: Noémie Lvovsky, Florence Seyvos
Cinematography: Agnès Godard
Editing: Michel Klochendler
Sound: Gabriel Hafner, Frédéric Ullmann
Cast: Ingrid Molinier (Inès), Julie-Marie Parmentier (Stella), Camille Rousselet (Marion), Magali Woch (Emilie), Jean-Luc Bideau (Emilie's father), Valeria Bruni Tedeschi (Emilie's mother), Marie-Armelle Deguy (Marion's mother), Christine Fersen (Stella's mother), Luis Rego (Stella's father), Marina Tomé (Ines' mother)

Les Sentiments (***Feelings***) (2003) (94 min., col.)

Production: Hirsch, ARP Sélection, TF1 Films Production
Script: Noémie Lvovsky, Florence Seyvos
Cinematography: Jean-Marc Fabre
Editing: François Gédigier
Sound: François Groult, Nadine Muse
Original music: Jeff Cohen and Philippe Rouèche
Animation: Guillaume Darou, Anaïs Vaugelade
Cast: Nathalie Baye (Carole), Jean-Pierre Bacri (Jacques), Isabelle Carré (Edith), Melvil Poupaud (François), Valeria Bruni Tedeschi (young mother)

Faut que ça danse! (***Let's Dance!***) (2007)(100 min., col.)

Production: Why Not Productions, France 2 Cinéma, Soficinéma 3, TSR, UGC, Vega Film
Script: Noémie Lvovsky, Florence Seyvos
Cinematography: Jean-Marc Fabre
Editing: Emmanuelle Castro
Sound: Brigitte Tallandier, Sylvie Mabrant, Nicolas Moreau, Emmanuel Croset
Original music: Archie Shepp
Animation: Anaïs Vaugelade
Cast: Jean-Pierre Marielle (Salomon Bellinsky), Valeria Bruni Tedeschi (Sarah Bellinsky), Sabine Azéma (Violette), Bulle Ogier (Geneviève), Bakary Sangaré (Mr Mootoosamy), Arié Elmaleh (François), John Arnold (Adolf Hitler), Daniel Emilfork (military doctor), Judith Chemla (medical student), Cécile Reigher (nurse) Michel Fau (psychiatrist), Jutta Sammel (Sarah as child), Michèle Gleizer (gynaecologist)

As Actor

Ma femme est une actrice (Attal, 2002)	Nathalie
Ah! si j'étais riche (Munz and Bitton, 2002)	Claire
Rois et reine (Desplechin, 2003)	Elizabeth
France boutique (Marshall, 2003)	Monique
L'un reste l'autre part (Berri, 2004)	Nicole
Le Grand Appartement (Thomas, 2005)	Charlotte Falingard
L'Ecole pour tous (Rochant, 2006)	Krikorian
Backstage (Bercot, 2005)	Juliette
Actrices (Bruni Tedeschi, 2007)	Nathalie
Un cœur simple (Laine and Bichet, 2007)	Nastasie
Copacabana (Fitoussi, 2008)	Suzanne
Coco (Elmaleh, 2008)	Brigitte
Les Beaux Gosses (Sattouf, 2009)	Hervé's mother
Ensemble nous allons vivre une très très grande histoire d'amour (Thomas, 2009)	Madame Adélaïde
Bus Palladium (Thompson, 2009)	military psychiatrist
L'Apollonide (Bonello, 2010)	Marie-France
Présumé coupable (Garenq, 2010)	Edith
Le Skylab (Delpy, 2011)	Aunt Monique

Laetitia Masson

Chant de guerre parisien (*Parisian War Song*) (1991) (13 min., col.)

Production: Quo Vadis cinéma
Script: Laetitia Masson
Cinematography: Caroline Roussel
Cast: Eva Ionesco, Eric Ambruster, Pascal Goblot, Foued Nassah

Nulle part (*Nowhere*) (1993) (52 min., col.)

Production: BVF Films
Script: Laetitia Masson
Cinematography: Antoine Heberlé
Music: Thibaut Saladin
Cast: Hélèle Fillières, Julien Rassan

Vertige de l'amour (1994) (5 min.)

Production: BVF Films
Script: Laetitia Carton, Laetitia Masson
Cinematography: Thierry Arbogast
Cast: Christophe Loir, Estelle Perron, Nicolas André, Nelly Barre

En avoir (ou pas) (*To have it (or not)*) (1994) (90 min., col.)

Production: CLP, Dacia Films
Script: Laetitia Masson
Cinematography: Caroline Champetier
Editing: Yann Dédet
Sound: Michel Vionnet
Cast: Sandrine Kiberlain (Alice), Claire Denis (Alice's mother), Arnaud Giovaninetti (Bruno), Didier Flamand (head of personnel), Roschdy Zem (Joseph), Daniel Kiberlain (Alice's father), Lise Lamétrie (Annette), Laetitia Palermo (Hélène)

Je suis venue te dire (*I've come to tell you*) (1996) (23 min., col.)

Production: Cuel Lavalette Productions, INA
Script: Laetitia Masson
Cinematography: Caroline Champetier (16mm, 35mm) and Laetitia Masson (Hi8)
Editing: Jean-Pierre Pruilh
Sound: Xavier Vauthrin, Pascal Rousselle, Laurent Thomas
Cast: Sandrine Kiberlain, Jean-Louis Loca, Mireille Perrier

A vendre (**For Sale**) (1998) (117 min., col.)

Production: CLP, Canal +, La Sept Cinéma
Script: Laetitia Masson
Cinematography: Antoine Heberlé
Sound: Michel Vionnet, Piotr Zawadzki, William Flageollet
Editing: Ailo Auguste
Cast: Sandrine Kiberlain (France Robert), Sergio Castellito (Luigi Primo), Jean-François Stévenin (Lindien), Chiara Mastroianni (Mireille), Aurore Clément (Lindien's sister), Roschdy Zem (bank manager), Frédéric Pierrot (Paris husband), Valérie Dréville (Paris wife), Mireille Perrier (Luigi's ex-wife), Samuel le Bihan (Pacard), Didier Flamand (mute man)

Love Me (2000) (125 min., col.)

Production: Ciné Valse, Canal +, studio Images 6
Script: Laetitia Masson
Cinematography: Antoine Heberlé
Sound: Philippe Amouroux, Vincent Guillon
Editing: Aïlo Auguste-Judith
Music: John Cale
Cast: Sandrine Kiberlain (Gabrielle Rose), Johnny Hallyday (Lennox), Jean-François Stévenin (Carbonne), Aurore Clément (Rose's mother), Salomé Stévenin (teenage girl / Miss Rose), Julie Depardieu (Barbara), Julian Sands (the sailor), Anh Duong (Gloria)

La Repentie (**The Repentant**) (2002) (125 min., col.)

Production: ARP, France 3 Cinéma
Script: Laetitia Masson
Cinematography: Antoine Heberlé, Georges Diane
Sound: Olivier Le Vacon, Jean Dubreuil, Philippe Amouroux
Editing; Dominique Faysse
Music: Jocelyne Pook
Cast: Isabelle Adjani (Charlotte), Sami Frey (Paul), Samy Naceri (Karim), Maria Schneider (Charlotte's sister), Claudine Mavros (Paul's mother), Georges Mavros (Paul's father), José Giovanninetti (Charlotte's father), Farida Amrouche (Charlotte's mother), Ari Päffgen (handsome stranger at wedding)

Pourquoi (pas) le Brésil (_Why (not) Brazil?_)(2004) (92 min., col.)

Production: Rezo films, CNC, Canal +
Script: Laetitia Masson
Cinematography: Crystel Fournier
Sound: Philippe Amouroux, Pierre André
Editing: Aïlo Auguste-Judith
Music: Benjamin Biolay, Jean-Louis Murat
Cast: Elsa Zylberstein (Laetitia Masson / Christine Angot), Marc Barbé (Paul, the husband / Pierre-Louis), Bernard le Coq (Maurice Rey, producer), Laetitia Masson (herself), Pierre Arditi (Haïm Cohen), Ludmila Mikael (beautiful woman), Daniel Auteuil (himself), Francis Huster (himself), Léonore Chastagner (Léonore), Christine Angot (herself), Alain Sarde (himself), Haïm Cohen (himself), Alexia Tansky (Valérie), Trice Lübeck (estate agent), Benjamin Biolay (himself), Pascal Bonitzer (himself)

Enculées (_Fucked (Off)_) (2008) (30 min., col.)

Production: Studiocanal, Sofilles production, Montpensier films
Scenario: Laetitia Masson
Editing: Jérôme Bréau
Cast: Hélène Fillières (Claire), Laetitia Masson (the director), Valentine Catzeflis (escort girl 1), Camille de Sablet (Claire's sister), Pierre-Félix Gravière (Claire's brother-in-law), Antoine Hamel (client), Rachel (girl x), William (boy x), Sylvie Gastambide (escort girl 2)

Coupable (_Guilty_) (2008) (147 min., col.)

Production: Rezo films, Rhônes-Alpes cinéma, Canal +
Script: Laetitia Masson
Cinematography: Antoine Heberlé
Editing: Aïlo Auguste-Judith
Sound: Ludovic Escallier
Music: Jean-Louis Murat
Cast: Hélène Fillières (Marguerite), Jérémie Renier (Lucien), Amira Casar (Dolores), Denis Podalydès (Louis Berger), Anne Consigny (Blanche Kaplan), voiceover: Michel Onfray

Petite fille (***Young Girl***) (2009) (television, 90 min., col.)

Production: Albertine Production. CRRAV, France Télévisions, TV5 Monde
Script: Laetitia Masson
Cinematography: Antoine Heberlé
Editing: Yves Langlois
Sound: Daniel Banaszak
Music: Jean-Louis Murat
Cast: Hélène Fillières (Sylvie Neige), Benjamin Biolay (Gabriel), Aurore Clément (Sylvie's mother), André Wilms (Sylvie's father)

La Superbe Live (**'*Superb*' *Live***) **+** ***Dans ta bouche*** (***In Your Mouth***) **(2010)** (portrait / 90 min., col.)

Production: Naïve, Camera lucida productions
Cinematography: Laetitia Masson
Editing: Alexandre Augue
Sound: Stéphane Larrat
Cast: Benjamin Biolay (himself), Coralie Clément (Biolay 1), Valerie Donzelle (Biolay 2), Alka Balbir (Biolay 3), Jeanne Chernal (Biolay 4), Aurore Clément (Rose Kennedy)

Marion Vernoux

Pierre qui roule (***Pierre on the go*** / ***A rolling stone***) (1991) (96 min., col.

Productions: La Sept ARTE, Anabase films, CNC
Script: Marion Vernoux
Cinematography: Pierre Boffety
Editing: Patricia Ardouin
Sound: Jean-Louis Garnier
Cast: Marianne Denicourt (Marie), Benoît Regent (Pierre), Philippe Fretun (the main in the toilets)

Personne ne m'aime (***Nobody loves me***) (1994) **(**98 min., col.)

Production: Bloody Mary Productions, Ciné manufacture, France 2 Cinéma, Télévision Suisse Romande
Script: Nicolas Errèra, Marion Vernoux
Cinematography: Eric Gautier

Editing: Jennifer Angé

Cast: Bernadette Lafont (Annie), Bulle Ogier (Françoise), Jean-Pierre Léaud (Lucien), Lio (Marie), Maaike Jansen (Dizou), Michèle Laroque (Cricri), Antoine Chappey (Pierre), John R. Pepper (the lover), André Marcon (Jacques), Boris Bergman (the man in the bar)

Dedans (*Inside*) (1996) (7 min., col.)

Production: Little Bear, LGP Films

Script: Stéphane Galas

Cinematography: Jean-Marc Fabre

Editing: Jennifer Augé

Sound: Mathieu Imbart

Cast: Eric Caravaca

Love etc (1996) (96 min., col.)

Production: Alicéleo, France 3 Cinéma, StudioCanal

Script: Marion Vernoux, Dodine Henry, adapted from the novel by Julian Barnes

Cinematography: Eric Gautier

Editing: Jennifer Angé

Cast: Charlotte Gainsbourg (Marie), Yvan Attal (Benoît), Charles Berling (Pierre), Thibault de Montalembert (Bernard), Susan Moncur (Susan), Daniel Duval (Yvon), Elodie Navarre (Eléonore), Marie Adam (Bernard's wife), Charlotte Maury Sentier (Catherine), Dominique Raymond (Marie's mother)

Rien à faire (*Nothing to be done*) (1999) (105 min., col.)

Production: ADR Productions, StudioCanal, CNC, Cofimage

Script: Marion Vernoux, Santiago Amigorena

Music: Alexandre Desplat

Cinematography: Dominique Colin

Editing: Jennifer Augé

Sound: Michel Casang, Marie Guesnier, Laurent Poirier

Cast: Valeria Bruni Tedeschi (Marie-Do), Robert Caravaca (young man on bus), Alexandre Carrière (Hervé), Patrick Dell'Isola (Pierre), Marion de Fachelles (Alice), Josette Hemsen (Josette Hemsen), Kelly Hornoy (Julie), Sergi Lopez (Luis), Chloe Mons (Catherine), Philippe Peltier (Robert), Farida Rahouadi (neighbour Marie), Florence Thomassin (Sophie)

***Reines d'un jour* (*A Hell of a Day*)** (2001) (100 min., col.)

Production: ADR productions, Canal +, CNC, France 3 Cinéma, Gimages 4
Script: Marion Vernoux, Nathalie Kristy
Cinematography: Dominique Colin
Editing: Lise Beaulieu
Music: Alexandre Desplat
Sound: Michel Casang, Bastien Guille
Cast: Valérie Benguigui (Stéphanie), Jane Birkin (Marlène), Clémentine Célearié (Michèle), Hélène Fillières (Marie), Philippe Harel (Antoine), Atmen Kélif (Jean), Victor Lanoux (Maurice), Sergi Lopez (Luis), Gilbert Melki (Shermann), Melvil Poupaud (Ben), Karin Viard (Hortense), Jonathan Zaccai (Pierre)

***A boire* (*Let's Drink*)** (2004) (90 min., col.)

Production: Compagnie Panoptique, ADR productions, France 3 Cinéma, Rhône-Alpes Cinéma, Canal +
Script: Marion Vernoux, Frédéric Jardin, Thomas Bidegain
Cinematography: Dominique Colin
Editing: Camille Cotte
Music: Nicolas Bogue, Alexandre Desplat
Sound: Valérie Arland, Marie Guesnier
Cast: Ludovic Abgrall (Jean-Pierre), Edouard Baer (Pierre-Marie Archambault), Emmanuelle Béart (Inès Larue), Jackie Berroyer (Mr Guibal), Marina Fois (Bénédicte), Atmen Kélif (Seb Abd Al Abbas), Pierre-Louis Lannier (the receptionist), Claude Perron (Mme Guibal), Jean-Michel Tinivelli (Patrick), Yves Verhoeven (Serge-André)

***Rien dans les poches* (*Empty Pockets*)** (2008) (2 × 110 min., col.)

Production: TF1 Video, Studio Canal, Chez Wam, CNC
Script: Marion Vernoux and Laetitia Trapet
Cinematography: Vincent Muller
Editing: Laure Mercier
Music: Nicolas Bogue, Quentin Sirjacq
Sound: Michel Casang
Cast: Anaîs (Vero), Nicolas Bogue (Lolo), Cécile Cassel (Anne), Stefano Cassetti (Maurizio), Alain Chabat (Rita), Emma de Caunes (Marie Manikowski), Emilie Dequenne (Judith Miro), Nicolas Duvauchelle

(Etienne Faber), Romain Goupil (Daniel Manikowski), Julien Honoré (Pierre Archambault), Clémentine Houée (Esther aged 4), Lio (Nicole Manikowski), Elie Semoun (Marco Abitbol), Louise Szpindel (Esther aged 15)

Index